# The PARADOX of POWER
## in a
## PEOPLE'S REPUBLIC of CHINA
## MIDDLE SCHOOL

# Studies on Contemporary China

THE POLITICAL ECONOMY
OF CHINA'S SPECIAL
ECONOMIC ZONES
*George T. Crane*

**WORLDS APART**
RECENT CHINESE WRITING AND ITS
AUDIENCES
*Howard Goldblatt, editor*

**CHINESE URBAN REFORM**
WHAT MODEL NOW?
*R. Yin-Wang Kwok, William L. Parish, and
Anthony Gar-on Yeh
with Xu Xuequang, editors*

**REBELLION AND FACTIONALISM
IN A CHINESE PROVINCE**
ZHEJIANG, 1966–1976
*Keith Forster*

**POLITICS AT MAO'S COURT**
GAO GANG AND PARTY FACTIONALISM
IN THE EARLY 1950s
*Fredrick C. Teiwes*

**MOLDING THE MEDIUM**
THE CHINESE COMMUNIST PARTY
AND THE LIBERATION DAILY
*Patricia Stranahan*

**THE MAKING OF A SINO-MARXIST
WORLD VIEW**
PERCEPTIONS AND INTERPRETATIONS OF
WORLD HISTORY IN THE
PEOPLE'S REPUBLIC OF CHINA
*Dorothea A.L. Martin*

**POLITICS OF DISILLUSIONMENT**
THE CHINESE COMMUNIST PARTY UNDER
DENG XIAOPING, 1978–1989
*Hsi-sheng Ch'i*

**CONQUERING RESOURCES**
THE GROWTH AND DECLINE OF
THE PLA'S SCIENCE AND
TECHNOLOGY COMMISSION FOR
NATIONAL DEFENSE
*Benjamin C. Ostrov*

**THE PARADOX OF POWER IN A
PEOPLE'S REPUBLIC OF CHINA
MIDDLE SCHOOL**
*Martin Schoenhals*

**CHINA'S ECONOMIC DILEMMAS
IN THE 1990s**
THE PROBLEMS OF REFORMS,
MODERNIZATION, AND INDEPENDENCE
*Edited by the Joint Economic Committee,
Congress of the United States*

**CHINA IN THE ERA OF DENG
XIAOPING**
A DECADE OF REFORM
*Michael Ying-mao Kau and
Susan H. Marsh, editors*

**DOMESTIC LAW REFORMS IN
POST-MAO CHINA**
*Pittman B. Potter, editor*

**POLITICS AND PURGES IN CHINA**
RECTIFICATION AND THE DECLINE OF PARTY
NORMS, 1950–1965
*Frederick C. Teiwes*

**MORNING SUN**
INTERVIEWS WITH POST-MAO CHINESE
WRITERS
*Laifong Leung*

**CHINESE FIRMS AND THE STATE IN
TRANSITION**
PROPERTY RIGHTS AND AGENCY PROBLEMS
IN THE REFORM ERA
*Keun Lee*

**THE MARKET MECHANISM AND
ECONOMIC REFORMS IN CHINA**
*William A. Byrd*

**CHINA, THE UNITED STATES, AND
THE SOVIET UNION**
TRIPOLARITY AND POLICY-
MAKING IN THE COLD WAR
*Robert S. Ross*

**AMERICAN STUDIES OF
CONTEMPORARY CHINA**
*David Shambaugh*

Studies on Contemporary China

# The PARADOX of POWER
# in a
# PEOPLE'S REPUBLIC of CHINA
# MIDDLE SCHOOL

## MARTIN SCHOENHALS

An East Gate Book

Routledge
Taylor & Francis Group

LONDON AND NEW YORK

**An East Gate Book**

First published 1993 by M.E. Sharpe

Published 2015 by Routledge
2 Park Square, Milton Park, Abingdon, Oxon OX14 4RN
711 Third Avenue, New York, NY 10017, USA

*Routledge is an imprint of the Taylor & Francis Group, an informa business*

**Library of Congress Cataloging-in-Publication Data**

Schoenhals, Martin, 1961–
The paradox of power in a People's Republic of China middle school /
Martin Schoenhals.
p.—cm. (Studies in contemporary China)
Includes bibliographical references (p. 204) and index.
ISBN 1-56324-188-9
ISBN 1-56324-189-7 (pbk)
1. Education, Secondary—Social aspects—China—Case studies.
2. Middle schools—China—Case studies.
3. Communist self-criticism—Case studies.
4. China—Social conditions—1976–
I. Title
II. Series.
LA1132.S36   1993
373.11′9′0951—dc20
92-38344
CIP

ISBN 13: 9781563241895 (pbk)
ISBN 13: 9781563241888 (hbk)

# Contents

# Acknowledgments

This book, and the research it reports, benefited greatly from the assistance of numerous individuals. I would first like to thank my doctoral dissertation committee: my advisor, Ward Goodenough, and the other members of my committee, Sandra Barnes and Kris Hardin. I also want to acknowledge the assistance of Anthony Wallace, my advisor prior to his retirement. During an ethnohistory seminar with him I developed some of the intellectual interests that led to my desire to study education in China. I am especially grateful to two additional readers of my manuscript, Frederick Erickson and Heather Peters. Dr. Erickson and Dr. Peters have supported me over the course of several years from the inception of this project to its completion. My research could not have proceeded without their help.

Scholars at other universities have also been very helpful. Lynn Paine gave generously of her time to discuss research possibilities with me, and it was she who suggested that I seek affiliation with a teacher training university in order to study its affiliated middle school. Heidi Ross shared many insights with me about Chinese education, based on her own ethnographic research at a Chinese middle school. Norma Diamond read a portion of my manuscript and made many valuable comments and suggestions.

Helpfulness is a Chinese virtue, and many Chinese friends gave tirelessly of their time and energy to help me with my study. Huang Shizhe, my language tutor at the University of Pennsylvania, was also the first one to guide me to a better understanding of Chinese culture. My friends, teachers, and students in the People's Republic of China were both the subjects of this study and the study's greatest facilitators. My desire to protect their anonymity prevents me

from naming them individually, although I wish that I could thank
each one by name.

The financial resources of a number of institutions supported various phases of my research. I would like to acknowledge the National
Science Foundation, for a graduate fellowship to support my graduate
studies and for a dissertation research grant to support my fieldwork in
the People's Republic. I would also like to thank the Wenner-Gren
Foundation for a grant to fund my fieldwork. A fellowship from the
University of Pennsylvania helped finance my graduate studies. The
dissertation year of a Mellon Fellowship in the Humanities supported
the writing up of my research.

Above all, I am grateful for the encouragement of my family and their
enthusiasm for my research. This book is dedicated, with love, to them.

# The PARADOX of POWER
## in a
# PEOPLE'S REPUBLIC of CHINA
## MIDDLE SCHOOL

# 1

# Introduction

I can still remember the day I arrived in the People's Republic of China to begin fieldwork for my anthropological study of a middle school. After stepping off the airplane in a driving rain, I went to the baggage claim area, loaded my luggage onto a cart, and wheeled off toward the reception room to look for my host. As I came down the ramp leading into the reception room, a crowd of Chinese converged on me from either side. Perhaps they were looking for their arriving friends and family, but perhaps too, I'm sure, they were interested in looking at me. This was my first realization that I was to be an object of curiosity to the Chinese because I was an outsider and a foreigner.

I avoided going out of my room that first week, not a commendable way for an anthropologist to act but necessary if I was to avoid being stared at by anyone and everyone I would encounter once I went out. Eventually, I learned to tolerate being stared at and to accept that, being a foreigner, I would be on display in China.

I also came to realize that the converse is true: The Chinese are always on display for foreigners. They present themselves as they wish others to see them and try to hide what is unflattering. Western researchers have encountered this phenomenon when doing short-term or survey research in China. They are often taken to "model" institutions, rather than typical ones, and are presented with a description of the institution's functioning that derives more from ideology than from reality. Such model institutions and the accompanying ideological descriptions of them are certainly interesting and worthy of investigation in their own right, yet a complete picture of China requires going beyond the image presented. And to do this requires long-term and intensive observation and residence in China, since it is by living in China, and by interacting with the Chinese in their communities, that one can penetrate beyond the displays to an understanding of how the Chinese really live.

## The Subject and Methods of This Study

This is a study of an urban middle school in the People's Republic of China, based on my thirteen months of observation of, and participation in, the school's activities. I began research in September 1988, left China following the Beijing Massacre of June 4, 1989, and returned to complete my research in late August 1989. I left China at the completion of my research in late December 1989.

The school I studied, which I will call Third Affiliated Middle School ("Third Affiliated" for short), is affiliated with Northeast University, the name I will use for a nearby teacher training university. I lived in housing for foreigners located at Northeast University and went to Third Affiliated four or five days a week, throughout my stay in China. My activities at Third Affiliated were various. I volunteered to teach several hours of English conversation each week as an extracurricular activity for the students and teachers of the school, so each day that I went to the school, I would teach at least one such forty-five-minute class. Also, during many of the days I was there, perhaps the majority of days, I was allowed to be present at some of the school's activities. I observed dozens of classes in a variety of subjects; attended student meetings, schoolwide assemblies, teacher preparation meetings, parent–teacher conferences, and students' extracurricular activities; and interviewed twelve students each for one hour in one-on-one private sessions. I interviewed about the same number of teachers, teachers of a diversity of subjects, each also for about one hour in private sessions. All interviews with teachers and students were conducted in Mandarin Chinese and were tape recorded.

Thus, my observation of, and participation in, the functioning of Third Affiliated was both long-term and intensive, since I was at the school several days each week during a thirteen-month period. I observed virtually all the activities occurring at the school, except for meetings of the Communist Youth League (Gongqingtuan), at which foreigners are not allowed. Being a teacher of spoken English at Third Affiliated over this period further aided my understanding of Chinese education, since it allowed me to experience how students react to their teachers. Of course, their reactions to me were not identical to their reactions to teachers who are Chinese. However, I was a teacher at Third Affiliated long enough and often enough for much artificial behavior to subside. I am fairly certain that this happened because all my experiences at Third Affiliated contrasted markedly with those I had during brief visits to other schools. In the latter case the Chinese displayed their schools to me as they wanted me to see them. At Third Affiliated I saw much about a school that approximated the way it really is.

My one disappointment at Third Affiliated was in not being able to have more relaxed and candid interactions with students. This was partly because students saw me as a teacher, and hence the majority of them avoided me just as they avoid their other teachers. (However, there were a few students with whom I became good friends.) Also, the Chinese do not often talk without restraint with those who are not their contemporaries, and I was twenty-eight during my research, more than ten years older than most of my students. The fact that I was a foreigner undoubtedly also accounted for some of students' restraint in interacting with me. For these reasons, many students were too shy or unwilling to talk with me, especially in private, and this is why I was only able to find twelve students willing to be interviewed.

The situation with teachers was quite different. Many teachers were quite open in telling me about both the positive and negative aspects of their lives as teachers. I made friends with several teachers and spent a great deal of time, both at Third Affiliated and in social situations off campus, with two in particular (described in more detail below).

Other experiences outside Third Affiliated complemented my experiences inside the school. At Northeast University I took four graduate courses in private sessions with education professors from the university, so I was not only a teacher in China but a student as well. Also, I visited many different schools in Northeast City, the city in which Third Affiliated and Northeast University are located. Most of these were just daylong visits. But my visit to a countryside school (described in Chapter 8) lasted for three days, and I visited one Northeast City middle school for several days during the course of several weeks, talking with teachers and students and auditing classes in a variety of subjects. This Northeast City middle school, which I will call Marketplace Middle School, differed from Third Affiliated in that Third Affiliated is an elite middle school with select students, while Marketplace Middle School is an average middle school with fairly typical students and teachers (except that the school is a frequent destination for educators from outside the school because it has guided its students to high achievement levels relative to their average ability). Of course, the school leaders tried to present the school in its best light, but, as it happened, one of my Chinese friends had done his student teaching there and he told me some stories about the school that I would never have heard from its administrators.

Finally, since this study of Third Affiliated is anthropological, I was interested in the relationship between what happened inside Third Affiliated and the wider sphere of cultural values guiding the lives of the school's students and teachers. My daily experiences living in China thus formed an integral part of my research, since these enabled me to understand Chinese culture better. I made several friends in China who helped teach me about Chinese views and values. Interacting with them and their families also provided valuable insights.

### An Introduction to Third Affiliated

Third Affiliated is a single school campus composed of both a junior middle school *(chuzhong)* and a senior middle school *(gaozhong)*. The junior middle school, like American junior high schools, has three grades, with students ranging in age from twelve and thirteen years old in junior grade one to fourteen and fifteen years old in junior grade three. The senior middle school, likewise, has three grades, with students ranging from fifteen to eighteen years old. (The similarity to the U.S. educational system is not coincidental. The Chinese educational system has, since its inception, been inspired by, and modeled after, American, Soviet, and European educational systems. See Cleverley 1985: 50–53, 127–40).

Third Affiliated is located in one of China's largest cities (the location of which within China must be concealed so as to protect the anonymity of my informants), a city I refer to as Northeast City. The combined enrollment of the junior and senior middle school grades is about 1,600 students. One of the most important characteristics of Third Affiliated, important especially because of its influence on the nature of the student body, is that Third Affiliated is a keypoint *(zhongdian)* school, often abbreviated in English as "key school." Key schools in China are schools selected to receive exceptional financial resources from the governmental body that finances the school. Third Affiliated is the most elite type of key school, a national key school, since a significant portion of its budget comes from the national government. (Northeast University also gives money to the school.) As such, Third Affiliated has a reputation for being the best middle school in Northeast City. Attending the school is considered an honor and a privilege, and most parents I talked with hoped their children would be able to attend Third Affiliated or one of the few other Northeast City key schools of comparable repute.

Key schools have select student bodies, chosen through examination. In Northeast City all students wishing to enter senior middle school take a citywide exam. Those scoring at the top usually attend Third Affiliated. (It should be pointed out here that less than half the middle-school-age population in China attends middle school, with 10 percent or less of the senior-middle-school-age population in senior middle school. Alternatives to senior middle school include the agricultural, vocational, and technical schools, whose student populations are increasing to the point of being as large as those of the senior middle schools (see Ethridge 1990: 192–93.) These figures are for all of China, rural and urban. The percentages of school attendance for urban areas alone are higher.)

Until 1988 recruitment for Third Affiliated's junior middle school was also highly selective. However, the district government of the district of Northeast City in which Third Affiliated is located directed the junior middle school component of Third Affiliated to recruit students on the basis of residence, rather than test scores. Thus, beginning in the fall of 1988, students entering Third Affiliated's junior middle school were all neighborhood children, both those who were academically proficient and those who were not. This change in students has led to increased discipline problems in the junior middle school.

The methods described above for selecting students are the primary ones, but additional methods are also used to recruit a number of students. While students selected through the above methods pay no tuition and have to pay only for materials and textbooks, Third Affiliated also accepts paying students. Charges per semester for these students total about 300 yuan (at the time of my research, 3.7 yuan equaled one U.S. dollar), a very high tariff that only wealthy Chinese families could afford. Thus, most of the paying students (called *jiedusheng*) are children of cadres based in Northeast City; paying students comprise about 25 percent of the students at Third Affiliated's senior middle school. Quite often such students have not attained top scores on Northeast City's citywide test for entrance into senior middle school. They are less academically proficient than students recruited through the examinations, and they often cause many of the discipline problems at Third Affiliated, a situation that Third Affiliated administrators described to me without hesitation.

Since Third Affiliated is affiliated with Northeast University, the school allows the children of Northeast University employees to attend Third Affiliated's junior middle school (but not Third Affiliated's senior middle school, which does not have such unrestricted enrollment for children of Northeast University employees) without paying tuition. One final group of students is those whose parents use their influence to get their children accepted tuition-free at Third Affiliated. One informant told me that officials at the local electric company and those at the local water company have threatened to shut off Third Affiliated's electricity and water unless the school reserves several slots for children of the utilities' officials. Needless to say, Third Affiliated complied.

Third Affiliated students, thus, come primarily from high-status and educated backgrounds. While I was not able to obtain schoolwide statistics on students' backgrounds, I asked many students about their parents' occupations. With the exception of grades in junior middle school enrolling only students from the neighborhood (many of whom are children of workers and of uneducated petty merchants), over half of Third Affiliated students are children of intellectuals, that is, children of university professors or engineers. (In China engineers are considered to be intellectuals.) About a quarter are children of officials. The last 15–20 percent are children of workers. Students come from all over Northeast City; those who live too far to commute every day, about 10 percent, live in dormitories at the school.

### Academic and Extracurricular Activities at Third Affiliated

School is in session from early September through June, with three weeks off for the Chinese New Year. The school week runs Monday through Saturday. School at Third Affiliated starts at 7:40 A.M. (There are minor differences between the schedules of junior and senior middle school. Below I describe the schedule followed by senior middle school students). Class periods last for forty minutes each, with ten minutes between periods. (Students stay in the same classroom for all their classes—it is teachers who move to different classrooms.) There are five periods in the morning. After the third period all the students in the school leave their classrooms and line up on the school's athletic fields for morning exercises. These exercises last for twenty minutes. After the fourth period the students do eye exercises in their classrooms. These exercises consist of rubbing the eyes with one's fingers using various motions. Lunch period is at about noon. The school kitchen cooks lunch for the students. About half the students buy lunch at school and half go home for lunch. After eating their meal, students study, play ball, or take naps. (It is Chinese tradition to take a nap after lunch.) At about 2:00 P.M. students return to their classrooms and sing in unison for ten minutes. There are two periods during the afternoon and then about an hour of extracurricular activities. Extracurricular activities include calligraphy, Russian language classes, oral English drill, astronomy, and so on. Sports—volleyball, badminton, basketball, and soccer—are also popular activities with many students. By about 5:00 P.M. most students have gone home for the day. Students average about two hours of homework per night. Many students study very hard, but others, as teachers often complained to me, do not study very diligently and often do not do their homework.

As for the teachers, they teach two periods every day, specializing in certain subjects, but rotating yearly to teach in different grades.

A typical classroom and class period are as follows. The typical classroom is much like a traditional American classroom. All students, about sixty in an average class, are assigned seats at individual desks facing the front of the classroom, where the teacher stands to lecture. There are eight rows of desks running the length (that is, in rows parallel to the classroom's side walls) of the classroom. Every two rows of desks are pushed together so that each student is paired with one other student and so that there are four row groups (xiao zu). Each student is paired with another student of the same gender if possible and in some classrooms all boys are assigned seats in one half of the classroom, with all girls in the other half.

Class begins as the teacher walks into the classroom and a student leader in the back of the classroom calls out to the class: "Rise!" They stand, the teacher says, "Hello, students," and they reply perfunctorily in unison, "Hello, teacher." The traditional practice of teachers doing most of the talking, and students most of the listening, has been attacked by educational policymakers and some teachers have experimented with new methods (especially having students divide into small groups to discuss a given problem). Nonetheless, the traditional method—in which the teacher lectures and/or asks simple questions to which students respond in unison—remains the norm. Teachers will also ask questions of individual students, who stand up to answer.

Third Affiliated students, as is true of students throughout China, study a prescribed curriculum with no electives, and the textbooks students use are, for the most part, ones used throughout the country. Subjects students must study are Chinese, English, math, politics, physical education, physics, chemistry, biology, history, geography, drawing, and music. The one choice left to students is whether they will major in a humanities curriculum *(wenke)* or a science curriculum *(like)*. This choice is made at the start of senior grade two and determines the proportion of science or humanities courses taken. Most students choose a science curriculum because it is believed to be a better route to a good occupation.

Students are graded in courses and take tests. However, grades are not that important since they do not determine whether one can enroll in a university. Rather, college attendance in China depends on passing the nationwide college entrance examination *(gaokao)*. Each summer the test is given throughout China to all senior middle school graduates. Those who pass will be assured of acceptance to a university; those who score higher have a chance to attend more prestigious universities. Those who do not pass may take the test the following year. However, if they are unable to pass, they cannot go on to college. With only a degree from a (nonvocational) middle school, an individual most likely will not be able to find a job and may remain unemployed for several years. Those with college degrees, on the other hand, will be guaranteed to be assigned jobs. Thus, taking the college entrance exam is the central, and most important event in the life of Chinese students at such schools as Third Affiliated. Students study throughout middle school with the main goal being to pass the college entrance exam, and many students suffer a great deal of anxiety as the date of the exam approaches. The exam is also very significant for schools, which are largely judged based on the percentage of students from the school who pass the college entrance exam. While only about a quarter of all students throughout China taking the college entrance exam pass (Edwards and Sun 1988: 220), Third Affiliated administrators boasted to me that about three-quarters of their students pass each year. This is one of the main reasons for the school's reputation and for the desire of Northeast City parents that their children attend the school.

The college entrance exam is one major distinguishing feature of secondary Chinese education. The other is the way in which students are organized for classes and many extracurricular activities. During their three years in junior middle school students are grouped into classes *(ban;* because of the ambiguity involved in using the English word "class," *ban* is used wherever "class" would be ambiguous), groups of about sixty students who stay together for all of their classes during their three years in junior middle school. In senior middle school students once again are formed into *ban,* as in junior middle school. *Ban* not only have all classes together but also participate in many activities together. For example, *ban* compete against each other in athletic contests held after school. Each semester Third Affiliated students have a daylong trip to some scenic spot. These trips are organized by each *ban,* and students travel to the spot chosen by their *ban* with other *ban* members.

All concerns of the *ban*—academic, social, discipline, and emotional—are the ultimate responsibility of one teacher, the class teacher *(banzhuren).* The class teacher is a regular subject teacher who also takes on the responsibility for guiding one *ban* over the course of the three years students of the *ban* are together. If a student is having academic problems, it is the class teacher who will try to help the student. If a student causes problems for a given teacher, that teacher will often tell the student's class teacher and let the class teacher deal with the student.

The class teacher is assisted by student leaders drawn from the *ban.* These student leaders are chosen in an election held by the *ban* each semester. Each *ban* has a studies representative *(xuexi weiyuan)* who is in charge of the study habits of the students in the *ban* and who helps less capable students with their studies; a propaganda representative *(xuanchuan weiyuan)* to communicate important news from higher up and to supervise students in the writing of wall newspapers (a form of propaganda displayed on public walls); an arts representative *(wenyi weiyuan)* who leads *ban* arts and entertainment activities such as singing; a livelihood representative *(shenghuo weiyuan)* to supervise groups of students who take turns cleaning the *ban*'s classroom; and an athletics representative *(tiyu weiyuan)* to organize extracurricular sports activities. In addition, for each major academic subject there is a student representative. The leader for the entire *ban* is a student known as the class monitor *(banzhang)*. The class monitor supervises the other student leaders and runs the weekly meeting of the *ban*. The class monitor is assisted by the assistant class monitor *(fu banzhang)*.

### An Introduction to Key Personages

I interacted with many Chinese as their student, their teacher, their colleague, and/or their friend. Names, of course, have been changed, and I have altered a few minor biographical details to further protect the anonymity of these individuals.

At Third Affiliated I became friends with two teachers named, respectively, Wu Laoshi and Zhou Laoshi. (Wu and Zhou are their respective surnames and *laoshi* means "teacher." I will use this form of address to refer to these and other teachers throughout this study.) Wu Laoshi is a woman, age thirty-one, who teaches biology at Third Affiliated and Zhou Laoshi is a woman, age thirty-eight, who teaches history there. Wu and Zhou have, in many ways, contrasting personalities. Wu is outspoken, a trait that often lands her in trouble with the authorities. She complains a lot and becomes indignant and angry easily; she is also very determined and hard-working, though relaxed and open with her friends, with whom she enjoys laughing about her misfortunes. Zhou is soft-spoken and less revealing of negative feelings. She usually has an air of pleasant agreeableness to her, though I never saw her hesitate to politely but forcefully challenge a lazy student or a misguided bureaucrat. Her kindness, mixed with polite resolve when needed, is seen as a highly desirable combination of traits by the Chinese, and Zhou is very well respected by teachers, school leaders, and students.

I taught many different *ban* at Third Affiliated but I eventually arranged my teaching schedule so that I could spend the majority of my time teaching the senior grade one *ban* of the English teacher Xu Laoshi. Xu Laoshi's students spoke English especially well, and I got along well with them. The Chinese tend to interact with outsiders and foreigners by explicitly or implicitly designating a few representatives to broker between the group and the outsider, and this pattern was evident in my dealings with Xu Laoshi's *ban*. There were two students, the *ban*'s two best students in English, with whom I interacted the most. If I had requests to make of the *ban* or of other students in the *ban*, it was to one of these two students that I turned to make my requests. The two students were quite different in character, although they got along well with each other. Wang Jianjun is a male student who excels in all academic fields and is a good athlete as well. Excellence in a broad range of endeavors is highly valued by the Chinese, and Wang Jianjun's well-rounded competence earned him much respect from his teachers and peers. In addition, Wang Jianjun is both humble about his achievements and very willing to help his peers if they have problems, traits that are also highly prized in China. Shu Shizhe, a female student, is also very bright and excels in all academic fields. She is very similar to Wu Laoshi: always complaining and criticizing various situations and people at high voice volume and speed. But she often tempers her criticism with a laugh, and much of what she says has the character of black humor.

One day in the fall of 1988 a small, shy, very intelligent, and intense twelve-year-old boy at Third Affiliated came up to me and asked if we could become friends. I agreed, and every Sunday thereafter the boy, Xiao Liu, and I would meet to play Chinese chess and badminton, and talk. (Xiao, literally "little," is sometimes used with the surname as an informal and friendly means of referring to a young person. I will follow this pattern in referring to my friends.) He knew a great deal about other countries; in his curiosity to know more, he would question me for hours about the details of life in the United States.

My friends my own age, all students at Northeast University, came from a variety of backgrounds. Two were children of workers (Xiao Chen and Xiao Yang), one was the child of an intellectual (Xiao Li), and one was the child of peasants (Xiao Zhang). Xiao Chen, female, is an excellent student and, like Wu Laoshi and Shu Shizhe, is intensely critical. Unlike Shu Shizhe, however, Xiao Chen does not temper her criticisms with a laugh, so she frequently alienates her friends because she offends them and their sense of face. Xiao Yang is an affable young man who is unsatisfied with his life as it is and is determined to do whatever it takes to improve it. (Such a determination to improve one's life-style, especially one's standard of living, was very common among many Chinese university students I met.) Xiao Zhang and Xiao Li are typical of the traditional Chinese scholar-gentleman, a type of person the Chinese lament is rare in China today: very honest, studious, humble, and helpful to anyone in need. Like Zhou Laoshi, however, both of these young men, despite their humility, can be extremely forceful and unrelenting in fighting for what they perceive as just and moral.

## Previous Ethnographic Studies of Chinese Education

Over the past decade, with the relaxation of restrictions preventing long-term research by Western scholars in China, a number of ethnographic studies of Chinese schools have been conducted. Heidi Ann Ross made an ethnographic study of the Shanghai Foreign Language School, a key middle school devoted to providing foreign-language training for outstanding middle school students (Ross 1987). She taught English at the school and talked extensively with the school's teachers and students; these conversations provide the most important source of data for the study. A major focus concerns the constraints placed on the school's teachers and students. Ross describes how teachers' lives are controlled both inside the classroom—where they must adopt teaching methods and content dictated by the state—and outside—by a working unit that has the power, for example, to forbid them from quitting their jobs. She also describes how students are constrained by school rules forbidding such activities as romantic relationships, by formal student organizations that compel students to think and act in a prescribed manner, and by the numerous assemblies and campaigns held at the school to urge conformity to national political values. Since the school Ross describes is a language school, much of the study also focuses on the methods of teaching foreign languages at the school.

Another work is Tani Barlow and Donald Lowe's book about their experiences living in Shanghai and teaching at the Shanghai Teachers College (Barlow and Lowe 1987). The authors use their experiences living and teaching in China to analyze a broad range of social and cultural issues, including the relationship among power, knowledge, and the status of intellectuals; feminism; age and the Chinese life cycle; sexuality; and the nature and implications of the Cultural Revolution. One of the authors' central concerns is to portray the intellectual and literary life of their students—the disinterest and disillusionment with politics, the fascination with existentialism, the attraction to American ideas and values, and so on. This portrayal is detailed enough to illuminate larger issues. For example, the book shows how the students tended to dichotomize and polarize their feelings toward social entities and historical time periods, so that the Cultural Revolution is viewed as a time of complete insanity and America is fantasied as being a perfect paradise.

Howard Gardner adds a valuable dimension to the study of Chinese education with his ethnographic account of arts education in China (Gardner 1989). Although his research is based on numerous brief visits to different classes and different schools rather than intensive, long-term observation at one school, the descriptions of classes are quite rich in detail. From his observations he draws several conclusions about Chinese arts education and Chinese education more generally: first, that class often resembles a highly polished performance; second, that teaching is seen as the transmittal of knowledge from the teacher to students; third, that the Chinese emphasize mastery of basic skills rather than creativity.

Several earlier books, while based on interviews with refugees rather than ethnographic fieldwork at a site in the People's Republic of China, deserve to be mentioned because of their highly detailed account of aspects of Chinese schooling. Jonathan Unger's book, which describes the years before, during, and after the Cultural Revolution, looks at shifts in the criteria used to determine which secondary students would be admitted to the Communist Youth League and to the university, and shows how students from different class backgrounds were pitted against each other in competition over college and Youth League admission (Unger 1982). Susan Shirk's book is similar to Unger's, as it too portrays the tension between different criteria used for university admission and the way in which competition for university admission affected secondary school students' relationships and their social strategies in the pre–Cultural Revolution era (Shirk 1982). Martin King Whyte describes the different kinds of group meetings held in pre–Cultural Revolution schools, their intended role in national political indoctrination, and the ways students sometimes manipulated the political rituals for their own purposes (Whyte 1974). Finally, several books have provided case studies examining conflicts between students and teachers, and among students, during the Cultural Revolution. Such works include Stanley Rosen (1982), Gao Yuan (1987), and Gordon Bennett and Ronald Montaperto (1980).

## Topics Covered in This Study

In this study I report Chinese cultural orientations I found to be particularly important in Chinese social life and the way in which these orientations are manifested in the experiences of students and teachers at Third Affiliated Middle School. In Chapter 2 I describe the major events I witnessed and the observations I made early in my stay in China that led me to form some of the conclusions central to this study. The chapter presents two related patterns: the centrality of evaluation and the centrality of criticism in Chinese culture. One aspect of criticism I note is the tendency among those of inferior status to criticize those of superior status. This phenomenon, and an analysis of the cultural values underlying it, is a major focus of my study. Since criticism of superiors was encouraged by Maoist ideology and practiced during the Cultural Revolution, a valid question is whether criticism of superiors really has any roots at all in Chinese tradition and culture. Chapter 3 reviews the literature on evaluation and criticism in China, showing that these orientations, and an ideology and practice of criticism of superiors both in society and in the classroom, can be found not just in Maoist China, but in traditional China as well. In light of Chapter 3, Chapter 4 considers the cultural foundations for criticism of superiors. I discuss the Chinese construct of face and how face leads to the legitimatization of the evaluation of others, even if those others are of higher status. Chapter 5 focuses on these issues in the classroom, as I analyze how face, criticism, and evaluation figure in educational pedagogy and discipline at Third Affiliated. Chapter 6 deals with socialization in the home, especially the role of criticism and face in parents' strategies for raising their children. Chapter 7 is on emotions. I discuss which emotions are prominent in the lives of teachers and students, what methods are employed in helping emotionally troubled youth, and how characteristics of Chinese culture help explain Chinese emotions and the nature of the response to troubled youth. Finally, in Chapter 8 I consider the relevance of my findings on Third Affiliated for a more general understanding of Chinese culture and education. I end by comparing the results of this study on face in China with those of anthropologists' studies of other cultures where face and shame are prominent. I argue that there is a paradox of power in cultures where face and shame are prominent and that this paradox accounts for why inferiors in such cultures have certain powers of evaluation, criticism, and shame that they can effectively use against their superiors.

\* \* \*

Note that the present-tense descriptions throughout this book pertain to educational policies and procedures for the years 1988–89.

# 2

## Evaluation and Criticism in Education and Social Life

### The Interest in Evaluation among the Chinese

Once, in a relaxed moment, I showed a set of photographs of my home and family to a Chinese friend. After looking through them and appreciating them, he told me he wanted to go back and rank them since, he explained, the Chinese believe that even among a set of good things, such as these pictures, one is the best, and some are better than others.

My friend's desire to rank my snapshots demonstrated what I had already observed since the start of my research: the fundamental role of evaluation in the lives of the Chinese. The Chinese spend a great deal of time determining who (or what) is the best and who is not. Such determinations are carried out informally, as by my friend, and formally, during the many competitions held to judge who excels at one activity or another. The competitive process generates excitement, as do the frequent discussions about how various people and things are ranked.

One incident exemplifying the intensity of excitement surrounding the evaluative process occurred at Third Affiliated during a performance of English-language plays written by students themselves. The students performed their plays before an audience of all the students in their grade and before three judges charged with ranking the plays from best to worst. I was one of the three judges. As the performance began, a large group of students huddled around me, watching eagerly to see how I scored their classmates. Each time I gave a score, the students surrounding me would all react to my evaluation. These discussions and debates (students not infrequently disagreed with my judgments) were loud, numerous, and spontaneous, a clear indication of the degree of interest in my evaluations.

Such interest in evaluation is quite common. As I began to teach English to students, I had them ask me questions. In almost every class there was one student who wanted to know which I thought was better, Chinese or American education. This was a question I was even asked during a lecture I gave to some university professors and graduate students. My friends were also often anxious to know how Americans ranked various things. Many people asked me which American universities were top-ranked, and they easily listed for me the top-ranked Chinese universities when I asked them this question. Sometimes I was asked who the best American educator was, or the best American anthropologist, and I was not sure how to answer. This confused my friends, and even upset them, since they said the Chinese all knew who was top-ranked for any given endeavor and they could not understand how an American could not know how things were ranked in his culture.

Soon after my arrival in China, people began instructing me in the relative merits of people and things. Our driver, I was told, was the best at the university. Third Affiliated was one of the best schools in the province. As I entered a roomful of students to coach them in English conversation, their teacher loudly identified for me and for them who had scored the highest on the English test. Another teacher recruited a student to accompany me to the bus stop and, as he approached, she made sure to tell me that his overall scores were only average.

As all of the above examples except the last suggest, the Chinese are especially interested in talking about those who are top-ranked and famous. Friends and acquaintances never failed to point out to me who (or what) was the best in a given category, and they talked about the merits of superlative people or things with near reverence.

### The Social Significance of Merit

The reason that evaluative rankings interest the Chinese so much is that they are very socially significant. Chinese status is in large part based on, and legitimated by, merit. Students often told me that they will listen to their student leaders at the school only if the leaders excel in whatever it is (academics, athletics, or the arts) that they are leading. It is commonly assumed that merit is a prerequisite to the ability to lead and influence people. Zhou Laoshi told me, for example, that the class monitor in one *ban* with which she was familiar was having a hard time organizing any activities, since he was a mediocre student and therefore could not persuade his peers to accept his leadership.

Even when there are other factors besides merit—such as age, gender, or political orientation—that are probably the real criteria for high status, the ostensible justification is often given in terms of merit. This appeal to merit was especially clear among Third Affiliated English teachers. Many older English teachers were clearly inferior in their knowledge of English to younger English teachers, because the older ones had studied Russian and only learned English by themselves after English replaced Russian in the Chinese middle school curriculum. Nonetheless, they clearly were the leaders among the English teachers. An older teacher was head of the English language department, and older teachers periodically required their younger colleagues to give open classes, so that the older teachers could evaluate and critique the teaching methods of their younger colleagues. Whenever I asked younger English teachers why older teachers, whose English was often mediocre at best, were called on to judge them, I was told that the school leaders felt that the years of teaching experience necessarily made the older teachers better. Furthermore, their grasp of English grammar was assumed to be better because of their long tenure, even though their actual oral English skills were clearly lacking. While it was quite evident that age was what gave the older teachers their status, deference to their merit—to their "experience" and excellent grasp of grammar—was the rationale usually given.

Since merit helps entitle one to a position of leadership, and justifies that position once attained, many Chinese lead a determined pursuit to cultivate their merits and have them publicly recognized. Fame, the public recognition of merit, therefore becomes a prime goal. The desire to be ranked highly and to become famous, though frequently unstated, stimulated the majority of people and institutions I came to know in China. Whenever I visited a school in China, its leaders, after an obligatory display of modesty usually consisting of a recounting of the school's earlier failures, would cautiously detail the school's current successes and high place in the rankings. Success was often measured in terms of the numbers of famous graduates the school had, since their personal fame was proof of the school's excellence. Telling a foreigner about the school's successes was an important event, since this, it was hoped, would spread the school's reputation abroad. In fact school administrators often commented among themselves in my presence, barely concealing their pride, that having an American hear about their merits was bound to make their school famous in America.

This desire for one's group to become top-ranked and famous operates at many levels in China. In fact the most common conversation I had in China, and one that I had with both intellectuals and workers (but more often with men than with women), was about the economic standing of various countries and the hope that China could move to the top of these rankings. Upon meeting someone in China they would usually talk at great length about America's premier economic status and express their longing for a similar high ranking for China. They easily admitted China's current inferior economic position but felt, as one student told me after such an admission, that China really should be number one.

Fame is a goal of individuals too, so teachers often use the prospect of fame to motivate their students. Xiao Yang told me that if a class teacher had a student who did not pass the college entrance exams, he or she might console the student by saying something like, "That's okay. Maybe you can still become a famous singer." Cultivating "talents," by observing the areas in which a student excels and then encouraging him in these endeavors, is the class teacher's most important duty, according to one experienced class teacher with whom I talked. Parents were especially eager to guide their children to fame. Third Affiliated once arranged for me to visit a former student who had won an international math award so that I could learn how Third Affiliated had cultivated his ability. I was accompanied by Zhou Laoshi, who later told me she wanted to learn what that student's parents had done to develop their son's talent, so that she could try the same with her six-year-old son. I later found out that Third Affiliated had engaged the mother of that student to give lectures to Third Affiliated parents on how they could guide their children to fame.

### Evaluation in Schools

The evaluative nature of Chinese culture, and the emphasis on fame, extends into the schools in unexpected ways. Not only are students evaluated, but the objects being studied are sometimes evaluated. In some contexts, and some subjects, determining who is good—learning who is good—becomes the goal of the class. Study that does not lead to an evaluative appraisal of something, or someone, is thought to be useless, as my graduate student friend Xiao Zhang told me.

I first became aware of this Chinese view of learning through misunderstandings about the aims of my own research. Despite my repeated claims to the contrary, my university advisors, Third Affiliated administrators and teachers, and my Chinese friends all thought that I had come to China to evaluate Chinese education and, finding it good, to spread news of its merits to America. For them research consisted of the evaluation of an object of study, and, in particular, the analysis of the merits of a virtuous object of study. My advisor at Northeast University, Shu Laoshi, arranged for me to visit "good" schools, and during these visits he would point out for me the many virtues of the particular school we were visiting. Sometimes other educational researchers would come on these visits too, as part of their own research, and their comments and questions showed that their own research was oriented toward discovering and reporting the virtues of each school we visited.

The Chinese view of learning and research is, thus, consistent with the evaluative nature of Chinese society. Research methods reinforce a social system largely based on merit, since the role of researchers is to help report the merits of the meritorious, thereby augmenting the merit-based reputations that earn status for an individual.

### Research as the Acclaim of the Virtuous

One particularly good example of the above view of research was an academic conference I attended in November 1988. The conference, which was held on the Northeast University campus and drew participants from all over China, was devoted entirely to the study of Tao Xingzhi, a major Chinese educator active in China during the first part of the twentieth century. What made the conference so different from a Western academic conference was that the participants did not take turns giving talks on various aspects of Tao's life and works. Instead, they took turns extolling Tao himself. One speaker listed all the famous people who had studied either with Tao or in schools he had established. Another speaker called on to summarize the results of the conference said with a great flourish, as if making a proclamation, that he had realized in the course of the conference that Tao was indeed a great man, even greater than Confucius himself. A common observation made by many was that for such a great man, Tao was not very well known. They felt that he should become better known in China and throughout the rest of the world, and they urged the conference participants to do more to propagandize (the word used was *xuanchuan*, which has less of a negative connotation than the English word "propaganda") Tao, in order to make his greatness more widely known. One participant even submitted a paper, the topic of which was how to propagandize Tao.

### Evaluation in Teaching

The following example, perhaps less obviously than the above example, shows how teaching and learning can be directed toward evaluating a famous person's work. It is taken from a graduate education class held at Northeast University. In the class were three graduate students and their teacher. The topic of conversation was the educational thought of John Dewey. In the selection below one student raises criticisms of Dewey's work that the professor, who admires Dewey, attempts to answer. (Due to poor recording conditions, it was not possible to transcribe this section word for word, even with the help of native informants. It has been transcribed nearly word for word, however, and I am confident that the text below captures the essence of the conversation.)

Student: Dewey talks about "education as growth" but "growth" suggests the individual, his environment, and so on. They're all natural things [versus education, which this student feels belongs to the domain of man and society]. So this "education as growth" [*she clicks with her tongue, the way the Chinese do to soften a sensitive conclusion*] just isn't quite right.

Teacher (in a patient, clarifying tone of voice): "Education as growth" means [that education] stimulates and accelerates the child's own, inborn abilities.

Student: I believe by "education" he actually means an external power that can develop what a child already possesses.

Teacher (correcting the student): He especially emphasizes internal things, not external things.

Student: Dewey says education is a kind of stimulus. This stimulus still plays a kind of external role, right?

Teacher: But this stimulus takes the child's inherent things as its base.

After a few more speaking turns the student raises a new criticism of Dewey. She says that his thought was too impractical and could never be put into effect in China or in America. The teacher admits that Dewey's ideals were not easily realized, but he says that Dewey is still renowned and influential:

Teacher: It is very difficult [to implement Dewey's ideals], very difficult. But there are still people in America who experiment with his ideas. In America Dewey's thought is rising and falling in popularity. One minute he's criticized, but the people who criticize him draw from his thinking. Dewey's influence is still great in America, and hasn't disappeared.

In the above passages a student negatively evaluates various aspects of Dewey, and the teacher patiently and with care refutes her points, suggesting that Dewey's thought really is valuable. He not only asserts its intrinsic value but also reiterates that Dewey is still influential in America. In this way he guides his students in the positive appraisal of Dewey and their recognition of his lasting renown.

### Studying as Studying the Good

Teachers, then, like researchers in China, reinforce the merit-based definition of status, since a common approach they use is to teach students to identify the merits of those considered meritorious. For many researchers and students alike, then, studying means studying the good.

This concept is actually reflected in the way the word "study" *(xue)* is used in Chinese. It can be used in a manner similar to the English word, to denote what students do. But it also has another meaning: "to analyze the merits of a meritorious person, and model your behavior after his." Parents or teachers, for example, will often point out a good student to a group of children, and then tell them to "study" from him, that is, learn how he has succeeded, and then do the same. The fact that both meanings are represented by the same word suggests that the first type of study, what students do, is often more like the second, evaluative, type.

This is not to say that all instances of teaching and research that I observed in China follow the same pattern. Math and the sciences, for example, are not taught using evaluation of their subject matter (though there is a heavier emphasis in such fields than in American science teaching on categorization, on assigning things to groups, and it is difficult to resist the temptation to see in this a reflection of another feature of Chinese social relations: the strong predisposition to assign people to designated groups). Evaluation is used to teach those subjects that have the greatest social consequences, particularly politics. In fact educational conventions allowing for evaluation in the teaching process, and the acclaim of those with merit, are very helpful in the Chinese government's efforts at political socialization. This is because values can be taught, and heroes worshiped, and it can all be done in the name of study and education. And to be able to claim that people have learned certain political values, rather than having had them forced upon them, is a much more effective way to ensure people's political allegiance.

## The Negative Side of Evaluation: Criticism in China

While those Chinese who excel—or, more precisely, who are judged to excel—win praise and fame, and the extolling of their virtues by even the educational system, those who do not excel often become the targets of negative evaluation and criticism. Since public reputation is so highly regarded, the threat to destroy it is a potent weapon, and virtually anyone can attack someone else by criticizing him, thereby challenging the reputation for merit on which his status is based. Criticism thus acts as a social leveler, since someone who unjustifiably tries to rise above the crowd can be criticized by the crowd, simultaneously thwarting his reputation and elevation in status; it is also used as a more general means of social control by institutions, authority figures, and parents, whose criticism of those under their authority is a kind of negative sanction. Criticism, then, complements positive evaluation, and it plays a similarly central role in Chinese culture.

Criticism takes a variety of forms and can be described by many different Chinese words, but the most commonly used word is *"piping,"* which translates as "to criticize." *Piping* means to express one's negative evaluation of a person to his face, with or without others present. The person may be criticized for his personal characteristics, behavior and actions, or performance of some endeavor, but a negative evaluation of his performance is only *piping* if it is a personal condemnation of the person and his ability. Thus, if a teacher tells a student in class that the student answered incorrectly, this may or may not be criticism, depending on the teacher's tone of voice. If, for example, the teacher tells the student the answer is wrong in such a way as to imply that the student is stupid, this may be considered criticism. Telling a student that his behavior is bad or inappropriate, such as telling him not to talk during class, is much more clearly *piping,* since it is necessarily the teacher's own negative assessment and condemnation of the student's actions.

Another common phrase is *"you yijian,"* which means "to have complaints." Unlike *piping,* in which the act is defined as publicizing one's complaints to their subject, Chinese speakers use *you yijian* to mean that they have complaints, whether or not they reveal them. Two other similar expressions are *"shuo huai hua,"* literally, "say bad things" (about somebody), and *"yilun,"* "talk about" (somebody or something, frequently meaning in a critical manner). Both of these are used to refer to the process of talking negatively about someone, usually behind his back.

Finally, there are the words *"ma"* and *"pipan." Ma,* "to scold or rebuke in an abusive manner," is, like *piping,* a negative evaluation of someone, but it is much more of an intentionally abusive act, and so the word *"ma"* has much more of a negative connotation than does *"piping." Pipan* is also a kind of criticism but more the kind represented by the word "critique." Whenever a Chinese theorist's thought falls from official favor, people will say that it has become the victim of governmental *pipan.*

In analyzing criticism the most important distinction to make is between open, public criticism and criticism or complaints told to the subject in private, or discussed in a private setting behind his back.

Because reputation cannot really be challenged if the criticism takes place in private, private criticism is common and does not pose as much of a threat (although the boundary between being criticized or complained about by a private group of people, and being publicly denounced, is ambiguous, so many leaders *do* worry about what is being said about them in private groups). Public criticism, by contrast, is potent and used sparingly, so as not to diminish its effect through overuse.

## *Criticism of Superiors by Their Inferiors*

In private, among friends, the Chinese complain and criticize quite frequently. Targets of criticism are often powerful persons or institutions. Ironically, I became aware of this tendency in the United States while observing my Chinese teacher, a Chinese woman who had been born in Beijing, and moved to Taiwan as a child and to the United States as an adult. A seemingly respectful, middle-aged woman who was an assistant in my Chinese class, she shocked me by saying some very negative things about her boss, our American professor, one day. She seemed to have no hesitation about letting her criticism of his ability be known to us, his (and her) students.

Much to my surprise I observed many similar cases in China in which those of inferior status criticized their superiors. (Since the English terminology having to do with criticism is not as rich as the Chinese, "criticize" and "criticism" are used loosely below in order to signify the various Chinese meanings described. Thus, "criticize" refers both to negative comments made behind someone's back and to negative comments made to them directly.) Criticism usually took place in nonpublic settings. It was very common for a small group of friends to sit around and complain about and critique their superior, who was not present. Sometimes an individual would go to a target of negative evaluation and, in private, make his critique known. Less often, an individual would criticize his superior in public. In all three situations, however, criticisms were made directly and boldly. The more people present as audience to the criticism, the more of an indignant and challenging air the criticizer assumed.

I observed criticism of a wide range of superiors: teachers, government officials, and family members. A memorable example was my twelve-year-old friend Xiao Liu's critique of a family member. Once when we were discussing China's population problems, Xiao Liu admitted that his father's older sister's daughter had given birth to a second child, in violation of China's one-child policy. Even though his cousin was nearly old enough to be his parent, Xiao Liu said he "scolded" *(ma)* her for having a second child, and he scolded her in the presence of her brother (Xiao Liu's father). In telling me this story Xiao Liu, a normally shy, studious boy, became quite angry and indignant about his relative's irresponsibility.

A very common target of criticism was the Chinese government. Throughout my research, both before the 1989 protests and after, the failings of the national government were a favorite topic of discussion. And as I found with any instances of evaluation in China, such discussions were of great interest to their participants. My Chinese friends were particularly excited to have me as an audience as they took turns describing for me the ills of the government—the government's failure to support education adequately, corruption and the need to have connections to get things done, China's mediocre economic development and the government's failure to solve this problem, and so on.

### Criticism of Teachers

Criticism of teachers was equally common. I was especially surprised, as were all the Westerners teaching English at Northeast and other universities, when our students or others came and criticized us and our teaching. Such criticism was not gentle, either. On the contrary, it was very direct and almost challenging, with the implied assumption that, once told, we surely had no choice but to mend our ways. One young American teacher I know was quite taken aback when representatives from his class showed up at his apartment halfway through the semester (the usual time for such visits) to present the class's decision that they write fewer papers. He tried telling them that only he should make that decision, but the representatives warned him that class attendance might dwindle (as it had for other American teachers in previous years) if he did not make amends. Another young teacher said she felt there was a certain arrogance to the students' demands, and a conviction in their correctness.

My students were equally bold in their critiques. Shortly after the first time I taught English to one class, a representative from the class approached me in private and, without any hesitation or embarrassment, told me the questions I asked to elicit discussion were too difficult, that many students felt they could not answer them, and that the students would rather play English-language games. Another class's regular English teacher turned to me one day before the start of the period and said that I was covering too little material per class period. A senior middle school grade two student in the front row, overhearing the conversation, indicated his agreement by saying, in a complaining tone of voice, "Too little. Too little." Wang Laoshi, a young Chinese literature teacher who was friends with many of the young teachers in my oral English class for teachers, told me in private, but quite directly, that the teachers were dissatisfied with the way I was teaching, and were losing interest.

Most teachers were subjected to some form of criticism (though, as discussed in Chapter 5, younger teachers, and females, were much more likely to be criticized), and virtually all students criticized their teachers. In fact, when I first began asking informants what kind of students criticized teachers, my informants expressed puzzlement at my question since, they told me as if I should have known better, all students criticize their teachers. Many of them criticize the teacher behind his back, and some go to him directly and ask him to change his approach. It is even common for students to go to the principal and complain about a teacher and request that the teacher be replaced by someone more competent. Regardless of the form criticism takes, I always found students to be forceful and direct in their critique, and unapologetic for making their complaints known.

During my first few months in China I witnessed a vivid example of student criticism during a meeting of students called together to evaluate their teachers *(pingjiao pingxue)*. Such meetings are held at Third Affiliated about halfway through every semester. At the meeting I attended there were about twenty students present (boys and girls) representing each of the *ban* in senior middle school grade one. The woman who called the meeting, and who sat at the head of the table chairing it, was a Third Affiliated administrator interested in collecting students' opinions of their classes and teachers. When each semester is over, students fill out written evaluations of all their teachers, but Third Affiliated administrators wanted to meet with student leaders as well, to hear opinions in person.

At first there was a certain shyness among attendees at the meeting—maybe due to my presence. Two boys who arrived late hesitated to enter the room, and the administrator had to coax them to come in. Students initially were not willing to talk, and laughed nervously. But the uneasiness soon passed, and the students engaged in unrestrained criticism. Each time the administrator mentioned a different class and teacher for evaluation, students would begin their criticisms. Their evaluative statements were always negative, with not one teacher being praised, and the students, contrary to their playful argumentativeness with each other outside class, never seemed to disagree with each other during this meeting. Students generally talked all at once, and some students talked among themselves, apparently complaining to each other, periodically coming back into the conversation. The few times that people paid attention were when one particular girl spoke. She had a very whiny voice and was the most vocally critical. She would begin a sentence at one pitch, and then restart the sentence at a higher pitch, a speaking pattern used, especially by women, to communicate overall dissatisfaction with something. The intensity of this girl's criticism seemed to attract and hold everyone's interest, since they would stop talking among themselves, and look at and listen to her whenever she spoke.

Following are some sample criticisms. About the computer class: "Totally uninteresting." "We can't comprehend class." "Makes some students fall asleep." "We don't get a thing out of it." About history: "Lacking in new content." They complained that the physics teacher skipped around too much, complained that the English test was too hard and included grammar they had not covered, and complained that they were overworked and got home too late at night. For each class there would often be one student who would say with exasperation: "We just can't bear it!"

The woman administrator listened to what students said and took notes, and was generally solicitous and supportive of their complaints. For example, they complained that one science teacher has his own methodology, and never listens to students' views. To this, she responded, with exaggerated patience, that they should try explaining to the teacher that there is more than one method, and so he should consider the students' suggestions. At the end of forty-five minutes, she thanked the students and told them she would pass on their criticisms to the teachers involved.

## The Public Criticism of Superiors

Not accidentally, all the examples cited thus far took place in nonpublic settings—among a small circle of friends or between one person and the target of his criticism.

Inferiors do criticize their superiors publicly as well, but such occurrences are not as common. Nevertheless, instances of the public criticism of superiors by their inferiors are highly socially significant, because public condemnation can destroy a high-status person's most valuable attribute: his reputation. In fact, it is because public criticism is so threatening that it is infrequently used, and only when really needed.

Perhaps one of the best recent examples of public criticism took place when Wuer Kaixi, one of the leaders of the 1989 student movement in Beijing, met with Chinese Premier Li Peng on May 18, 1989. The meeting, which was televised, began with comments by Li Peng in which he noted the youthfulness of Wuer Kaixi and the other students with whom he was meeting. Youth are generally expected to be subordinate to their elders in China, so Li Peng's comments were undoubtedly meant to remind the students of their position. Despite the inferiority of the students' status, Wuer Kaixi interrupted the premier at this point in the conversation, shouting at him that there wasn't time for such talk (Han and Hua 1990: 242; Yi and Thompson 1989: 168–69).

Because the presence of a foreigner in an audience makes a public situation even more public, I rarely had the opportunity to witness a student openly criticizing a teacher. But I am aware of the following two instances. The first happened to me one day when due to scheduling confusion I arrived five minutes late to a Third Affiliated class I was supposed to teach. As I walked into the classroom, a male student called out, "You're late." The second was told to me. One day a young, female Third Affiliated teacher said in class that most members of the Communist Party are bad. A male student, whose father is a party member, stood up and said, directly, "Teacher, you are wrong." He then said she had "gone crazy." The teacher cried all day and night. Hearing this, the class teacher for that class went to the boy's father and told him what his son had done. The father went and saw the teacher and apologized to her for his son's actions. The class teacher also talked to the boy directly to see if he would apologize, but he would not, since he still maintained that the teacher was wrong in what she had said.

## *Chinese Views on Criticizing Superiors*

A very important question to ask is to what extent the criticism of superiors by inferiors is accepted in China. That is, to what extent is it considered normal, or even appropriate behavior, rather than the behavior of maladjusted individuals? The conventional image of Chinese society as hierarchical might at first lead one to conclude that criticism of superiors would be intolerable. While the conventional image of a hierarchical Chinese society is correct in many ways, the boldness of challenges to superiors, and the frequency of criticisms of them behind their backs, suggest the need for a finer analysis.

When I first noticed that students could be very critical of their teachers, and quite bold when they came to them privately to complain about their teaching methods, I decided to ask some teachers I knew how they felt about students who came and criticized them, expecting that they must surely find such students annoying. Instead, most teachers told me that they really like students who criticize them privately. They explained that teachers know all students are criticizing them, so they regard those who are willing to reveal their complaints directly to their faces as their friends. They see this as evidence of having gained the trust of these students. Students confirmed this view. They told me that it is usually the good students and those with good relationships with their teachers who will approach them with complaints. In an atmosphere of widespread criticism, direct, private criticism becomes a friendly act when compared with its alternative.

But what is the view of public criticism of teachers? This is a very complex and important issue, which will be taken up in greater detail in Chapter 4. In essence, there are covert and overt values that encourage those of inferior status to criticize their superiors. There is a very strong emphasis placed on anyone's right to criticize anyone else if that person's views or actions are "wrong" or bad. Part of this emphasis derives from modern Chinese political movements, since the Communists have often sought to fight their opponents by defining their views and actions as "wrong," and encouraging the disenfranchised to criticize these "wrongs." But there is a cultural dimension to this phenomenon as well. Inferiors and superiors are allowed, even expected, to appraise each other, and this means that if the evaluation is a negative one, and negative enough, it can be expressed publicly. Those who step out of line can be criticized publicly, whether from above or below.

## Criticism from Above

Criticism from above means the use or threatened use of criticism by powerful individuals or institutions to discipline and punish those under their authority. Although criticism is used in many institutions—schools, the workplace, the political arena, and the family—as a means of social control, this section is primarily concerned with criticism in the schools (its use in other domains will be treated in later chapters).

When teachers encounter discipline problems in their classes, there are a number of things they can do. Some—such as fining students, terminating class early, awarding prizes to the most disciplined class (see Chapter 5 below)—do not directly involve criticism. But in many cases criticism is central to control.

As discussed above, it is necessary to distinguish between private, individual criticism, and public criticism. Criticism of a student in front of other students makes a student feel a loss of face, a very serious emotional injury in China, so public criticism is reserved for only major offenses. This means, for example, that if a student is talking during class, considered a relatively minor offense, the teacher will be reluctant to criticize the student by name. Rather, the teacher will often say something like, "There are some classmates talking in class, and this makes it very difficult for other students to hear." Or, the teacher may choose to criticize the student privately. Sometimes the teacher will approach the student after class, outside the classroom, and reprimand him. Many teachers, however, prefer to notify the student's class teacher, since the class teacher is the one ultimately responsible for all discipline problems of the class (even including any discipline problems arising while some other teacher is teaching). The class teacher then might criticize the offending student in private.

The exact course of such private criticisms depends on the offense and on the discipline habits of the teacher. There has been much advocacy in modern China of the need to temper the absolute authority of teachers, and one proposed reform has been for teachers to "talk reason"(jiang daoli) with minor offenders. Many Third Affiliated teachers used this approach in their private criticisms of students. Often the teacher, or class teacher, would bring up "reason," usually the unquestioned assumption that the student's highest goal (and that of his parents and teachers as well) was his or her future academic success, primarily acceptance into an elite university. The teacher might then simply say that being unruly during class was clearly antithetical to this goal, thus demonstrating the negative implications of the student's behavior.

Not all teachers would "talk reason" with a student. For many teachers, the potency and power of criticism in China was reflected in the potency and power of their manner when criticizing. Some teachers could be quite fierce when criticizing—other teachers and students would point them out to me, and I could well imagine their ferocity. But the following incident, told to me by a friend, serves best to illustrate just how critical teachers can be toward their students.

At Marketplace Middle School (see Chapter 1) teachers had a practice wherein if one teacher began to criticize a student in the teachers' office, any teachers present could join in the criticism. A female student once passed a note to another girl in class, asking to borrow meal tickets. The class teacher, a middle-aged woman known for her strictness, discovered the note passing and had the girl come to the teachers' office, where my friend just happened to be sitting. The class teacher made the girl face the wall and then criticized her in a very harsh, scolding tone: "You're the only one in the class who broke the rule against writing notes and the only one to think of eating during class [implying the girl's selfishness, considered a highly negative trait]. May you die of hunger!" The class teacher then turned to another teacher present in the office and said with disgust, "Her mother doesn't control her [the student]." That teacher then concurred: "I know her mother. Her mother is just like her, overly bold [boldness is generally a male virtue, so this implies an attack on the mother's and the daughter's femininity] and disobedient [also usually considered to be a male trait]." Yet another teacher present in the office chimed in: "That kind of student [referring to the "disobedient" girl] should be made to stay here. You shouldn't let her go home for lunch. Let's just see if she dares to act up again in the future." In the end, they did not let the girl go home for lunch, and she was reduced to tears.

Wondering if teachers at an elite key school such as Third Affiliated would refrain from the harsh criticisms used by teachers at non-key Marketplace Middle School, I decided to talk with Wu Laoshi. Wu refuted my hypothesis, citing specific examples of harsh Third Affiliated teachers. Only some teachers are as unyielding in their criticisms as the Marketplace teachers described above, but every school, Wu assured me, has at least some such teachers.

## Self-Criticism

Another way in which criticism is used for discipline is the self-criticism *(jiantao)*. The self-criticism, as its name implies, is an admission of one's wrongdoing, and a promise to avoid making similar mistakes in the future. The person responsible for punishing the student (usually the class teacher) will make the student write down his self-criticism. It may then be given to the teacher in whose class the student was unruly. Or the class teacher may make it public, by having the student write it in a place for all at the school to see (Third Affiliated had public blackboards, on which students were sometimes required to write their self-criticisms), or by compelling the student to read his self-criticism in class. Self-criticism's value as a form of punishment lies in the fact that the student is not only criticized, but criticized by himself. Of course, since students must write the self-criticism whether they want to or not, they are usually not sincere in their admission of wrongdoing, but this does not seem to matter. What matters is that they are made to give the appearance of a confession, a confession that is often made public. What the student believes in his heart, yet never makes known to others, may soothe his psyche somewhat, but it cannot repair his all-important public reputation.

I was able to obtain a copy of a self-criticism written by a Third Affiliated student that contains many common characteristics of such documents. It was written by a student who swore at a teacher in class when she called on him to answer a question. The teacher did not criticize the student during class, but afterward she described the incident to the boy's class teacher, who then had him write the following self-criticism for his teacher. I have translated it below:

> Teacher X (teacher's name):
> Last Friday during your class you [the student uses the polite form of "you"] called on me to answer a question. I, however, could not answer. At that time you kind-heartedly advised me that I must study diligently, yet underneath I was still reluctant, and offhandedly said some dirty words. At that time, even though you were angry, you continued class so as not to interfere with class for other students. I, however, did not understand the teacher's [Teacher X] frame of mind, and didn't pay any attention to you. Today, after Teacher Y [the student's class teacher] talked with me, only then did I realize that my behavior at the time was

truly excessive, truly disrespectful to the teacher, indeed the kind of behavior that makes people mad. I hope you won't be too angry, and I earnestly ask you to let me continue coming to your class, forgiving me this time. From now on, during your class I will earnestly pay attention, and will remedy my past disrespect toward you.

Student: (Student's name)

### Public Criticism

Sometimes the offenses of students at Third Affiliated are serious enough to justify criticizing the student in public. And the most serious of public criticisms is the "all-school criticism" *(quanxiao piping).* The all-school criticism is just what its name suggests: All the students, teachers, and administrators from the school are called out onto the playing field, and a student (or students) who has committed some very serious offense is criticized there, in front of everyone. For especially serious offenses, the fact that the student is subjected to an all-school criticism is noted in his permanent file *(dang an),* which will follow him as an adult wherever he goes to live or work. By criticizing a student in front of the entire school, and sometimes entering a record of this in his file, an extremely wide circle of people is informed of a student's misdeeds. The all-school criticism, therefore, is among the worst of all punishments a student could be made to endure. (There are other severe punishments as well, such as expelling a student or transferring him to a school for juvenile offenders, but these actions are often preceded by, and announced at, an all-school criticism.)

The all-school criticism at Third Affiliated that I witnessed was called to criticize six male students accused of fighting. The fight had taken place several days earlier, when a senior grade two student cut into the lunch line. That day senior grade three students were on lunch line duty, so one of them grabbed the student by the collar and pulled him out of the line. The next day the senior grade two student got five of his friends to go with him and beat up the senior grade three student. (Enlisting one's supporters to beat up an enemy is a common practice among Chinese youth.) The student and his five friends were caught, and it was they who were the targets of the all-school criticism.

The first step was a forty-minute assembly of all students in senior grade two, and all teachers, to decide how to deal with the offenders following the all-school criticism. During this assembly it was the teachers who were charged with making this decision, and the students formed the audience to the decision making. One alternative was to expel the offenders. Another was to put them on probation, and expel them if they committed offenses in the future. A third possibility was to make them write self-criticisms and read these in front of their *ban*.

Immediately after this assembly, all the students and teachers in the school filed out onto the playing field and sat down in chairs that they had brought with them from their classrooms. The six offenders sat with classmates from their *ban*. The atmosphere seemed somewhat perfunctory, and a number of students in the audience were reading books. The administrator in charge of "thought education" *(sixiang jiaoyu)* stepped up to the microphone and said she would analyze the problem at hand so that other students in the audience could be educated. Most students respect student cadres, she said, but some do not (a reference to the fact that the student beaten up was, as a lunch line attendant, a student cadre). Some students say bad things about student cadres behind their backs. Also, she said, most tuition-paying students (see Introduction) are okay, but some are not. (The offenders were all tuition-paying students.) The offending students' class teacher then spoke. He described their previous wrongdoings: one had stolen a bike, one had cursed a teacher, and one had stolen a small sum of money. As each of these previous offenses was described, students in the audience laughed. In the end an announcement was made as to what was to be done with the students: A warning *(jinggao)* was to be entered in their files. With this announcement, the criticism of the students was over.

## Chapter Summary

This chapter describes the widespread role that evaluation plays among the Chinese. Who is good and who is not good is an issue of great interest in China, interest that stems from the social significance of merit. The significance of merit lies in the fact that it is a major basis on which people earn and justify positions of power. Cultivating and preserving a reputation for merit thus becomes a critical goal.

The chapter then analyzes education's role in reinforcing meritocracy. In many instances, research and teaching are devoted to discovering and extolling the virtues of virtuous people. Education thus serves to consolidate the reputations upon which status is often based.

The second half of the chapter considers negative evaluation—criticism. Surprisingly, inferiors can often be very critical of their superiors, and this occurs in the schools, where students often complain about and criticize their teachers. Used in this way, criticism has the potential to lower the status of high-status people. However, criticism is also used by high-status people themselves. Authority figures and institutions punish those under their authority by criticizing them privately, and in severe cases, in public.

Evaluation, and criticism in particular, are so central in Chinese society that they have played a very important role in modern Chinese political movements. In fact, the widespread use of criticism in the political domain seems to suggest that criticism is an offspring of politics, making it a new political phenomenon rather than an old, cultural one. To determine whether or not this is true requires an examination of pre-Communist China for historical examples of evaluation and criticism; this topic will be covered in Chapter 3.

# 3

## The Historical Background of Evaluation and Criticism

The tie between status and merit in China has a long history, which the present chapter will explore. Historical writings are supplemented by those of anthropology to arrive at a full illustration of the significance of merit in Chinese tradition.

One special focus of this chapter is the evaluation and criticism of superiors by their inferiors. This phenomenon has been a hallmark of post-1949 China, especially during the Cultural Revolution. Given this, it might seem that its existence during my research resulted from prior political criticism campaigns like the Cultural Revolution. This is, in fact, partly true. But the frequency of its occurrence in contexts that were not overtly political led me to suspect that it must have a cultural/historical derivation as well, so I sought examples in pre-Communist China.

### Merit in Traditional China

#### *The Ideology of Meritocracy in Historical China*

Unlike the ancient Greeks, the ancient Chinese had no concept of equality of people. Confucius and his followers, as well as adherents of all other schools of thought except the Taoists, advocated the necessity of a hierarchy of men (P. Ho 1962: 2–4). But all the schools of thought also sought means to solve the inherent injustice such a hierarchy can create. Confucius's solution was to choose rulers based on their merit. He believed that if the government was composed of wise and virtuous men, social harmony would prevail (P. Ho 1962: 5). In order to make virtue, rather than wealth or inherited status, the real basis for choosing leaders, Confucius advocated educational opportunity for all without regard to social class, and he offered instruction to his disciples irrespective of their social background (P. Ho 1962: 6). His ideal was thus a hierarchical society in which all men had an opportunity for education, with those demonstrating their excellence in study and virtue occupying the top level of the hierarchy (P. Ho 1962: 6).

Confucius's successors continued to expound meritocratic ideals. The third-century B.C. Confucian thinker Xun Zi said:

> Although a man is a descendant of a king, duke, prefect, or officer, if he does not observe the rites of proper conduct and justice, he must be relegated to the common ranks; although he is a descendant of a commoner, if he has acquired learning, developed a good character, and is able to observe the rules of good conduct and justice, then elevate him to be minister, prime minister, officer, or prefect. (Quoted in P. Ho 1962: 7)

Mo Zi made a similar analysis and concluded that "ranks should be standardized according to virtue . . . " (quoted in P. Ho 1962: 7).

Centuries later, views similar to those of Confucius and his followers were still being articulated. Wright gives an interesting account of such views during the Tongzhi Restoration of the mid-nineteenth century (Wright 1957). She writes that Restoration statesmen were "positively obsessed with the idea of 'human talent' " (Wright 1957: 68). In true Confucian fashion they believed that good government would result only if men of high ability occupied leadership positions, and, conversely, they attributed China's mid-nineteenth-century problems to the failure to educate men properly and to install in office those demonstrating high ability. (This analysis is amazingly similar to my Chinese friends' explanations for contemporary China's problems—that China's current low level of economic development results from China's failure to value education adequately, and to put men of education and talent into office.) One Restoration statesman, Zuo Zongtang, wrote:

> Chaos in the Empire results from the fact that civil government is not properly maintained. That civil government is not properly maintained results from the fact that men of ability are not in office; that men of

ability are not in office results from the fact that men's hearts are not upright; that men's hearts are not upright results from the fact that learning is not expounded. (Quoted in Wright 1957: 68)

## *Meritocratic Ideals in Practice: The Examination System*

Consistent with their meritocratic ideals, the Chinese developed institutions to ensure, at least in principle, that leadership positions would be filled with meritorious men, rather than men qualified only by wealth or class background. The Han government sought men of talent for government service through the recommendatory system. After 134 B.C. provincial and local authorities were asked on a regular basis to recommend meritorious men as candidates for government service (P. Ho 1962: 10). This system was later discontinued, and during the Tang Dynasty a competitive examination system was established to select men for official positions (P. Ho 1962: 11, 12). With only a few qualifications, discussed below, the examination system was to become the primary means for selecting government officials until the examinations were terminated in 1905.

Over time the way in which the Chinese defined the concept of merit narrowed down, until by the Ming–Qing period merit was believed to consist of, or to be reflected by, one's knowledge of the classics and theories of administration, and one's literary attainments (P. Ho 1962: 11). Correspondingly, the examinations became a test of textual and literary ability. They were conducted on district, provincial, and metropolitan levels, with a candidate successful at one level allowed to proceed to examinations at the next higher level. The first exam, conducted at the district level, required two "eight-legged" (a particular kind of stylized, essay form, consisting of verse and prose) essays on subjects from the Confucian Four Books, and a short poem. The wrong use of words, violation of rhyming rules, or poor calligraphy could disqualify a candidate at this level. In the second of the three sessions at the district level the candidate was made to write from memory one or two hundred words from a portion of the Kangxi Emperor's Sacred Edict. Exams at higher levels were similar, demanding essays on the classics and on history and government, as well as the composition of poetry. Only a select number of candidates were allowed to pass at any given level, so only those of outstanding ability (according to the examiners' concept of ability) could successfully pass the exams at the highest level, the triennial metropolitan exams given in Beijing (I. Hsu 1975: 103–6).

The purpose of the examinations was to determine who was genuinely meritorious, and then assign such people to positions in the government bureaucracy. The examinations were the primary way to secure a position as an official, so the Chinese official class was thus largely composed of men of merit, as defined by the examinations (I. Hsu 1975: 103, 109; P. Ho 1962: 256; Menzel 1963: x). Furthermore, the better the examination results, the better the chances of winning a good government position. While those passing only the district exams were rarely appointed as officials, those passing the provincial exams had a better chance, and those passing the metropolitan exams were guaranteed an official appointment. Those with the highest metropolitan scores achieved membership in the Hanlin Academy, from which the very highest officials were chosen (Borthwick 1983: 2; Menzel 1963: x).

Since being an official has always been the highest status position one could attain in Chinese society, and wealth alone was no match for the power of the official (I. Hsu 1975: 96; F. Hsu 1981: 187; P. Ho 1962: 44–45, 51; Marsh 1961: 1), the examination system was one that conferred high status on the basis of merit, and gave even a poor peasant the opportunity to rise to the top levels of society. Of course, in practice the system did not always work according to its ideals. Members of the "degraded" class of people (all those—such as beggars, hereditary servants, entertainers, and prostitutes—below the status of ordinary commoners), though numerically small in number, were not allowed to take the examinations until about 1800 (P. Ho 1962: 18–19; Chang 1963: 22). The poor who were allowed to take the exams often could not afford the money to hire a tutor to teach them the classics (Chang 1963: 23). Sons and brothers of officials had a separate higher quota assigned to them in the exams, making it easier for them to pass (Chang 1963: 22–23). And, finally, offices and titles were sold, so a wealthy person could buy his way into the bureaucracy, a practice of relatively low frequency that became predominant after the mid-nineteenth-century Taiping Rebellion forced the government to sell offices at a previously unprecedented rate (P. Ho 1962: 48–51).

Despite these unmeritocratic practices, the majority of evidence documents the relatively high rates of social mobility, both up and down, in China (P. Ho 1962: 257–58; F. Hsu 1963: 46–47; Kracke

1963: 6–7; Wakeman 1975: 22). (One author, Marsh 1961: 187–89, concludes that it was difficult for commoners to get into the bureaucracy but that, once there, they had as good a chance to be promoted as the sons of officials). Popular ideology reflected the ideals and realities of this social mobility. Many sayings and popular literary works contributed to what has been called a Chinese version of the Horatio Alger myth—the belief that even a man of humble birth could, by diligent study, pass the examinations and rise to the top stratum of Chinese society (Marsh 1961: 2–4; P. Ho 1962: 86–89; C.T. Hu 1984: 15). One proverb held: "A bequest of chests of solid gold is not as valuable to your descendants as teaching them a basic classic" (quoted in P. Ho 1962: 87). Another: "Generals and ministers were not originally blue-blooded, and so a man of ambition should aim high" (quoted in P. Ho 1962: 87). And in an "exhortation to learning" by a Song emperor: "In books there are houses of gold; in books there are thousands of bushels of grain; in books horses and carriages abound; in books can be found women with complexions of jade" (quoted in C.T. Hu 1984: 15).

*An Additional Significance of Merit*

Anthropological research demonstrates that merit had another significance as well. The public recognition of one's merit was the basis for fame, glory, and the all-important Chinese concept of face, values at least as important to the Chinese as wealth or occupational status per se.

Much of the special emotional salience of merit-based fame for the Chinese lay in its connection to ancestor worship (the worship of a man or woman by his or her children and other patrilineal descendants). Ancestor worship was the universal religion in China (F. Hsu 1981: 248), and despite the Communists' hostility to traditional religion in general, it is still practiced in much of rural China (Baker 1979: 206–11). Worship took a variety of forms, including the holding of séances to communicate with the deceased, annual visitations to graveyards to supply the deceased with food, money, and clothes, and the maintenance of a shrine in the center of the house, where incense was burned daily as an offering to the deceased and to other patrilineal ancestors (F. Hsu 1967: Chapter 7). Being worshiped by one's offspring was so important to the Chinese that unmarried people and childless couples would go to great lengths to obtain fictive or adoptive offspring so that they would have someone to worship them after their death. Deceased individuals lacking real or fictive offspring to provide sacrificial offerings to them were condemned to a life of wandering as a "hungry ghost" (Baker 1979: 74–82).

While those with offspring were guaranteed of being worshiped after their deaths, whether or not they would be remembered and honored by more distant patrilineal descendants depended on a number of factors. This is where the importance of earning merit-based fame comes in: A man famous for his merits and virtue while alive would be the source of much glory for his offspring and lineage, so they would worship him with that much greater reverence. Becoming famous was thus a way to achieve symbolic immortality.

Hsu describes the great attention given to meritorious ancestors. A family home, for example, prominently displayed plaques showing the honors won by its ancestors during their lifetimes. Ancestors alive ten or more generations before the living one were included, and the family had such a desire for honor that it even fabricated imagined or alleged honors for its ancestors if the real deeds were not glorious enough (F. Hsu 1967: 28–29). Lineages kept genealogical records, with the rich compiling extensive multivolume records on outstanding ancestors and their achievements. Achievements for male ancestors primarily included examination honors and high posts in the official bureaucracy, and the demonstration of filial piety and harmony in family and community. Female virtues recorded were chastity and faithfulness to husbands and attentiveness to parents-in-law (F. Hsu 1967: 232–37).

The achievements of outstanding ancestors were not only maintained in written form but were reported orally as well. The tales of excellent ancestors were told after meals, at family gatherings, and during Ancestor Festivals, enabling even illiterate men and women to become familiar with the achievements of their ancestors (F. Hsu 1967: 235–36). A grandfather might call his family around to listen to stories from the lineage book—stories of the family's many ancestors who had worked and studied hard, and earned exam honors and the resulting positions as officials. The stories often ended with an exhortation to remember the ancestors' achievements and emulate their good deeds (M. Yang 1945: 138–39).

As the discussion above illustrates, lineages maintained a connection to past generations by recording and remembering the merits of the ancestors; merit thus helped preserve the intergenerational continuity of the lineage, and contributed to the prestige of the lineage, since the ancestors' achievements lent glory to the lineage as a whole (which is why lineages spent so much attention recording the merits of outstanding ancestors). Any meritorious member of the lineage brought glory to the whole lineage, and descendants' achievements could even bring glory to the ancestors (F. Hsu 1967: 8, 264, 267–68; M. Yang 1945: 141). Merit bound the generations of the lineage together through glory shared in each others' accomplishments, giving the lineage as a whole its prestige.

A reputation for merit was the primary basis for the prestige of the lineage and family. While wealth was sought after by the Chinese as one component of family prestige, wealth alone was insufficient for a family to become famous and earn the respect of the community (M. Yang 1945: 51–52). Yang describes how a sense of family honor—face—was more important than family wealth. A family might say: "Money, property, these are insignificant in comparison with our family's face!" (quoted in M. Yang 1945: 170). A family's reputation was very important, and families, especially from the middle and upper classes, had a great desire to be admired and talked about throughout the local region. Families and lineages earned their reputations in large part by having members who excelled at studies, passed the examinations, and became officials. A family with a member who passed the exams would be addressed by the title used for a successful exam candidate, and in some cases the family even placed a special pair of flagpoles outside its door to mark off its status as the family of someone who had done so (M. Yang 1945: 50). The importance attached to merit over wealth, or more specifically scholarship over trade, is illustrated by the fact that Chinese genealogies were filled with descriptions of the scholarly and official attainments of lineage members, but made no mention at all of trading or commerce despite the importance of such activities in communities such as the one Hsu studied (F. Hsu 1967: 236).

## Merit in Mao's China

Since a lineage's prestige derived largely from the fame it and its members enjoyed for their outstanding merits, it is not surprising that the destruction of lineage power and Mao Zedong's more general assault on the traditional sources of authority in China required an attack on merit and the pursuit of fame. (Anti-fame sentiment actually has precedents in premodern China. The Taoist-minded Chinese disapproved of the importance attached to fame, and they said, "Family fame or clan honor is nothing but the dew of the early morning, or a cloud on the dry sky." [Quoted in M. Yang 1945: 53.]) The following passage, which was used in *Quotations from Chairman Mao* (see Mao 1967: 208), is from a 1942 speech Mao gave. In this passage Mao criticizes the pursuit of fame by connecting it with the failure to follow the party:

> Those who assert [that is, pursue] this kind of "independence" [independence of the party] are usually wedded to the doctrine of "me first" and are generally wrong on the question of the relationship between the individual and the Party. Although in words they profess respect for the Party, in practice they put themselves first and the Party second. . . . What are these people after? They are after fame and position and want to be in the limelight. (Mao 1965 [1942]: 44)

Mao's anti-fame sentiment was especially strong during the Cultural Revolution. During that time one group of Red Guards proposed eliminating names of authors, players, and directors from all performance and literary credits, so as to block the road to personal fame; in this spirit collective authorship was required of all scholarly articles until 1972 (Cleverley 1985: 169, 203).

Mao also attacked merit and meritocracy. Shirk argues that merit is not as amenable to political control as what she calls "virtuocracy," the awarding of opportunities on the basis of political virtue (Shirk 1982). By shifting away from reward based on merit to a system of reward based on one's demonstration of such political virtues as political commitment and activism, the Chinese government could better consolidate its power and promote adherence to its campaigns for social and political change (Shirk 1982: 4, 10–11).

Mao's struggle to replace meritocracy with virtuocracy can best be seen in the policies he advocated for recruitment of students into universities. Given the importance of academic credentials to the Chinese, any rewards he was to give to the politically virtuous would have to include the opportunity to earn those credentials. Mao and his followers thus fought to award university enrollments to the politically virtuous— either those of good family class background or those who, perhaps in spite of a bad class background, demonstrated politically virtuous thoughts and deeds. The Maoists criticized such meritocratic practices as the college entrance examinations for perpetuating the dominance of bourgeois groups. Not everyone agreed with Mao, and there was a persistent conflict between "the two lines on the educational front," meaning between those, like Mao, who wanted to base college admissions on political criteria and those, such as Liu Shaoqi, a high-level leader purged in the late sixties, who wanted academic criteria. Admissions criteria shifted between political criteria and academic criteria from year to year, but there was a trend, which reached a climax during the Cultural Revolution, toward giving supremacy to political criteria (Shirk 1982: 17–18, 41–53; Unger 1982: 12–15).

The shift away from meritocracy reached its climax during the Cultural Revolution. College applicants no longer took academic examinations for admission to college, and school grades were not taken into consideration in the admissions process. Grades and exams were replaced by a system of recommendations, whereby workers or peasants at each workplace recommended who should be allowed to attend college. Candidates were recommended for admission based not on academic, but on political qualifications, such as work attitude and commitment to political activism (Shirk 1982: 45).

Schools also adopted antimeritocratic educational policies. The Maoist "line" in educational practice had maintained that examinations and grades should be dethroned (T. Chen 1974: 35). Mao criticized the way tests had been traditionally administered, and he called for such changes as open-book tests, group discussion among students of possible answers to test questions, and allowing students to copy each other's test answers. He believed that groups of students should grade each other's work, or that students should make up their own exams and grade themselves (Chu 1980: 364–67). Some of Mao's ideas were in fact carried out immediately before and during the Cultural Revolution. Schools gave open-book and collective exams. Grades were not published, and no one ever failed. Students were encouraged to work together in an atmosphere of mutual help (Cleverley 1985: 196–97; Unger 1982: 79–82, 180–81).

With Mao's death and the assumption of leadership positions by those who, like Deng Xiaoping, had opposed the Maoist educational line, meritocratic principles emerged in China once again. By 1978 the exam system had been fully restored (Shirk 1982: 46). This restoration means that access to university education and to the high-status jobs requiring university educations is once more awarded (for the most part—there were rumors of a return to Maoist entrance criteria as I left China in 1989) according to academic merit.

## Criticism in Communist Chinese Society

Criticism and self-criticism have been used by the Chinese Communists as central methods of political indoctrination and social control. The 1956 constitution of the Chinese Communist Party includes the following statement: "No political party or person can be free from shortcomings and mistakes in work. The Communist Party of China and its members must constantly practice criticism and self-criticism to expose and eliminate their shortcomings and mistakes so as to educate themselves and the people" (quoted in Lewis 1963: 160).

Mao's writings are full of references to the importance of criticism (see Mao 1976). For example: "There is no construction without destruction. Destruction means criticism and repudiation; it means revolution. It involves reasoning things out, which is construction. Put destruction first, and in the process you have construction" (quoted in Chu 1980: 288). Mao rejected the use of compulsion by administrators to force people to adopt Communist ideals and practices and instead advocated "the method of discussion, of criticism," to change people's beliefs (Chu 1980: 291). He stated that anyone had the right to criticize anyone else, and he encouraged such criticism (Chu 1980: 295; Mao 1976: 265). In fact Mao admitted that he, like all people, had shortcomings, and so he remarked, "If you say you cannot argue against or criticize me, the Chairman, I think you are wrong" (quoted in Chu 1980: 295). (Of course, this was Mao's rhetoric; in reality, he was often intolerant of those who criticized him and even encouraged people to criticize him so that he could identify his enemies. This was one of Mao's reasons for encouraging criticism during the Hundred Flowers campaign of 1956–57, following which at least 300,000 critics of Mao and the Communist Party were branded "rightists" and punished harshly for their supposed crimes. See Cleverley 1985: 138–39; I. Hsu 1975: 796.) His call for people to criticize him and other Communist leaders seemed to appeal both to a sense of daring and to a sense of duty: "Have the guts to touch the tail of the tiger—the high officer" (quoted in Chu 1980: 293). Also: "Thoroughgoing materialists are fearless; we hope that all our fellow fighters will courageously shoulder their responsibilities and overcome all difficulties, fearing no setbacks or gibes, nor hesitating to criticize us Communists and give us their suggestions" (Mao 1976: 258). The challenge to the Communists to accept criticism was equally strong: "If we have shortcomings, we are not afraid to have them pointed out and criticized, because we serve the people. Anyone, no matter who, may point out our shortcomings" (Mao 1976: 265). Finally, Mao strongly encouraged his comrades to criticize themselves as well: "Conscientious practice of self-criticism is still another hallmark distinguishing our Party from all other political parties. As we say, dust will accumulate if a room is not cleaned regularly, our faces will get dirty if they are not washed regularly" (Mao 1976: 259).

Criticism has been used as a political resource by the Chinese Communists since their early years, and they have continued to use it frequently. The extent of the Chinese reliance on criticism makes them unique among ruling Communist parties. Although in the Soviet Union the Bolsheviks did meet in small cells to study political texts and party programs and criticize each other, the Communist Party of the Soviet Union never relied on such small group criticism meetings to mobilize adherence of the masses to its programs. Its reliance instead on coercion and command by external hierarchies of power contrasts sharply with the significant use by the Chinese Communists of mutual criticism in small groups to educate and mobilize the masses (Dittmer 1974: 338; Whyte 1974: 24, 27–28, 34–35).

The Chinese Communist practice of criticism can be traced back at least as far as the Long March of 1934–35 (Chu 1980: 303). It became more extensive during a 1942–44 Communist campaign to build unity among the party's disparate leadership. During that campaign party members, leaders, students, and intellectuals engaged in daily group study of party documents, criticism of each other's past attitudes and actions, and declaration by group members of their allegiance to official policies (Whyte 1974: 32–33; Dittmer 1974: 315–16; Selden 1969: 107–10).

Criticism was central to subsequent political campaigns as well. It was used during several movements in the 1950s, including the Hundred Flowers campaign of 1956–57, when intellectuals were called on to voice criticisms of cadres. It was a weapon against cadres again during the Four Cleanups campaign (also called the Socialist Education Movement) of 1962–66, a campaign to rectify corruption among cadres. During the Cultural Revolution criticism reached new levels. One example of criticism during that time was the Mao Zedong Thought Propaganda teams. These teams were sent to schools to carry out "struggle-criticism-transformation." They organized discussions to criticize "revisionist bourgeois ideology" among party members and to confront teachers, school administrators, and students with their political failings (Chu 1980: 287–88, 303–5).

## Types of Criticism

Small group criticism, the first type adopted by the Chinese Communists (described above), continues to be an important method of political indoctrination. Cadres, students (including secondary students), soldiers, ordinary workers, urban residents, and others are all organized into small groups based on where they work or study, or where they live. Although the groups do not always function exactly as they are supposed to, in principle they are small groups of around ten members each (Whyte 1974: 39) that meet at least once a week for two to three hours of political study (during political movements the groups have met for longer daily sessions—Schurmann 1959: 53). The focus of the study session is often a party document articulating a given policy or ideology. After the document is read, all the group members, whose attendance at study sessions is mandatory, are expected to comment on it. It is anticipated that in this process many will vocalize their confusion about the document or their negative attitudes toward it. When negative views are expressed by a group member, all the other group members are called on to criticize him, and he is also expected to make a self-criticism of his own negative views. In this way the opposition to a party policy or ideological viewpoint is supposed to be overcome through criticism and persuasion. Sometimes a document is not the object of study; instead individuals will take turns criticizing other group members, and themselves, for attitudes or actions that are seen as contradictory to Communist policy or principle. One Third Affiliated student, for example, was criticized in his Communist Youth League small group because he had failed to stop when he collided with another Third Affiliated student on his bicycle, a demonstration of his unsocialist, selfish tendencies. Poor study or work habits are another common focus of criticism. (Most of this discussion of small group criticism is based on discussions with my informants. For a full treatment of the subject see Whyte 1974. Also see Unger 1982: 184–87; Chan et al. 1984: 78–82; Shirk 1982: 38–39, 91–94, 150–51; and Schumann 1959. Issues covered above are summarized in Whyte 1974: 2–3.)

By making individuals critically examine their attitudes and actions in a small group, the pressure of the small group can be used to enforce compliance with party policy and ideology. The fear of being criticized, face-to-face, by all the members of the group, and isolated from the group for one's "erroneous beliefs," is a powerful means, especially in face-conscious China, of encouraging individuals to confess their errors and profess (even if not genuine) a conversion to the "correct" attitude. The collective effect of these public declarations of belief in the party makes it very difficult for any individual to continue to vocalize opposition to party policy (see Whyte 1974: 53–55; Selden 1969: 106–8; Schumann 1959: 57; Solomon 1969).

A second type of criticism common in Communist China is public criticism. In public criticisms, sometimes called "(mass) criticism meeting," or "struggle sessions," a crowd of people was gathered to publicly denounce someone seen as an opponent because of his transgressions against them and/or their principles. Targets of criticism were usually forced to be present during these denunciations, a painful process since crowds of criticizers sometimes numbered as high as 100,000 (Thurston 1987:122). Targets of criticism and those criticizing them have included the following: former landlords or corrupt local officials criticized by their fellow villagers; primary school, middle school, and university teachers and administrators criticized by the schools' students; and prominent intellectuals, party cadres, and those of formerly elite class background criticized by fellow urban dwellers (criticism in villages: Chan et al. 1984: 19–20, 37–40, 41–66, 71–73, 118–20, 138–40, 146, 149–50, 158–62, 208–10, 242–43; C.K. Yang 1959: 192–93; in schools: Bennett and Montaperto 1980: 36–42; Gao 1987: 50–60, 75–76; Thurston 1987: xiii–xiv, xvi, 121–22; Chan et al. 1984: 111–12; Kwong 1988: 16, 27; Unger 1982: 115–16; Cleverley 1985: 201; in cities: Bennett and Montaperto 1980: 75–76; Liang and Shapiro 1983: 77–79, 120–21; Fairbank 1986: 336; Kwong 1988: 76; Thurston 1987: 112–13, 117–18, 122–24).

Given the sensitivity to face and public reputation in China, and the corresponding difference between private and public criticism, the public version differed significantly in tone from the more restricted contexts of the small group criticism. While the latter was a collegial process among supposed equals, public criticism was an attack on one who was seen as both an enemy and a criminal, and its purpose was less to reform him than to delegitimate and destroy him (Dittmer 1974: 352–54). Many authors have described in great detail the cruelty of the victimization that could occur during public criticism. (Thurston [1987] cites many examples; see also Bennett and Montaperto 1980: 38–39).

Since public criticism has such power to delegitimate someone, it has been used by the Communists as a prime weapon during political campaigns to attack and remove from power such pre-Communist elites as landlords, intellectuals, and petty powerholders. In fact public criticisms were generally not spontaneous occurrences but affairs orchestrated by Communist functionaries during political campaigns to combat their opponents and opposing ideologies. Government organizers sought to turn the envy and outrage of the masses against the elites who were a supposed threat to both the supremacy of the masses and the Communist government.

Chan et al. (1984) give a good account of how public criticism was arranged by government officials and carried out by villagers against their local leaders. In 1965 during the Four Cleanups campaign, a political campaign to "clean up" the corruption of local rural officials (1984: 37), a work team of cadres was sent to Chen Village, the village Chan et al. studied (1984: 41). In preparation for their attack on local leaders the work team spent days interrogating Chen villagers about the malpractices of their local leaders. When enough information was gathered to document the corrupt transgressions, the cadres were confronted one by one by poor peasant representatives who raised the charges against them in face-to-face struggle sessions. Accusations were hurled at each target for hours until each finally confessed. Each accused person was then brought before the peasant masses in struggle meetings. The crowd numbered in the hundreds, but the cadre work team had previously cultivated a group of activists to lead the attack. The accused was led out onto the stage with his head bowed and wearing a placard stating his crime. Activists would stand up and yell charges of denunciation against him, and other audience members were gradually aroused to join in. Once the momentum of criticism was established, it was virtually unstoppable. Some accused leaders were subjected to several nights of these struggle sessions until it was felt that they had been sufficiently humiliated (see Chan et al. 1984: Chapter 2, especially pp. 54–64).

During the Cultural Revolution public criticisms occurred with greater frequency and ferocity than ever before. As in Chen Village, the accused, usually intellectuals or cadres charged with taking the "capitalist road," were brought before crowds numbering as high as 100,000 (Thurston 1987: 122). They wore placards announcing their crimes and often cone hats as well, and they were sometimes paraded through the streets like criminals. In the struggle sessions they were not only criticized and denounced by people shouting such slogans as "Down with the Soviet Revisionist Spy, Down with [person's name]," but they were sometimes humiliated and harmed in other ways such as being spit on or made to "ride the airplane," which meant to assume a body posture with head bowed and arms out like wings. Sometimes the victim was hoisted up in the air in this position by a rope. Other forms of torture were also employed and sometimes caused the victim to lose consciousness (Gao 1987: 50–60, 75–76; Liang and Shapiro 1983: 79, 120; Thurston 1987: xiii–xiv, 112–13, 117–19, 121–24, 228–29; Fairbank 1986: 336).

A third form of criticism is the "big character poster" *(dazibao)*. The first large-scale writing of big character posters took place during the Hundred Flowers campaign (Dittmer 1974: 317), and poster writing has occurred during various politically active times since then, including during the 1989 Democracy Movement. Big character posters, as the name implies, are large sheets of paper on which political slogans and rhetoric are written. They are posted on walls or presented in some other very public context for all to see and read.

Big character posters were an especially integral part of the activities during the Cultural Revolution, and many authors (for example, Gao 1987: 34–36, 40–50, 54–57, 67–69, 71–75; Liang and Shapiro 1983: 44–55; J. Chen 1975: 230–35, 306–7) have described the writing of big character posters during that period. The poster writing in the Cultural Revolution was so extensive that public spaces were covered with the posters (Liang and Shapiro 1983: 46; J. Chen 1975: 230, 232). It was even reported that 100,000 posters were written at Beijing University in one week (Kwong 1988: 16). The posters were often vehicles for criticizing other people. Individuals, including those of superior status, such as bosses and teachers, were attacked by name in

the posters, accused, sometimes falsely, of actions or orientations an-
tagonistic to Mao and the Maoist revolution (Gao 1987: 40–50, 54–57,
67–69, 71–75; J. Chen 1975: 230–35, 306–7; Liang and Shapiro 1983:
44–55). The content was inspired by, and often conformed with, the
rhetoric of the *People's Daily* and *Red Flag,* the main party organs,
and the tone of the language was exaggerated and poetic (J. Chen
1975: 230–31).

Finally, there is the use of the media as an instrument of criticism.
One of the best such examples of this occurred during the Cultural
Revolution in the "great repudiation" campaign launched against the
high-level Chinese leader, Liu Shaoqi. Liu was seen as an enemy of
Mao and a "capitalist roader," and in 1967 the Politburo officially
decided to attack him through the media (Dittmer 1974: 158). For two
years, with the peak occurring in the spring of 1967, Liu was criticized
in countless articles of both the official and Red Guard press. More
than 3,000 polemical articles were written blaming Liu for the evils
that the Cultural Revolution was supposed to correct (Dittmer 1974:
94, 161).

### The Ideology and Practice of Criticism of Elites by the Masses

Mao insisted that criticism was important and that the ultimate right to
criticize belonged to the masses. Since they were the "masters," the
proletarians had the authority to criticize everyone and everything
(Chu 1980: 301–2). Consistent with this philosophy, Mao encouraged
the masses to challenge traditional elites by criticizing them. During
the Cultural Revolution, for example, Mao waged war against the establishment by calling on the young, especially students, to attack their
establishment superiors (Fairbank 1986: 319–20). He and his supporters organized the formation of the Red Guards, young high school and
university radicals who were encouraged to, in the words of a big
character poster Mao wrote, "Bombard the Headquarters," and seize
power from the "revisionist" members of the establishment (Fairbank
1986: 328–29, 337).

Maoist policy during the Cultural Revolution sanctioned and supported the antiestablishment actions of the Red Guards and others
seeking to challenge those in power (Kwong 1988: 8–9, 17, 25, 31–
32). During the Cultural Revolution most central and provincial leaders were purged and criticized. The Red Guards played a key role in

these purges by criticizing leaders in wall newspapers, mass struggle sessions, and Red Guard newspapers. These attacks were not only consistent with the central government's decisions on which leaders should be denounced and purged but were, in fact, partially conducted under central government directive (Kwong 1988: 74–76). Another example of the direction of mass criticism from above is the government work teams, which visited young people, even those in their early adolescence, like Liang Heng, and attempted to persuade them to write reports criticizing their rightist parents. The work teams also organized mass meetings of the relatives of people who the work teams thought should be criticized. These relatives, young children as well as older adults, were told that if they did not criticize their relatives, *they* would be criticized (Liang and Shapiro 1983: 61–65). My informants had similar recollections. They told me that they criticized their teachers during the Cultural Revolution because if they had not done so, they would have become the targets of criticism due to their reluctance to criticize others. Criticizing others (except for Mao, who was to be worshiped) was seen as a revolutionary duty. Those who tried to obstruct mass criticism and the assault on targeted teachers were themselves publicly denounced (Bennett and Montaperto 1980: 40; Unger 1982: 113).

The young and those of lower status, acting with the encouragement of official policy and ideology, criticized selected targets of superior status frequently during many of the political campaigns waged in Communist China. While campaigns in the 1950s and early 1960s were characterized by poor peasant denunciations of local elites (see above), in the Cultural Revolution the young, and especially students, played the role of leading criticizers. Mao had said, "students are encouraged to criticize teachers" (quoted in Chu 1980: 304), and so teachers, as well as school administrators, were often the targets of students' attacks (see, for example, Liang and Shapiro 1983: 45–51; Bennett and Montaperto 1980: 36–42, 48–49; Gao 1987: 39–76; Kwong 1988: 15–23, 27, 35; Unger 1982: 111–13, 115–16, 180; Chan et al. 1984: 111–12; Thurston 1987: xiii–xiv, xvi, 121–22; Cleverley 1985: 201).

After the party Central Committee issued the May 16 Circular in 1966 calling for the criticism and repudiation of "those representatives of the bourgeoisie who have sneaked into the Party, the government, the army, and all spheres of culture . . ." (quoted in Bennett and

Montaperto 1980: 36), attacks against teachers began. In the senior middle school attended by Bennett and Montaperto's Red Guard informant, the principal targeted two teachers, one previously denounced during the Anti-Rightist campaign of 1957 and the other a teacher from a "bad" (that is, landlord, or other formerly high status) family background. The principal denounced the two teachers in an all-school meeting, after which students plastered the walls with big character posters denouncing them. Criticism centered on the bad-class-background teacher's wearing of pretty dresses and the other teacher's failure to participate in politics. The teachers were also subjected to struggle meetings. Every three or four days the principal would call a general school meeting where each class of students would be given the opportunity to confront and abuse the accused teachers. Crowds of students forced the teachers to wear caps and collars with inscriptions such as "I am a monster." The students organized into "control monster teams" to smear black paint on the teachers and force them to clean the toilets. They yelled slogans and accusations at the teachers and continued to confront the teachers for days until they finally admitted their mistakes. Later, the principal, afraid that he might become the victim of the students' attacks, tried to deflect their criticism of him by calling for a new round of criticism against several additional teachers (a strategy my informants believed Mao himself had used in calling for mass criticism of various groups during the Cultural Revolution so as to redirect the focus of criticism away from him. While it was by no means true that all instances of inferiors criticizing superiors in the Cultural Revolution were incited from above—see, for example, Bennett and Montaperto 1980: 41–42, for a discussion of independence in student attacks on teachers—direction or sanctioning from above, often for political reasons, was a common phenomenon). Eventually, though, a work team of sixteen outsiders entered the school and, in an all-school "mobilization meeting," called on everyone to write big character posters against the principal and other party leaders (Bennett and Montaperto 1980: 35–41, 47–49).

While only a limited number of teachers were chosen to be struggled against, all of them, according to my informants, were criticized in big character posters their students wrote about them. Liang and Shapiro (1983) cite some examples of the content of big character posters students wrote about teachers at Liang's school. One showed swarms of flies buzzing around the head of a teacher who was often faulted for wearing perfume. The caption read, "Why does it stink? It is the stink of Capitalism!" Liang and his friends criticized another teacher for boasting of his use of Soviet teaching methods, proof of his surrender to the Soviet Union. They illustrated their big character poster with a man standing in front of a blackboard holding chalk in one hand and a Soviet flag in the other (Liang and Shapiro 1983: 47). My informant, Xiao Yang, at the time only nine years old, told me how one teacher, who had had a running feud with another teacher before the Cultural Revolution began, convinced Xiao Yang to write a big character poster against her enemy. In this poster Xiao Yang falsely accused the target of having extramarital affairs. Such false accusations were common in big character posters. Although targets could respond with their own big character posters denying false rumors, the damage to their reputations was often already done.

### Criticism in Pre-Communist China

Many scholars have noted that Communist practices of criticism are consistent with the cultural values and social practices of pre-Communist China. They have pointed out, for example, that the practice of shaming a person by criticizing him before others, both in small groups and in mass public meetings, is as effective as it is because the Chinese, traditionally, have been very sensitive about being shamed publicly. One who is shamed in public loses face and is alienated from the group, both traumatic experiences in a society known for the value it places on face and association with the group (Fairbank 1986: 336; Whyte 1974: 21–22; Solomon 1969: 318–19, 326–27). It has also been argued that the Communist practice of dealing with a transgressor by seeking his self-criticism and the confession of his political crimes derives from traditional moral and legal codes. Since Confucianism stressed the importance of educating and transforming a transgressor, rather than merely punishing him, Chinese legal codes accordingly affirmed the value of the wrongdoer's conversion to correct ways, as signaled by his admission of guilt. If he confessed, punishment was waived or lessened, but if he would not confess, torture was applied until he did (Dittmer 1974: 338–39).

Many Communist criticism practices were not only consistent with cultural values but actually continued pre-Communist practices. Just as victims of the Cultural Revolution were taken through the streets wearing placards announcing their "crimes," in the past criminals had been dragged through the streets on the way to the execution ground in order to provide a concrete example of the consequences of transgression for the crowds of people gathered to watch the spectacle. In a 1927 article Mao had reported that the peasants paraded landlords through the street and forced them to wear dunce caps (Kwong 1988: 64; Thurston 1987: 118). While it is also true that the Communists undoubtedly practiced criticism to a much greater extent than had ever been done in the past, the evidence presented above shows that their actions were by no means without precedent.

### Pre-Communist Criticism of Superiors

Neither was the criticism of superiors by their inferiors unprecedented. A certain tension existed (and still exists, I believe) in Chinese culture between the value placed on hierarchy and compliance with the wishes of superiors and, on the other hand, the tolerance and even approval of criticism of superiors by those beneath them in status. Pye (1988) argues that there were two opposing political cultures in traditional China, high Confucian culture and a blend of Taoism, Buddhism, and localized systems of belief. The former endorsed hierarchy and authority while the latter glorified the rebel and his challenge to authority (1988: 39–40). Underlying these two political cultures was a more fundamental polarity in Chinese culture that Pye characterizes as the "acceptance of the legitimacy of venting emotions over any form of mistreatment by authority and a sense of the propriety and wisdom of controlling feelings and accepting one's situation fatalistically" (1988: 54).

There were even prescriptions for protest within Confucianism itself. In Confucius's words, "How can he be said to be truly loyal who refrains from admonishing the object of his loyalty?" (quoted in Houn 1965: 63). When asked how a prince should be served, Confucius said, "Do not deceive him, but when necessary withstand him to his face" (quoted in Houn 1965: 63). When asked if filial piety meant for the son to obey his father's orders, Confucius responded:

> How can you say this! How can you say this! . . . When confronted with unrighteousness, the son cannot but remonstrate with his father and the minister cannot but remonstrate with his ruler. Therefore, when con-

fronted with unrighteousness, remonstrate against it! How could merely obeying the father's orders be considered filial piety? (Quoted in Hucker 1959: 195)

Thus Confucius rejected the notion of unconditional obedience to authority and called on people to remonstrate with errant rulers or parents. Confucius and his followers were so insistent on this that remonstrance became not just a right of officials but a manifestation of their duty to their leaders (Hucker 1959: 196; Goldman 1981: 3). (During the student protests that occurred during my fieldwork I heard very similar sentiments. Many students felt that it was their obligation to criticize and protest against China's leaders.)

Both Mencius and Confucius sternly rebuked rulers to their faces (Houn 1965: 64; Hucker 1959: 194). Even before Confucius remonstrance had been institutionalized; Confucius referred to a great remonstrator who had bravely sacrificed his life in the service of admonishing the last Shang emperor (Houn 1965: 61). Until the Song Dynasty there were two groups of remonstrators. The first was composed of officials who, either on their own initiative or in response to a call to consult the throne, admonished the emperor. The second was composed of "talking officials," who played no role in the empire other than to talk or criticize. Within the second group there were those charged with admonishing the emperor, while a second group, the censors, was to impeach corrupt or incompetent officials. During the Song Dynasty a few structural changes occurred in the system but its function remained intact throughout subsequent dynasties (Houn 1965: 61–62).

The system of remonstrance was a regular and accepted part of the Chinese government. All the rulers professed adherence to it, and none dared repudiate it. Some rulers were not receptive to particular criticisms, and they were often condemned for this reaction, while those who were tolerant of criticisms made of them were praised (Houn 1965: 61). Many emperors even actively encouraged their subjects to admonish them (see Houn 1965: 66–68). Upon the death of his chief critic a Tang Dynasty emperor fell into a deep sorrow and remarked: "In my life I used three mirrors. One of bronze to adjust my dress; the records of history to correct the mistaken policies of the present; and Wei Cheng [his deceased critic], who served to reveal the faults of my character. Now I have lost the best of my mirrors" (Houn 1965: 67).

This Tang emperor's tolerance of dissent won him the admiration and acclaim of later generations, and he was cited as a model to be emulated by later rulers (Houn 1965: 67).

Of course, not all emperors were so tolerant of dissent. Remonstrance could be extremely hazardous since a displeased ruler might fire or even kill his critics (Hucker 1959: 201–2; Houn 1965: 66). Critics of even intolerant emperors persisted with their criticisms nonetheless and were even emboldened by the resistance of their leaders (Hucker 1959: 202; Houn 1965: 62), in part because those critics killed by their emperor for their criticisms could earn posthumous fame as a result of their martyrdom (Houn 1965: 65–66; Hucker 1959: 200). In addition remonstrators supported each other, so that if one was banished or killed for his criticisms, others would take his place and continue his remonstrances (Houn 1965: 62–63).

### Dissent in the Pre-Communist Classroom

Occurrences of criticism of superiors by their inferiors were not limited to the political sphere. In schools students sometimes challenged the authority of their teachers, and prominent among these challenges was criticism. Following are some examples:

Before the Cultural Revolution, even before the Communists assumed power in 1949, students wrote big character posters attacking their teachers. One older Third Affiliated teacher told me that in his middle school in the early 1940s, if a student believed a teacher was, for example, too strict, the student would write and post a big character poster saying something like: "Down with Teacher X." Such posters were by no means the actions of delinquent students but, in fact, were usually written by good students.

In his autobiography the famous scholar Guo Moruo recounts an incident in which the author and his fellow classmates united to criticize and defeat a teacher. The incident occurred in 1907, when Guo, in his mid-teens, was attending a Sichuan Province *xiaoxue,* a Chinese-run (that is, non-missionary) school. While *xiaoxue* now refers to a primary school for preteens, at that time it was a school where the majority of students were probably in their teens, with some students considerably older.

The author and six other students once decided not to give the food ladle to an older student known for overeating, thereby preventing him from serving himself lunch. After lunch the students were confronted about this by a teacher, who sternly asked: "Why didn't you give him food?" One student responded: "What do you mean, not give him food? We put the food on the table." The victimized student said pitifully: "You took the ladle, and didn't give it to me." An audience of students, who had gathered outside the window of the room where this conversation was occurring, laughed. Teacher: "You little things. What are you laughing at!" The students outside scampered away and then later returned. Teacher: "Why didn't you give him the ladle?" Student: "For eight people there's only one ladle. He [the older student] is too unintelligent. When the ladle didn't come to him, he could have used his bowl [to scoop out the food]." Teacher (to all seven accused students): "You little things! You're the only smart ones. You don't fear dying young." Students outside the window laughed again. Student: "We usually can't keep up with him. He usually hoards the food for himself. Today he couldn't beat us this way, and came to tell on us."

At this point the teacher unexpectedly slapped this student on the face, and the student started crying. Guo stood up for his fellow student and said: "Teacher, you're too mean." The students outside chimed in: "Yes, mean! Mean!" Guo continued: "In this civilized age still beating students!—Too inhumane. That shows your contempt for students' human dignity." The students outside and inside then formed together to clamor angrily at him. The teacher, seeing his "might overturned," stood up and walked into his room. After this incident of resisting the teacher, Guo became a school leader (Guo 1979 [1928]: 79–81).

In the biography of the Chinese general Fang Zhimin there is a story about how Fang and his classmates protested against their teacher and principal in various clever ways. Fang, in the early 1920s, was in his late teens and was a student at a Jiangxi Province technical school (also not a missionary school). One of Fang's teachers at that school irritated Fang and his classmates with his simple-minded lectures. For example, the teacher explained the English word "water" to the class by saying: " 'Water' is what we drink. It is what is in the oceans." Believing this teacher to be a "good-for-nothing" whose irresponsible teaching methods showed that he was just out for what he could get for himself in whatever way he could get it, Fang decided to go with several classmates to present a petition about this teacher to the school principal. They told the principal that several of the school's teachers were both ignorant and incompetent and they politely asked him to exchange teachers. The principal replied that the students, in speaking that way, were harming the teacher's respectability.

Fang became increasingly angry after leaving the principal's office. It then occurred to him that the school would have an evening party to commemorate the ninth anniversary of the 1911 Revolution. Fang decided to write his teacher into a play and mock his "Water is water" style. They gave the actor playing Fang's teacher a line in which he confused two simple characters, telling his class that the *li* of *xingli* was the *li* of *zheli*. The actor playing the teacher then added the teacher's famous line to the class: "Does everyone understand, or not?"

All the students in the audience roared with laughter and started talking about the teacher. The teachers in the audience, including the target of the satire, left quietly and angrily. The principal rebuked Fang, saying he hoped that Fang would concentrate on his studies in the future. But Fang countered that he could not study with such a bad teacher.

Fang then decided to investigate corrupt practices at the school. He hoped to find that the principal had taken funds from the school construction budget and used them to build a mansion for himself. Such a revelation, Fang thought, would arouse public indignation against the principal. (It is interesting that Fang chose to investigate his principal's misdeeds as a means of delegitimating and overthrowing him. This was the same tactic frequently used by the Communists in their attack on elites. See above, on public criticism in Chen Village.) The principal heard about Fang's plans and put up a notice to expel Fang and several other students. This ignited all the students, and led the student organization Fang had formed to call for the expulsion of the principal and the issuance of four resolutions: (1) to go on strike; (2) to dismiss the principal and have him prosecuted; (3) to reveal the school's corruption; (4) to demonstrate and submit petitions to relevant government offices. The students mounted protests at the principal's house. Other schools followed the lead of Fang's school and set up their own organizations calling for an end to the "old" and "dark" Jiangxi Province (Z. Zhang 1983: 18–22).

The resolution described above by Fang and his classmates to go on strike was not unusual. Just as a performer who loses his audience is disgraced, so a teacher whose students refuse to attend his class loses face. Therefore, student strikes were, and still are, a significant means of protest. While not actual criticism, such strikes do communicate the students' disapproval of their teacher or school.

An interesting account of strikes as a means of protest is contained in the autobiography of the director and playwright Tao Dun. In 1924, 23-year-old Tao was a middle school student at Shandong Province Middle School (also not a missionary school). His English teacher that year was not very good, so the students asked the school for a new teacher. After the school leaders refused, the students stopped attending the English teacher's class. Out of sympathy for their colleague, all teachers in the grade stopped teaching. Tao and his classmates then asked the principal to end the teachers' strike. He refused, leading the students to call their own strike of all classes at the school. In response to the student strike, the school authorities hurriedly begged well-liked teachers to mediate the dispute with the students. The school admitted its mistakes, and Tao took responsibility for writing a manifesto to criticize the school for its handling of the whole incident (Tao 1987: 108).

A history of a missionary middle school established by the Yale in China Association has several references to student strikes (see Holden 1964: 50–52). Shortly after the school's opening in 1906, for example, a few students once refused to stand in chapel for hymn singing. Angered by this, the school leader, an American, struck the table. The students then all left the school, and within hours the school was empty (Holden 1964: 50). In the ensuing years the students' challenge to school leaders became more forceful, and in 1926 they submitted a set of demands, among which was the right of the Student Union to call for the dismissal of any teacher at the school (Holden 1964: 159).

A final example comes from a short reminiscence about an incident in 1945. The class in which the author of the reminiscence was a student got a new teacher, a young woman (female teachers were still rare at that time) in her twenties. The author, spurred on by his classmates, asked the teacher how to pronounce five characters that the students had looked up in an old dictionary and purposely chosen because they were obscure. Their motive was to "test" the teacher, believing that if she could not answer, she was no good. (Asking difficult questions to test and embarrass a teacher is still a common tactic of students. See Chapter 5.) The teacher in fact could not answer. The author, feeling even more arrogant, read out the characters. The teacher's face became entirely red. The author haughtily left class, and other students followed, leaving the teacher alone in class (Y. Zhang 1985: 245–46).

## Chapter Summary

This chapter considers the historical background of the prevalence of evaluation and criticism in China. Unlike other societies where status was determined at birth, Chinese ideology held that society's elite positions (essentially official positions in the bureaucracy) should be awarded on the basis of merit. The determination of who was outstanding thus became an important concern of society, and Chinese individuals, in their pursuit of high status, exerted much energy to cultivate and demonstrate their merits.

The ideology of meritocracy was systematized in the examination system. People who scored highest on the exams were assigned the highest positions as officials. Although antimeritocratic practices did exist, the exam system still provided a high level of opportunity for those of lower status to rise to the top levels of society by virtue of their intelligence and diligent study.

Judgment of merit was not only important in recruiting people for elite positions but was also a central idiom of Chinese religious worship. Ancestor worship was, in large part, ritualized recognition of the merits of ancestors. Individuals thus sought merit-based fame both for occupational reasons and because it guaranteed them a kind of immortality that comes from being remembered by one's descendants. Also, fame based on one's merits and virtues brought status to one's family and lineage, which is another aspect to the significance of merit.

Because merit in traditional China was so important in justifying the status and power of an individual or group, the Maoist attack on traditional elites also entailed a repudiation of traditional meritocratic notions. University recruitment strategies were correspondingly changed so that those demonstrating the greatest commitment to revolutionary values, rather than those scoring highest on academic tests, gained acceptance to college. Such new university recruitment policies went up and down in favor, reaching their greatest manifestation during the Cultural Revolution. The post–Cultural Revolution return to recruitment by academic examination signals a return to meritocratic principles and shows the strength of such traditional principles despite a concerted Maoist attack against them.

This chapter then covers a history of the use of criticism by Chinese Communists. Mao, in his writings, accorded criticism a significant role in the society he sought to fashion, and criticism, in fact, was prevalent in Communist social and political campaigns from the early stages of the Communists' struggle for power. Criticism took different forms, including small group criticism, big character posters, press criticism, and public criticism or struggle sessions, and the tone of the criticism depended on the degree to which it was conducted in public. In small group criticism, which occurred only among the restricted context of one's presumed peers, all participants were considered equal and the goal was the rectification of their thinking. In the more public forums of the other three types of criticism, one person was singled out as a target, and criticism was more a weapon of attack and punishment.

One characteristic common to all forms of criticism was that inferiors often criticized superiors, and they were sometimes even officially sanctioned and directed to do so. In schools, students wrote big character posters attacking their teachers and abused them in public criticism meetings.

This chapter concludes with a discussion of the antecedents of Communist criticism in the pre-Communist era. Communist criticism was an effective resource precisely because it responded to traditional cultural values placed on face and the public recognition of merit. Therefore, not surprisingly, Cultural Revolution tactics such as parading an opponent through the streets had occurred in pre-Communist China as well.

Most importantly, the criticism of superiors by inferiors also had pre-Communist precursors and was ideologically justified and systematized in the institution of remonstrance. There are examples in the literature demonstrating that even in the classroom, students would challenge and criticize teachers and administrators whom they thought were incompetent, unfair, or corrupt.

Because criticism, and in particular the criticism of superiors, has a pre-Communist history, it becomes important to analyze its cultural underpinnings. This is the aim of the next chapter, in which the logic of face is discussed, along with how it can account for such phenomena as the criticism of those of high status by those with lesser status.

# 4

## The Centrality of Face

The concept of face is probably the feature of Chinese culture most familiar to Westerners. That most Westerners have heard about the Chinese concept of face is not accidental. Face is central to Chinese culture, and anyone who has contact with Chinese society cannot help encountering the manifestations of its importance.

The word "face" has come into common usage in English, having acquired a meaning in English that approximates what *mianzi* (face) means to the Chinese. English speakers will often use the phrase "saving [X's] face" to mean the act of arranging a delicate social situation in such a manner that any negative critique of X is muted. We also talk of "losing face" and mean "to be humiliated by the exposure of one's weaknesses." Chinese speakers most frequently speak of face in the negative, as something lost. *"Diu mianzi"* and *"diu lian"* both mean "to lose face" (although the latter is more serious). The meaning includes the English usage of "to lose face" and means, more broadly, to feel publicly humiliated because of an action displaying your incompetence or immorality to others. (This definition, as with the one that follows, will be elaborated on below). *"Mianzi,"* or "face," refers to the sense of psychological and social well-being that comes from the public recognition of your merits and virtues.

The Chinese concept of face is thus intimately connected to evaluation and criticism. This chapter's discussion of face is an elaboration of the previous treatment of evaluation since face is one more facet of the Chinese emphasis on evaluation.

### A Description of Face and Its Significance

Face is central in Chinese individuals and thus in their collective culture. All Chinese adults are expected to have a sensitivity to face, that is, to be able to feel the hurt that comes from public humiliation, and to desire to protect oneself from public dishonor. Having this sensitivity is so fundamental that any adult who does not seem to have *lianchi,* a "sense of honor and shame," is considered practically inhuman. One of the gravest ways you can insult someone is to say that he has no sense of shame, or that he does not want face *(bu yao lian).*

The reason that it would be so degrading for a Chinese adult to lack a sense of shame is that this would mean such a person was outside of society and unresponsive to its norms. Such a person could not be shamed and therefore could not be controlled. Public shaming, as the many examples in Chapters 2 and 3 demonstrate, is a primary means of control. Whether in schools, the workplace, or anywhere else, the Chinese will frequently handle discipline problems by publicly humiliating major offenders. Once, while talking to Xiao Li about how to solve discipline problems at the workplace, he told me that the best solution was to take a really bad offender and criticize and/or punish him publicly as a lesson to others. (The Chinese often say that criticizing an offender in public is done to provide a lesson in morals for the audience to the criticism. This is no doubt a partial motivation but the other motivation—public criticism as punishment—is equally true. However, in order to portray themselves as benevolent educators rather than as malevolent punishers, Chinese authorities less frequently admit the punitive motivation for public shaming.)

Since face is so central in social control, the Chinese place fundamental importance on it. They expect any mature adult to have at least a minimal sensitivity to face and, as described above, they hold in contempt anyone who lacks such sensitivity. (Only children are not obligated to have a sense of face and shame, as described below.) The socialization process encourages young people to develop a sense of face as they mature, a topic discussed in greater detail in Chapter 6. Furthermore, the Chinese treat each other's faces with respect for their precious value. This means, almost paradoxically, that although the Chinese can maintain social control by making offenders lose face, this happens with relative infrequency (except during exceptional times such as the Cultural Revolution), and instead the Chinese will try to protect the face of all but major offenders. This is because, as my informants told me, if people were publicly criticized and made to lose face all the time, they would no longer be sensitive to being shamed and then could no longer be disciplined by this method. Thus large-

scale public humiliation is used for discipline purposes, but it is reserved for exceptionally bad offenses (although what actually constitutes a major offense is not always clear and requires a certain degree
of judgment.) In everyday life the importance of face is maintained by
norms obligating all adult Chinese to respect each other's faces, just as
they must respect their own. An important aspect of this mutual face-
saving is the prohibition against public criticism of others for minor
errors.

Interestingly, the converse of mutual face-respect also holds true.
There is a general feeling that if someone is unjustifiably disrespectful
of your face—upsetting the usual balanced reciprocity—then you can
justifiably be disrespectful to his, a kind of reciprocal disrespect. As
Xiao Chen told a superior, "If you disrespect me, then I will disrespect
you." Or as one teacher lectured her students: "If you don't respect
other people, they won't respect you." One consequence of mutual
disrespect is that the person who is made to lose face will often become angry and indignant at the person making him lose face, and he
will often set out to recover his own face by seeking revenge on his
victimizer. The Chinese Communists appealed to this psychological
dynamic by repeatedly calling attention to the humiliation of the Chinese
people by their enemies. By stirring up feelings of self-humiliation the
Communists were hoping to also provoke popular anger toward the
people's victimizers (Pye 1968: 71).

While all Chinese must have a basic respect for their own and each
other's faces, some individuals and classes of people have more sensitivity to their own face than others, and one is expected to be somewhat more protective of their faces. (This variation in face-sensitivity
is subtle, as is the response it evokes, and is not as basic a principle of
Chinese society as the general reciprocal obligation to honor face described above). Informants frequently told me, for example, that females
are more easily shamed and more sensitive to face. Interestingly, one
informant said this is true among young women, but at about thirty to
fifty-five years of age the difference in face-sensitivity between males and
females diminishes. Informants also said the elderly, of whom more is
expected, are more vulnerable to loss of face. Because of this, they told
me that they believed individuals should be more careful in criticizing
both older people and females. There is also some indication that intellectuals and those who are more intellectually inclined are more sensitive to loss of face through public criticism. Third Affiliated, unlike

other schools with less outstanding students, did not post exam results for all to see. One teacher told me that is because Third Affiliated students are good students, so if the score of a student not doing well on an exam were publicized, this student would be more embarrassed than would an average student without a reputation to uphold.

The one category of people who are not under an obligation to be aware of their own and other's faces is children. Face is a social value and hence is seen not as something people are born with but as something they must learn. Children have little or no awareness of, nor sensitivity to, their own or others' faces. As an individual enters puberty *(qingchunqi),* he begins to develop a keen sensitivity to his own face and a strong aversion to being publicly criticized, yet he still is not fully responsive to, or obligated to be responsive to, the faces of others. Only in adulthood does an individual become fully sensitive to face, his own and those of others, and only then is he held accountable to fully display this sensitivity.

The recognition that face must be learned came out clearly in my interviews with informants. The greatest consistency among answers from different informants emerged in response to comparison between the criticisms of them voiced by teachers and parents while the informants were adolescents and such criticism while they were preteenage children. They uniformly answered that when they were children, their parents and teachers would openly and often harshly criticize them since, informants said, children have little knowledge of face. But as they entered adolescence, adults began to be sensitive to their youngsters' faces, because of the growing awareness that adolescents have of their faces. I observed this to be the case. When I visited families with children around five or six years old, I frequently saw their parents criticize them, and sometimes harshly. While I felt a strong imposition of parental will on adolescents, they were never criticized in my presence, even though I knew, from what informants had told me, that they were criticized when no visitors were present. That children, in contrast to adolescents and adults, were thought not to have much sensitivity to face perhaps best reflects and reinforces the importance of face in China. It means that being sensitive to one's own face and the face of others is seen as one of the clearest markers that an individual has become a mature adult. For an adult to lack this sensitivity would mean he was like a child, immature and hence degraded.

## *Losing Face*

Since it is taken for granted that every mature Chinese person will have face, it is usually talked about not in the positive but in the negative sense, as something that can be temporarily lost. This can happen when a person's sense of psychological and social well-being is harmed by the public display of his immorality or incompetence. In the case of the former, this can happen when moral transgression is revealed, or when one is publicly criticized for a moral transgression such as, for example, when a teacher criticizes a student, in front of the class, for talking during class. A very common example of losing face because of incompetence is when a student is called on in a foreign-language class to answer a question, but speaks inarticulately or cannot speak at all. Such a situation will especially lead to loss of face if the student is normally adept at foreign languages. This illustrates a very important point about loss of face: losing face involves the failure to live up to what is expected of you. If the public learns that you have violated a moral standard to which you should have conformed, this can lead you to lose face. If you have an established reputation but fail, in some context, to live up to it, this can also lead you to lose face. The implication of this is that those of whom more is expected—those who are famous, those who are older—are more vulnerable to losing face than are those without a reputation, or the young. The famous singer who sings poorly on a given occasion is especially vulnerable to losing face. The honored professor whose sexual improprieties are revealed is similarly vulnerable. In the words of a traditional maxim: "A tall thing is easy to break; a white thing is easy to stain. The white snow in spring can hardly find its match; a high reputation is difficult to live up to" (quoted in Cleverley 1985: 157). As a result, higher-status people, of whom more is expected in terms of both their competence and morality, are subjected to a greater burden to perform competently and to adhere to moral standards.

As with criticism, the terminology in Chinese for describing loss of face, shame, and embarrassment is quite rich. For losing face, the two most important expressions are *"diu mianzi"* or *"diu lian."* The latter, the more serious, is more likely to be used in the case of a moral transgression. Merely feeling embarrassed or ashamed *(bu hao yisi,* or *xiukui)* may not necessarily lead to losing face. Similarly, an awkward social situation may make you feel *bu hao yisi,* but would not usually make you lose face. Also, if you have a certain ability but cannot display this ability in a given situation, you lose face, whereas if you have no ability, then your performative failure only makes you feel shame *(xiukui)* rather than loss of face.

There are a number of parameters to loss of face that deserve analysis. First, face is lost when an individual feels that he has fallen beneath what the group expects of him because of a public display of his incompetence or immorality. Feeling that he has fallen beneath group expectations, the individual experiences the pain and isolation resulting from the withdrawal of group esteem. Loss of face is, thus, fundamentally an emotional reaction (usually temporary) of a person who has failed to live up to others' expectations. If he is publicly humiliated but feels no sense of humiliation, then he has not lost face. If others learn of his wrongdoings, but he is not aware that they know about them, then he has not lost face. His faults must be made public, and this must happen in such a way that he knows that they have been made public and is affected by this knowledge.

This brings up a second issue. Face is usually lost, especially in cases of incompetence, in a situation that is performative. Such situations are by no means always actual performances in the Western sense of the word. (Classrooms, for example, are not performative settings in the Western concept, but they are a prime performative arena for loss of face by teachers and students in China.) However, the contexts in which face is often lost in China resemble performances because many of the characteristics found at performances are present. As at a performance, there is an audience and a person performing a task whose successful outcome depends on his skill. The performer is often one deemed worth watching, someone with a reputation. Those who comprise the audience are usually less skilled than the performer. Finally, the performer's self-esteem, his face, rises or falls with the audience's reaction. It is through the audience's reactions—whether or not they laugh at the performer, whether or not they attend to his performance, and so on—that the performer learns whether he has secured or lost public respect. The audience and its reactions thus play a significant role in whether or not a performer loses face.

Third, there must be a genuine public audience. If you perform for yourself and fail, you will not lose face. More importantly, if you perform incompetently before your family, you will also not lose face. You can only lose face when your incompetence is made public and becomes known to outsiders. Usually, this means you lose face when just about anyone but family sees you perform incompetently, friends included. However, the insider/outsider distinction is flexible, so that sometimes friends can be considered insiders, and losing face occurs among non-friends. Sometimes all Chinese are insiders, and losing face means having your incompetence known to foreigners. The stakes involved escalate as distance between the performer and his audience grows. Chinese often feel much greater loss of face, for example, when performing incompetently before a foreigner than when doing so before Chinese. The one important qualification to this pattern is that a performer will not lose face if there is no relationship between him and his audience because he is anonymous and among total strangers. If, for example, you are excellent at riding a bicycle, but fall down from your bicycle in the street, you will not lose face if the people who see you are total strangers and have no idea who you are. If you are anonymous to them, they can have no expectations of you, and their seeing you fall cannot harm your reputation. One consequence of the above is that an outsider can have a great deal of power. Unless you are in an anonymous situation, it is the person outside your given social group whose esteem you most want, and it is he who, at the same time, can cause you the greatest loss of face if you fail in his presence.

Fourth, you can cause loss of face for others. If you fail a university exam, then you might say that you have lost your parents' face *(diu fumude lian)*. You can even lose China's face. When a Chinese student studying in the United States, for example, does something embarrassing, his fellow Chinese classmates might remark that he has lost China's face.

Finally, just as all adults have sensitivity to face, but some are more sensitive than others, so every adult can lose face, but some have more at stake. Those who are more sensitive, or those who have an outstanding reputation, will be more vulnerable to losing face.

### Examples of Loss of Face

Many of the following examples are drawn from actual events that happened to my informants, and they are therefore not outstanding examples, but rather typical ones. An example of a serious offense being made public and leading to loss of face happened at Northeast

University. Two students at Northeast were found to have violated sexual standards, one of the most serious offenses in China. It turned out that one male college student would sometimes bring his girlfriend to his dorm room and engage in sexual relations with her. His roommates eventually turned the couple in to the school authorities, and both of them were expelled from Northeast for having had premarital sex. This was especially devastating to the expelled female student, a first-year student from the countryside who earlier that year had been sent off to college with a big ceremony in her village. Her mother, feeling that she too had lost face, committed suicide. The girl did the same, and finally her father killed himself. This example illustrates how making public the transgressions of one person can lead to loss of face for the whole group to which he belongs.

An informant told me of another incident that also demonstrated this. My informant once went to the Foreign Guest House at Northeast University to visit her friend, a foreigner. The attendant on duty prevented her from entering, which was an unfair violation of his authority at my informant's expense. Later, when my informant met up with her foreign friend, she told her what had happened. My informant was eventually rebuked by the head of the housing department, who cited a Chinese saying, "The ugliness of the house shouldn't be let outside" (jiachou buwai chuan). In other words, my informant should not have let outsiders know about the faults of the inside; she should not have told a foreigner about the abuses of the Chinese attendant.

Another way to lose face is to perform incompetently, relative to your reputation, in front of others. If a person talented in many endeavors except, say, singing, is asked to sing at a party, and then sings poorly, this can lead to loss of face. If a person with a college degree and a person with a graduate degree do the same job at a work unit, and the former achieves more than the latter, the latter person will feel he has lost face since, judging by their respective degrees, he should have been the one to do better. If a student stands in class and corrects a teacher's mistake, the teacher will feel loss of face, especially if he is older and/or more sensitive about his face. If a teacher calls on a student, and the student cannot answer the question, the student may feel loss of face.

A third way to lose face is to be shown to be weak, and men are especially vulnerable to losing face this way. If a man's friends come to visit and his wife asks him to do the laundry, something women in

China traditionally do, he will lose face. Many Chinese, especially men, feel that if they lose a fight or an argument, or if they lose a fight and fail to be revenged, then they will lose face. During my stay in China the owners of two small restaurants where I ate once got into a fight. In the end one owner told me his competitor would not be returning to his business. The reason was that the owner and six friends had beaten the competitor up in the street and forced him to kneel in public and ask for forgiveness. The competitor felt such an intense loss of face that he could not bear to return to the neighborhood where his lucrative restaurant was located, so he closed it.

There are still other forms of weakness considered to lead to loss of face. If a teacher, employer, or parent orders you to do something in a forceful and abrupt tone of voice, this can hurt your self-respect (zizunxin), which is nearly as serious as harming your face. Being cheated by a merchant can endanger your face, and anyone so cheated will try very hard to seek retribution. This is also true if someone robs you in the street. Also, yielding to others when, for example, boarding a bus, can lead to loss of face. A Chinese newspaper article explained:

> People in China rarely give others the right of way. When they want to go through a door, they do not usually care about the person on the other side . . . Giving precedence to others is usually considered a loss of face. "Who are you and why should I make way for *you?*" they would say. People make way for their superiors, elders, colleagues or friends, but never for strangers, because they do not want to look inferior. . . . [A Chinese person] will not give precedence to anyone in the street if he does not want to look inferior. (Lao Hu 1989)

One last way in which face can be lost concerns requests. If you ask someone to assist you in some way, and that person refuses, this will often make you lose face. This is especially true if the person is someone with whom you have a good relationship, friends included, and someone therefore whom you thought would help you. Their refusal violates your expectations about the quality of your relationship, and makes clear to both of you that they do not esteem you, and your mutual relationship, as highly as you had thought.

### Protecting, Promoting, and Giving Face

While face is usually conceived of in the negative sense, as something to be lost, it also has a positive side, as something that is given, protected, and promoted. I have already defined the main meaning of "*mianzi*," face, as the sense of psychological and social well-being coming from the public recognition of one's merits and virtues. Since having one's merits publicly recognized also often leads to the attainment of high status, face and status are connected, and thus a second meaning of face is authority. Authority, in turn, gives a person many connections *(guanxi)*, so if you say someone's face is "big," this usually means that he has a great deal of authority, and/or that he has many connections and is good at getting things done. To specify the antithesis to lost face and shame—that is, the sense of pride itself resulting from your merits and virtues—the Chinese usually use words other than *mianzi*. A teacher at a key school whose students all fail the college entrance exam, for example, will lose face *(mianzi),* and if they all succeed, he will obtain honor and glory *(guangrong, guangcai).* Any major achievement or award in a competition can bring a person glory, and such glory also extends to the group to which he belongs. Having money itself cannot bestow glory since it is an honor only bestowed by others, and hence cannot be bought or acquired in transactions.

As previously discussed, all adult Chinese are expected to be sensitive to face. To describe a lack of this sensitivity the Chinese often say someone "does not want face" *(bu yao lian)*. However, describing the presence of this sensitivity is more complicated. Someone who is sensitive to face and shame is said to have a strong sense of "self-respect" or "pride" *(zizunxin)*. This is, of course, a very desirable trait. But someone who goes beyond this—who not only avoids shame but actively pursues glory—evokes ambivalent feelings in the Chinese. Such a person, one "paying much attention to face" *(hen jiang mianzi* or *yao mianzi),* takes too active an approach to face. He is seen as trying too hard to acquire glory, the positive, non–social-controlling variety of face, rather than expending his efforts, as he is supposed to, to avoid shame and loss of face. Such near self-evaluation is disfavored, since it conflicts with the power of members of Chinese society to evaluate each other.

While pursuing glory too actively is condemned, glory itself is highly esteemed, thus many Chinese individuals and institutions manifest outward modesty while covertly pursuing and promoting their faces and their glory. This process is especially familiar to any foreigner who has visited China, since glory comes from making your merits known to outsiders, and, therefore, foreigners, the supreme out-siders, are prime candidates for any Chinese desiring to enhance his reputation and glory. Advertising your merits to outsiders is called *xuanchuan*, a word that means "propaganda" but is closer in tone to "advertising." In Chapter 2, I referred to my prime encounters with *xuanchuan*, which occurred when I was taken to visit schools. Such visits that always took a similar form. In the introduction to the school given by its administrators and experienced teachers, the school repre-sentatives would talk first about how inadequate the school's educa-tional practices were in years past. This discussion allowed them to display the required modesty, yet cast their inadequacies as a thing of the past. They would continue with a discussion of how, through the hard work of a dedicated faculty, the school had transformed itself into an outstanding institution; they would then cite the many accomplishments of the school, its students, and teachers, while concealing its faults.

I was able to see this promotion of face at work especially clearly in my visits to Marketplace Middle School. The administrators there did not know that I had a friend from Northeast University student teach-ing there. My friend had no stake in protecting Marketplace's face, since he was only a temporary member of the school, so he told me quite honestly what was happening there. His version of events was quite at odds with that told by the administrators. They professed to be telling me everything about the school, even its faults, yet they failed, for example, to tell me that in between two of my visits several stu-dents had tried to break into a school office at night to steal an exam answer key, and that in the process one of these students slipped from the balcony in front of the office and fell to his death. The school administrators were protecting and promoting the school's glory by concealing its faults from a foreigner. This practice is very common whenever any foreigner goes to visit any institution in China. In fact it is also common whenever any Chinese who is not a member of a given institution goes to visit that institution. Xiao Zhang told me that he experienced the same problem studying schools in China that I had: Whenever he visited one they would only reveal their merits to him.

Not only can you promote your face, but others can also promote your face for you, an action that, unlike promoting your own face, is not looked down on. One way in which others can promote your face is by protecting you from criticism or loss of face. For example, if you do not force someone who is not good at singing to sing a song at a party (Chinese often take turns singing at parties), then you are protecting him from losing face, or, simply, protecting his face *(baohu mianzi)*. If a teacher waits until after class to criticize a misbehaving student, rather than criticize him in front of all his peers, then the teacher is protecting the student's face. Others can also give you face *(gei mianzi)*. When a student answers a question in class incorrectly, his classmates often laugh at him. In such a situation, a classmate who might rise and say to the laughing students "What's funny about this?" would be giving face to the student being laughed at. A leader who accepted an invitation to come to the house of a middle- or lower-status person would be giving that person face. Another very important way to give face is to praise someone in front of others. This is something the Chinese do quite often, since praising someone and giving him face makes him feel good, and this, in turn, predisposes him to honor whatever request one might make of him. Officials at Northeast University regularly praised our drivers in front of us because, they told us, this was the best way to guarantee that the drivers would be cooperative in the future. Whenever Shu Laoshi accompanied me on my visits to schools, he would always praise the school administrators with whom we were meeting in front of all others present, including me. They would always be quite obviously pleased at the public praise. That this praise was probably often insincere did not matter; public praise is not valuable in itself but is valuable because it gives face to its recipient. In political study meetings participants are often required to *bao tai,* to express their opinions of the government and the Communist Party. They always will say that they support the party and praise it. In many cases they really loathe the party, but the insincerity of their statements is inconsequential. By publicly praising the party they are giving it face, whether or not, in private, the praise is genuinely felt.

One variant of giving face is *jiu mianzi,* "rescuing face." If someone criticizes you and later turns around and praises you, they are rescuing your face. You can also recover your own face. Since face is an emotional reaction stemming from a humiliating situation, if you forget the feelings of humiliation, then you have recovered your lost face.

As the above discussion suggests, protecting and promoting your own face and that of others often requires a certain measure of insincerity and even of untruthfulness. For example, since you can lose face if someone denies your request, the Chinese infrequently directly deny requests made of them, even when they have no intention of fulfilling such requests. Instead, they will invariably promise to fulfill the request and then proceed to do nothing. When the person making the request reiterates it, they are often told that there are unforeseen delays preventing carrying out the request, but that, after the short delay, the request will still be honored. This process of delays can carry on for weeks and months. Foreigners visiting China become quite familiar with this phenomenon. During my first year in China many of the foreign residents in the Foreign Guest House at Northeast University complained that the building was not being heated, as had been promised in their contracts. Members of Northeast's Foreign Affairs Office, with whom we foreigners were on good terms, nonetheless refused to tell us the truth (as we were finally later told by one young university official): The Guest House and Foreign Affairs Office were at odds with each other, and the Guest House made trouble for the Foreign Affairs Office by violating promises made by the Foreign Affairs Office in its contracts with foreigners (in this case, a promise to supply heat). Instead of telling us this, they said the heating coal was on a slow barge working its way up from southern China. Needless to say, by the time I left China one year later, the barge had still not arrived.

Chinese will sometimes also misrepresent the truth in order to promote their own face. Institutions will often falsely boast about their accomplishments. After a visit to a school for juvenile delinquents I was asked my opinion of the school. Since I was impressed with the school, I told its leaders that I thought the school was impressive. The next day my friends told me that I had been quoted on the provincial television station as saying that the Chinese schools for juvenile delinquents are much better than similar American schools, because the American schools for delinquents are run by the police. (I, of course, did not say this.) A few days later I was quoted again in a local newspaper. The quotation attributed to me was so different from what I had actually said that I had to look up many of the words I had "said" in the dictionary, since the quotation exceeded the limits of my Chinese vocabulary.

### Face and Evaluation

#### The Limits on Who Can Evaluate

Since face and evaluation are central to social status and social control, rights of evaluation—who can and cannot evaluate—are socially structured and are not given to any and all people. Above all, you are not supposed to praise yourself. If you were allowed to praise yourself and were not dependent on others to give you esteem, then Chinese society would be deprived of an important means of control. My informant, Xiao Chen, often a nonconformist, was one who did not abide by the Chinese prohibition of self-praise. She thought highly of herself and would announce her merits to others. She once said to a classmate and the leader of a small group of student teachers that she had taught a practice class quite well. He responded angrily, "Of what use is it to evaluate yourself? I don't think you're the best." Later, a teacher took Xiao Chen aside and instructed her in the dangers of self-praise, she told her that she should admit her weaknesses to others but not advertise her own strengths.

As the above example illustrates, the societal proscription of self-praise is complemented by a requirement to display modesty and self-criticism. In many contexts, Chinese will engage in a kind of formulaic modesty. Whenever I visited an institution, its representatives invariably claimed, "Our conditions are truly inadequate." After I audited a teacher's class, the teacher always asked me for my criticisms and admitted that he had much left to learn. In my Chinese-language class at an American university, our teacher, who had recently arrived from the People's Republic, came into class one day, his head hung low as he confessed that our section had the lowest test scores; he took the blame for our poor performance and asked us how he could remedy his ineffective teaching approach. Needless to say, the class did not know how to respond since teachers who self-criticize before their students and ask their students how they can improve are uncommon in America. But for the Chinese, modesty and self-criticism are expected.

There are good reasons to self-criticize in China. One astute informant told me that self-criticism is a form of self-protection, because if you criticize yourself first, then criticism of you by others is made more difficult. Xiao Li told me that if a leader in the workplace asks you if you can do a given task, you must say, "I'm no good—I can't." Only after much persuading will you agree to give it a try. That way, if you fail, no one will criticize you. If, however, you willingly volunteer for a task, or agree to do it the first time you are asked, others will accuse you of "trying to become famous" (xiang chuming). If you succeed, they will still praise you, but if you fail, they will criticize you, and you will lose face.

To try to show off your skills, or "to put yourself in the limelight," is called "*chu fengtou*" in Chinese. While showing off is acceptable if you are genuinely meritorious, showing off when you are clearly unskilled is widely condemned. Someone who tries to show off and fails is seen not only as a failure—which in itself makes an individual in China vulnerable to ridicule—but also as a selfish fool. The failed show-off is viewed as selfish because he threatens society's right to evaluate him, and foolish because he appears ignorant of, or insensitive to, modesty and face. The failures of the person who has tried to show off elicit much more laughter from others than do the failures of the modest person; since being laughed at by others is a prime way to lose face, the show-off is much more vulnerable. The show-off also attracts more attention, and is thus more vulnerable to criticism. Xiao Chen, my show-off informant, was warned about this by sympathetic friends, who told her that by not hiding her merits she would be watched more closely by others eager to find her faults. This phenomenon is articulated in a traditional Chinese saying: "The bird that sticks its head up gets it chopped off" *(qiang da chu tou niao)*. Since Xiao Chen failed to heed her friends' advice, she was often criticized by her classmates and was, more generally, unpopular among them. At Third Affiliated the incompetent show-off was among the most unpopular of all types of students.

Despite the strong hostility in China to the incompetent show-off, many people still try to display their talents. This is because while a failed display will lead to condemnation and criticism, a successful one can help you cultivate your reputation. Thus I often perceived a certain tension in many Chinese individuals between the desire to show off and the recognition of the requirements of formulaic modesty. One solution to this tension adopted by many is to both self-criticize and self-praise, but in such a manner that the former is overt and obvious while the latter is subtle yet, nonetheless, present. As described above, in my visits to schools administrators would always mention the faults of the school first and only then, with a certain degree of feigned embarrassment, mention its merits. Many individuals adopted this strategy. One student told me that China is clearly the most backward nation in the word. He then added that, with time, it would become the world's greatest. I found the combination of pride and humility, or pride intentionally concealed by humility, to be a quintessential characteristic of most Chinese I met. In addition, the more formulaically self-critical someone was, the more covertly proud he seemed to be. This association of pride and humility can be explained by face. *Lianchi,* as defined at the start of this chapter, is both a sense of shame and a sense of honor. Without honor, an individual would have no face to lose. Without a sense of shame, an individual would not be capable of losing face.

### Who Evaluates and Who Gets Evaluated

The right to explicitly evaluate someone's competence or performance—that is, the right to issue a public judgment, which will be widely accepted, of someone's potential or performed talent—belongs to high-status persons, who are often themselves considered superior in competence. Whether in academics, athletics, the arts, or other fields of endeavor, those of superior status are the ones charged with evaluating. In the classroom, for example, it is the teacher who decides whether a student has answered a question correctly or not.

However, given the intense interest of the Chinese in evaluation, those of inferior status still find ways to evaluate others, even others who are of higher status. There are many ways in which inferiors can implicitly evaluate the competence or morality of others. One such means is staring. As most foreign visitors to China know from personal experience, the Chinese stare a lot, and there is no general belief, as in the West, that staring is impolite. The reason staring is permitted, and sometimes even encouraged, is that it is an important means by which the general public can implicitly evaluate someone, and a means by which they can indirectly cause someone to lose face. By staring at someone, a crowd of people can communicate its disapproval of that individual and his actions. As one Third Affiliated student wrote in her English diary about her classmates' reaction when they discovered that she might be dating a boy, something middle school students are not allowed to do: "That was the darkest day in my junior middle school life. As soon as I entered the classroom, I felt a lot of sights like sharp arrows shooting into me. There were indifferent, surprised, taking-pleasure-in-others' misfortunes, sights everywhere." (I made minor corrections in the English grammar of this passage.) As this passage illustrates, being stared at can be very painful. This is because being stared at can lead to a feeling of loss of face. Staring at someone makes him aware that his actions are being observed, communicates public disapproval for his actions, and creates a barrier between him (the person watched) and the group (those who watch him)—all key factors in loss of face.

Just as staring at others is quite common in China, so is laughing at others, something for which I never heard anyone be scolded. Laughing at someone is another means of implicitly evaluating them and making them vulnerable to  loss of face; so isrefusing to pay attention to someone's public performance, if that performance is deemed incompetent. (In the next chapter I show how this happens in the classroom when students think a teacher is no good.)

Of course, in any society inferiors are able to implicitly evaluate their superiors in the same ways described above for China. However, implicit evaluation is validated in China in a way that it is not in many other societies, because of the role implicit evaluation plays in the creation and destruction of face and reputation. Recognition for merits and talent is frequently gained in a public, performative context, before an audience whose reaction confirms its appreciation. The audience's reactions are also instrumental in making one lose face because of incompetence, since it is through others' reactions that the performer becomes aware of failure and loss of others' esteem. In cases of immorality as well it is the reactions of others that communicate loss of societal respect, leading to loss of face. Thus the reactions of the audience witnessing performative displays of merit, and watching and judging the morality of social actors, are central to the dynamics of reputation and face. This is true even if the audience is inferior in status to the performer (which is often the case). Since societal control over individuals' faces is central in China, even the highest superior is required to depend on others to give him face, or make him lose face, and for a high-status person these others will most likely be his inferiors. So the reactions of an audience of inferiors to the actions of a superior are considered to be a valid measure of his merit and morals, and a legitimate means to make him lose face if he performs incompetently or acts immorally. This gives inferiors a culturally accepted and sanctioned role as the implicit evaluators of their superiors.

So the power of superiors to explicitly evaluate inferiors is balanced by a sanctioned right of inferiors to implicitly evaluate superiors. An additional check on the evaluative power of superiors is simply that they are more often the targets of evaluation than inferiors, more likely to be on stage, and hence more often vulnerable to loss of face. There is in China an interesting asymmetry in who gets evaluated. As you age and/or gain status, you are not only not freed from the burden of being evaluated, but are even more likely to be evaluated. You are watched more closely, and your immoral behavior becomes a cause for more gossip and negative evaluation than would generally be the case if you were of lower status. This asymmetry also holds true for judgments about talent. If you are of higher status, people will pay more attention to your displays of merit and will be more eager to witness your performances in order to verify that you are as good as you are reputed to be. I experienced this phenomenon firsthand. As a doctoral student, and as a native of the United States, the country the Chinese most admire, teachers at Third Affiliated believed that I surely had a great deal of educational expertise. Shortly after my arrival at the school, many teachers asked to audit my oral English class to observe both my methods and my skills. When I explained that I had come to study Chinese teaching methods, and so wanted to see them teach, they were reluctant, explaining that since I must be more skilled at teaching than they, it was more appropriate that they be my audience than that I be theirs. Despite my supposed expertise, teachers who audited my course did not hesitate to criticize my teaching. I learned that the performance and actions of those with status and merit are the most closely watched and those people are the most closely judged. While inferiors are judged too, less is expected of them, so they are more often in the audience than on stage.

One additional manifestation of the heavier evaluative pressure on superiors is the Chinese tendency to credit superiors for the successes of their inferiors and blame them for their failures. Praise or blame for an inferior's accomplishments is awarded less to the inferior himself than to his superiors. For example, a student who passes the college entrance examination wins glory for himself. But he wins even more glory *(zheng guang)* for his school, his teachers, and his parents. Diligent students would often say that their motive for studying was to repay the effort their parents had put into raising them by passing the college entrance examination, thereby winning glory for their parents and teachers. It was commonly accepted that a student's achievements were "for the teacher's glory." Similarly, a very intelligent student at a key school who fails the college entrance exam is an embarrassment not just to himself, but even more to his parents and his teachers, who are seen as having failed every bit as much as the exam candidate. I knew a number of parents who were truly dejected because their children, who were intelligent and who had gone to key schools, did not pass the college entrance exams. It was common in such a situation to say that the child who failed a major test had lost his parents' face *(diu ta fumude lian).*

Many Chinese practices reflect the fact that praise and blame for an inferior's achievements, or lack thereof, are awarded to his superiors. For example, schools and teachers base their reputations on the achievements of their students. Whenever I visited a school, a major component of the presentation of its administrators was a description of all of the "talents" *(tiancai)* that the school had cultivated. At Third Affiliated administrators closely monitored the percentage of its students who passed the college entrance exam, since the school's traditionally high percentage of such students was the primary basis for the school's high reputation. If a teacher adopted a teaching technique that other teachers, or the principal, felt was not consistent with preparing students for the college entrance exam, they would pressure the teacher to abandon that technique. Teachers were also judged on the basis of their students' exam results. Twice each semester, after midterm and final examinations, the school would calculate the scores for each teacher's students, and all teachers for a given subject in a given grade would be ranked based on their students' scores. This practice prompted one teacher to tell me that she believed the exams were meant less as a test of the students than as a test of the teachers, a nice articulation of the Chinese tendency to focus the evaluative spotlight on superiors.

Holding a superior accountable for his inferior's performance is a tradition of long standing in China. Whenever I asked an informant to explain the phenomenon, he would invariably say, "That's the way it's always been in China," and quote some traditional idioms as evidence. Many of these sayings reflect the fact that a child or student must be nurtured to greatness, so that if he fails to become great, it is the fault of his father or teacher. The famous *Three Character Classic* includes the following: "A father is in the wrong if he gives birth to a son but doesn't teach him, and a teacher is lazy if he is not strict with his student" *(Yang bu jiao, fu zhi guo. Jiao bu yan, shi zhi duo); and,* *"Famous teachers give rise to good students" (Ming shi chu gao tu);* as well as, "When those above behave unworthily, those below will do the same" *(Shang liang bu zheng, xia liang wai).*

Crediting superiors with their inferiors' achievements was institutionalized in Chinese tradition in the practice of ancestor worship. As Hsu summarizes: "Those who fail to do well reflect upon the conduct of their ancestors, and their ancestors share the disgrace of their failing to do well" (F. Hsu 1967: 264). Xiao Li said that the desire to earn glory for one's ancestors, while not as strong as in traditional China, is still a factor. A son will study hard in order to earn honor for his father. Hsu suggests that one reason people may give credit for their successes to their ancestors is to avoid the arrogance of claiming that their achievements derive from their own superiority (F. Hsu 1967: 267–68). This may explain the crediting of superiors with their inferiors' accomplishments in contemporary China. A successful student, in order to avoid arousing his classmates' jealousy and avoid being seen as one trying to put himself in the limelight, may attribute his success to the efforts of his teacher and parents. Likewise, his teacher and parents, who must also refrain from advertising their own merits, are nonetheless entitled to brag indirectly by reporting the accomplishments of their students or children.

### The Power to Make Someone Lose Face

The power to evaluate someone is significant, but evaluation becomes even more potent if it leads to loss of face. The question thus becomes: Who has the power to make others lose face?

As in the case of evaluation, inferiors and superiors have complementary powers. Superiors can publicly criticize or negatively evaluate someone, causing the target to feel a loss of face. However, the public before which he will most easily lose face is a public of his status peers or inferiors. While you can lose face in front of an audience of people superior to you in status, the emotions of losing face are more likely to be engendered when you are criticized before an audience of equals or inferiors. The rights of explicit evaluation may generally belong to superiors, but the power to make someone feel he has lost face belongs to an audience of his equals or inferiors.

This is because of the nature of face. Loss of face is both the loss of a public group's esteem and estrangement from the group as a result of your temporary degradation. If the public group witnessing your failure consists of your superiors, a group generally considered better than you in merit and often virtue as well, you may lose their esteem, but you cannot become estranged from them since you were never accepted as their equal in the first place and were not a part of their group. Thus your failure does not lead you to experience the real pain of loss of face—estrangement from the group to which you belong.

If the audience consists of your status equals, however, then your failure lowers your standing in their eyes and threatens your place among them. This feeling is intensified when the audience consists of inferiors. You might have failed at what even they could have successfully accomplished, so you not only experience temporary estrangement from your own group but fall below it into a lower-status group—this is the real loss in loss of face.

Your loss is others' gain. Inferiors who witness your failure may feel emboldened by it. They may believe that they could have succeeded where you failed, and may feel justified in looking down on you, even though your status exceeds theirs. Looking down on others, *qiaobuqi*, is a common phenomenon in China. One main situation in which others will look down on you is, as just indicated, if you fail at something that your inferiors could have done successfully. In this case inferiors (but not superiors) can, and often do, look down on you. For example, a college student may look down on a graduate student who is unable to answer a question that he, the college student, could have answered. If, however, the roles were reversed, with the college student unable to answer a question the graduate student could answer, then the graduate student could not look down on the college student. The latter situation is consistent with what we might expect given their respective educational levels and so cannot be a justification for anyone's arrogance. But the former situation conflicts with expectations, leading the graduate student to lose face and status and the college student to feel emboldened and justified.

The one main situation when the above pattern is reversed is when someone is judged on position rather than performance. A high-status person may not be able to look down on a low-status person as a result of that person's failures, but he can look down on such a person because of his low position. For example, primary and secondary school teachers in China are underpaid and have little status, causing many people to look down on them. Similarly, a graduate student may look down on a college student because his own education level is higher.

In general, then, you lose face in front of equals or inferiors, and they feel most justified in looking down on you for your failures. The same pattern also holds true for age. Older people are vulnerable to losing face before a crowd of younger people, but a young person failing before a crowd of his elders is not very vulnerable to losing face. Thus the hierarchical Chinese social system has an intrinsic tendency to invert temporarily—temporarily raising the status of inferiors above superiors—whenever a high-status person fails to perform in a manner consistent with his perceived ability and status before a crowd of his inferiors.

## The Toleration of Criticism of Superiors by Inferiors

Despite the official downgrading of Mao and Maoism after his death, the Maoist ideology described in the last chapter, calling on everyone to criticize themselves and others, remains in force in China. Evidence of this is a story in a magazine I saw for middle school students, the moral of which, according to the author, was that concealing others' "mistakes" (that is, their moral transgressions, in this case cheating by a student) harms everyone and damages the collective honor. The article ends by saying that a model youth should criticize himself and others (Zhao 1984: 59). Perhaps this ideology should not be considered as much Maoist as Chinese, since many informants whom I knew to be opposed to Maoism were nonetheless firm advocates of the importance of anyone's right to criticize anyone else, even his own superior in cases of severe moral transgressions. Xiao Li, for example, told me a story to illustrate the view that superiors can make mistakes and so should be willing to accept the criticisms of their inferiors. Xiao Li's story was of how his aunt had asked him to help persuade her daughter (Xiao Li's cousin), an educated woman who was dating an uneducated peasant, to switch her romantic interests to an educated man. Xiao Li talked first with another cousin, the young woman's brother. This cousin is Xiao Li's inferior in status because of his age (Xiao Li is married and in his late twenties while the male cousin is in his late teens). Nonetheless, he took Xiao Li to task for old-fashioned ideas and, specifically, for Xiao Li's failure to recognize the legitimacy of emotions in dating and love. Xiao Li conceded that his cousin might be right, told him he would think about the issue, and decided to interfere no longer in the romances of his female cousin. In telling me this story Xiao Li stressed that inferiors, such as his male cousin, can sometimes be right, and that if they are right, they should not hesitate to criticize a superior, just as Xiao Li's male cousin had criticized Xiao Li.

Many informants articulated similar views. Given the Western view of a strictly hierarchical China, I was surprised to find that when I asked if a superior ought to be obeyed all the time, informants answered in the negative. They told me that if a superior is "wrong," that is, if his commands are faulty or immoral in some sense, then inferiors need not obey him, and should correct the superior's mistaken beliefs. This view was invoked as well during the student protests of spring 1989. Many of my friends said they believed that it was their duty to oppose the government and call government officials to account for various immoralities, particularly their participation in corrupt practices. In justifying their involvement in the protests as a duty, my friends were echoing the Confucian view, described in the previous chapter, that a man must rebuke his ruler if the ruler's actions are faulty. In true Confucian fashion my friends told me that they were willing to sacrifice their careers, even their lives, in order to criticize the government for its malfeasance.

Early in my stay in China I noticed a certain asymmetry in the call to criticize. There was less ideological encouragement for superiors to criticize inferiors than for inferiors to criticize superiors. (This is not to say, however, that inferiors were in reality always free to criticize their superiors. They were not, since, as discussed below, they risked retaliation from their superiors.) Teachers almost universally told me that they welcomed their students' criticism because it helped them improve their teaching. Of course, I knew that teachers were not really as tolerant of criticism as they appeared, but they felt it necessary to make a pretense of their receptivity. Students, however, seemed under no similar obligation to display their willingness to be criticized by their teachers. When I asked them their attitude toward teachers who criticize students, they told me that they dislike teachers who criticize them too much, especially those who criticize unfairly. They said students believe such teachers are "inexperienced." As one student summarized, a student who criticizes unfairly can be forgiven, but a teacher, who ought to know better, would not be forgiven. I doubt that the students' responses to my question merely reflected less pretense among them than among teachers. In fact, I usually found that teachers were more open and honest with me about how they felt than were students, so the difference between teachers' and students' toleration of criticism is probably attributable to a cultural ideology that is more tolerant of inferiors criticizing superiors than of the reverse.

In some ways criticism of superiors by inferiors is not only tolerated but even encouraged. Inferiors who criticize superiors attract the attention and respect of their peers. In Chapter 2 I described a meeting held at Third Affiliated to give students a chance to air their opinions of teachers to an administrator, where there was one female student who expressed fierce criticism. Other students at the meeting, who were engaged in private conversations with each other, stopped talking to listen when this student spoke. Her indignation clearly caught their attention. A similar dynamic was evident at an academic conference I attended. One man used the conference as an opportunity to express his anger at the central government in defiant and indignant terms. Whenever he spoke people listened carefully and commented to each other what an interesting and forceful speaker he was. When some time was left over near the end of the conference, he was the one whom people persuaded to give an additional short speech.

I asked many students their opinion of a student who publicly criticizes a teacher. I had expected most students to say, even if they felt differently, that they would dislike a peer who openly criticized a teacher, believing such a student to be disrespectful of the teacher's authority. Instead, students told me that they greatly admired a student who dared to criticize the teacher (even though they did not generally like a student who was abusive to the teacher by, for example, swearing at him). They regarded such a student as brave, honest, and active *(huoyue)*, all important virtues among the Chinese. Even most teachers said they liked such students. Teachers know that all their students criticize them behind their backs, so they feel that those who criticize them publicly are being open, honest, and even amicable by helping the teacher realize what his pedagogical weaknesses are.

Of course, the fact that students admire the bravery of a peer who publicly criticizes a teacher demonstrates that in many cases the inferior's criticism is not without adverse consequences. Despite an ideology encouraging superiors to accept inferiors' criticism of them, in reality superiors sometimes become very angry when criticized. While they may not have the weapon of ideology on their side, they often possess the social and even physical power that comes with their high status, which they will sometimes use in retaliation against a critical inferior. This was Mao's tactic when, during the Hundred Flowers campaign, he encouraged criticism and then shortly thereafter persecuted those who had spoken out against him and his policies. Given the risks of inferiors' criticism of superiors, it is a phenomenon that is ideologically tolerated and sanctioned but one that does not occur as often as ideology might lead one to expect. In fact, in the classroom the vast majority of public criticisms for moral transgressions are issued by the teacher against transgressing students, and students in China live in genuine fear of the public criticism of their teachers.

Nonetheless, the ideal of criticism of superiors by inferiors is sometimes realized in China. Chapter 2 cites a number of illustrative examples. Following is another, included here because the way in which Xiao Li analyzed the incident for me is so revealing about why criticism of superiors by inferiors is culturally tolerated.

Shortly before I left China in 1989, the leaders of Marketplace Middle School invited me to give a lecture in Chinese to all the teachers at the school about American education. During the question-and-answer session after my presentation, I was truly surprised by the challenging tone of voice used by several teachers when they asked me questions. Since I tape recorded the lecture and the questions, I was later able to transcribe the exchanges I found most challenging. The following is one such exchange, with a middle-aged female teacher:

Teacher (asking forcefully): If students [in the United States] don't do their homework, what happens?

Author: If they don't do their homework, it is reflected in lowered grades.

Teacher: Do you [using the plural form of "you," meaning "you Americans"] have any students who don't want to study, students who are extremely hard to educate?

Author: If the situation is really bad, a school social worker will be called in.

Teacher: You just said [She says the following considerably more slowly, as if imitating and mocking me] "Psychological experts have full-time responsibility for those students [that is, students who don't want to study]." You mean to say there are that many psychological experts to take responsibility for those students?

In this exchange the teacher spoke quickly (except when imitating me), at high volume, and with a defiant flourish. (I attempted to be merely informative in my tone, since I did not see this lecture as an arena for confrontation.) She seemed to involve her fellow audience members in the challenge against me, since as her challenge to my answers seemed to grow more successful, she would look around the room for audience reactions confirming the correctness of her position. In another exchange she asked me if we have morals education in the United States. I tried to explain that we have no unified national morals education, but after a few questions she thought she had caught me in a contradiction. She turned to her fellow audience members and said, in a lowered, self-satisfied voice, "They do too have morals education."

I decided to play the tape of these exchanges for Xiao Li to see if he felt, as I did, that this teacher, and a few others, were being impolite to me by adopting a confrontational tone in a situation where I would not, ordinarily, have expected confrontation. He first sought to justify the way she acted. He said that even when he goes to hear a famous professor or scientist speak, he believes it is perfectly acceptable to argue with the lecturer. Furthermore, in such circumstances one should argue with a resolute and self-confident tone, since this is the best way to get others in the audience to listen to what you have to say. If you are too polite, and indirect in your questioning, your fellow audience members will tune you out.

I said that I was surprised that lecturers do not mind being challenged by someone in the audience. Xiao Li said that sometimes they do mind, but that they must forgive the challenger. The reason is that, as in my lecture at Marketplace Middle School, the teacher in the audience was my inferior, or at least she considered herself so because of the difference in our educational levels. Xiao Li explained further that since she considered herself my inferior, she felt that she could act the way a child acts in China: She could criticize others, even her superiors, without any awareness of their face.

I heard a similar explanation for why middle school students can often get away with criticizing their teachers, even sometimes criticizing them openly. One of my informants was both a good student and a merciless public criticizer of her teachers when she was in middle school in the mid-eighties. She did not hesitate to stand in class and tell the teacher that he had taught something incorrectly, or had "not explained clearly at all." I asked her why she had not criticized her teachers less directly. She said it had never occurred to her at the time to use a gentler approach since, during middle school, she was too young to know about being sensitive to others' faces. She also told me that her ignorance of face was accepted because of her age. She and other students who criticize teachers without regard to face can be forgiven because no one expects middle school students to know about being sensitive to others' faces, but a teacher lacking face-sensitivity toward his students cannot be forgiven since adults are supposed to be fully sensitive to face.

As the explanations from the above informant, and from Xiao Li, indicate, those who are of lower status are held less accountable for being sensitive to others' faces than are those of higher status, and inferiors are thus freer to criticize their superiors than superiors are to criticize their inferiors. This is especially true for adolescents, who are beginning to develop their own face-awareness but are not yet held accountable for respecting the faces of others.

Thus, while all Chinese other than children are under a general obligation to mutually respect each other's faces, this obligation is asymmetrical. Because sensitivity to face must be learned, adults and people of high status are held more accountable for respecting others' faces (except when someone commits a serious violation of the moral code) than are the young and those who are metaphorically young— those of lower status. One manifestation of this is that the common Chinese refrain—that if someone does not respect you then you are free to disrespect him—is usually said by an inferior about superiors. The burden of respect and sensitivity to face falls most heavily on superiors.

That the burden of being sensitive to others' faces is lighter for inferiors helps to explain why inferiors are sometimes less restrained in criticizing than are superiors, but there are still additional explanations for this phenomenon. I often saw arguments on the street, usually between strangers who had gotten in each other's way when trying to board a bus. If the dispute was between a man and a woman, which seemed at least as common as fights between people of the same gender, the woman would frequently be the more aggressive one, sometimes expressing unrestrained ferocity and rage. (Such raging of women against men was an equally common occurrence in traditional China. See Wolf 1974: 157, 159–61.) The man, in response, would back away and say, or gesture so as to indicate, "Okay, okay." Xiao Li confirmed that this is a common pattern and explained it to me as follows. He said that people who consider themselves to be of higher status believe that it lowers them to argue with someone of lower status. By refusing to argue with women in the street, men, who consider themselves to be of higher status than women, are actually showing that they look down on the women who try to argue with them. The same principle even applies between countries. Xiao Li pointed out that China willingly argued with the Soviet Union in the 1960s because the Chinese regarded the Soviet Union as their equal. But when relations with Albania temporarily soured in the 1970s, China refrained from an open dispute because Chinese leaders believed that open argument with the Albanians would mean that China accepted Albania as its equal, which it was not willing to do. One consequence of this refusal to debate with an inferior is that it gives inferiors a certain freedom to argue their case against, and even criticize, their superiors, since inferiors know superiors are reluctant to condescend to argue back.

## Chapter Summary

This chapter discusses face and its central role in Chinese culture and Chinese social relations. Face, an individual's feeling of well-being coming from the public's recognition of his merits and virtues, is central to social control in China, since it is by giving or taking away public esteem that the public is able to control an individual. Because of its centrality to the maintenance of societal order, all mature Chinese are expected to be sensitive to face, that is, to be able to feel the hurt that comes from public humiliation and loss of face, and to desire to protect their own faces from public dishonor. All mature Chinese are also obligated to respect the faces of others, that is, to only hurt an individual's face if his faults truly justify it. To do otherwise would dilute the public's power to shame individuals due to overuse of this power. Children are exempt from these obligations. Since sensitivity to face must be learned, children are not obligated to be sensitive to their own or others' faces.

The most common dynamic of face in China is loss of face. Face is lost when a person's sense of well-being is harmed by the public display of immorality or his incompetence. Face is often lost in a performative context when a person (the performer) performs badly before a public audience who can witness and react to his incompetence. The audience reaction communicates a lowered esteem.

There are many different types of circumstances that can lead to loss of face. Face can be lost when moral transgressions are publicly exposed and/or when one is publicly criticized for moral wrongdoings. Face can be lost when one performs incompetently, relative to his/her reputation, in a public setting. If a person is weak in some way, face may be lost. And, finally, if someone denies a request made of them, then the requester may lose face.

Face also has a positive side. People can promote their own face by advertising to the public their merits and virtues. Others can also promote your face for you, by publicly praising your merits and virtues while concealing your faults.

The final four sections of this chapter deal with the relationship between face and evaluation. Since control over others' faces, and the ability to evaluate them, is central to social control, self-praise threatens the power that society has over individuals. Chinese society therefore prohibits self-praise and requires modesty and self-criticism. Those who are not meritorious, and who fail, but show off anyway, violate societal stipulations on self-evaluation and are subject to public ridicule.

The power to evaluate competence lies with those other than yourself, but this power is balanced between inferiors and superiors. Superiors have the right to explicitly evaluate one's performance, but since the reactions of an audience, usually of inferiors, are central to the dynamics of face, reactions of laughter, refusal to attend the performance, staring, and so on are culturally validated. This gives inferiors a role as implicit evaluators of their superiors' merit and morals. This is a role that inferiors often play, too, since superiors are more likely to be on stage as the targets of evaluation, and inferiors are more often in the audience as implicit evaluators.

The power to make someone lose face is also balanced between inferiors and superiors. Superiors have the power to evaluate you negatively in public, but it is this public whose lessened esteem for you actually causes you to lose face. If the public consists of your inferiors, you will be much more likely to lose face than if they are your superiors, since the former case is a greater threat to your social standing and to your membership in a group. If inferiors witness your failings, they may believe that they could have succeeded at where failed, leading them to look down on you. As a result, their status temporarily rises while yours declines, leading to estrangement from your status peers.

Finally, inferiors have the power to explicitly condemn someone for their immorality or incompetence. While superiors do not in reality always tolerate such condemnation from their inferiors, there is a cultural ideology that at least legitimates inferiors to criticize immoral superiors, and that requires superiors to accept such criticism.

The chapter ends by explaining why criticism of superiors' morality and competence by their inferiors is culturally tolerated. Inferiors, especially the young, are less obligated to be sensitive to others' faces than are superiors. As a result, they can criticize directly and even unfairly, and yet still be excused for being insensitive to face. Superiors would not be excused for similar insensitivities.

Since the classroom is a prime arena for contact between inferiors and superiors, and one in which there is evaluation of both morals and competence, the classroom is an important domain in which to observe the operation of the principles described in this chapter. The next chapter attempts such a description, focusing on face and evaluation in the classroom.

# 5

## Face, Criticism, and Evaluation in the Classroom

### The Classroom as an Arena for Evaluation and Face

This chapter examines the fundamental role played by evaluation, and by face, in the Chinese classroom. While schooling entails a great deal of evaluation—both of students and of teachers—in any Western country, evaluation is more integral to daily interaction in the classroom in China than is the case in, say, an American classroom. Students and teachers in China are evaluated not only by processes, such as tests or student evaluations of teachers, which are separate from the everyday routines of learning and teaching in the classroom, but by each other every moment they are in class.

This became apparent to me during my own teaching in China. The ability to speak English well is highly valued in China today and is one of the key markers of a person of high status, so students are very attentive to how well they, and their classmates, speak English. During English conversation class whenever a student hesitated in responding to a question I had asked, or stuttered with nervousness or confusion, other students in the class would frequently burst out laughing. Sometimes I saw an entire class rocking back and forth in their seats with convulsions of laughter in response to the incompetence of one of their classmates. Teachers were not spared this embarrassment either. A number of times, for example, teachers whose standard Mandarin Chinese was not very good, tried (often for my benefit) to lecture to students using standard Chinese. As soon as the teacher mispronounced a word, revealing his lack of facility in standard Chinese, students immediately responded by laughing. Being subjected to such derision is, of course, very humiliating. Students know this and sometimes therefore laugh all that much harder. One female student told me that middle school and college male students like to sit in the back of the classroom and laugh at the mistakes their female counterparts make in answering the teacher's questions. I never heard anyone reprimand students for laughing at their classmates, and it seems fair to say that such laughter is generally tolerated.

An interesting illustration of how widespread laughing at others' incompetence is in China, compared with America, came in a speech I heard given by a Chinese actor who had recently returned from America. His speech, given before the entire student body at Third Affiliated as an extracurricular activity, was a humorous discussion of cultural differences between America and China. The actor noted that Americans do not laugh at mistakes the way the Chinese do. In America he was shocked that the audience failed to laugh at a mistake he had made in the course of his performance. In China, he said, the audience would have laughed. The actor really aroused the Third Affiliated students' appreciation of the comical nature of American customs when he told them that he stepped on an American girl's foot and *she* said she was sorry. Such behavior is strange to the Chinese because they expect witnesses of incompetence to make a person vulnerable to the humiliation of his errors, rather than politely making him feel he has done nothing foolish.

Another common manifestation of the evaluative nature of classroom interaction in China is the way the level of noise in the classroom from students carrying on their own, private conversations *(jiang hua)* while the teacher is lecturing varies with the competence of the teacher's lecture. If a lecture is good or particularly interesting to the students, all of them will listen attentively and not carry on their own conversations. If students think a lecture is bad, however, virtually the entire class will not pay attention, usually by talking among themselves. Thus whether students *jiang hua* (from now on, I will use this Chinese expression rather than its more cumbersome English equivalents) reveals less about those students (as it might in America, where good students are not supposed to *jiang hua*) than about their teacher. If a teacher is bad, there is little stigma attached to students who *jiang hua*. Since a bad teacher, or a bad lecture, is not worth listening to, even good students in China can, and do, *jiang hua*. Xiao Li, a very polite and dutiful young man, told me without any compunction that he and his college classmates at one of China's most famous universities would *jiang hua* throughout the lectures of one of their professors, whom they considered incompetent. In such a situation there is not much the teacher can do, since the *jiang hua* is usually seen as a reflection of his incompetence. In such situations teachers often give up lecturing and leave the class; sometimes they burst into tears. At Third Affiliated I was told about a number of different teachers, often young females, who cried during class because the level of noise prevented them from doing any teaching. In the example cited above Xiao Li's professor was a young man, and he too, finally, broke down and cried during class. Xiao Li and his classmates then felt sorry for him. Although they did not revise their estimation of his abilities, they did decide from that point on to try to tolerate his incompetence.

Even good teachers become the victims of *jiang hua* if a particular lecture, or teaching technique, is judged by students to be inadequate. In my own teaching I found *jiang hua* to be an exceedingly accurate barometer of how my students felt about a particular lecture or teaching method. I noticed that if I told lively stories about my life in America, and if I spoke clearly yet introduced many new words into the lecture, then students would sit in rapt attention, and some would even nod as I spoke in order to show their approval. After such lectures, students and teachers would confirm that they had genuinely enjoyed the class. However, the minute I used a sentence that was too complex, or talked about a subject that was not so interesting, students would immediately start to *jiang hua*. I taught many classes in which I could make myself heard only by shouting. Many of my students felt English conversation was a "waste of time" since the college entrance exam does not test students' facility in spoken English, and therefore many of these students would not pay attention. I saw quite a few students doing their homework during class, and once noticed students in the front row playing cards. Students would especially *jiang hua* whenever I called on other students to respond to my questions, a reaction different from, but clearly related to *jiang hua* during the teacher's lectures.

Thus evaluation is central in the Chinese classroom because the teacher and students whom the teacher calls on are constantly being differentially evaluated by the class as a whole. By laughing, *jiang hua,* or quietly paying attention, the class immediately communicates to a teacher or a student whether he has succeeded or failed. The evaluative nature of interaction in the classroom is even reinforced by several factors. First, laughter is a particularly potent evaluative response from the Chinese because of the frequent association between it and criticism. I once saw a young boy of about five years old resisting whatever it was his father wanted him to do. The father issued a typical Chinese criticism to his son: "If you don't behave, people will see how foolish you are and will laugh at you." I also noticed that several parents of young children laughed at their children when they were misbehaving, or would scold them while other adults would laugh at the child.

A second factor intensifying the evaluative nature of the classroom is the common practice among many students of deliberately asking the teacher a difficult question in order to "test" *(kao)* the teacher's knowledge and ability. In Chapter 3 I cited an example from around 1945 in which the students picked five difficult characters from an old dictionary and asked the teacher how to pronounce them. When she could not answer successfully, the students left the classroom. One of my students, a funny yet somewhat haughty boy, once asked me a very difficult question about English grammar. When I could give only a partial answer, he proudly recited the full answer for me. Other foreign teachers I talked to also said their students asked deliberately difficult questions in order to test the teachers' ability. Because of this practice, even today some Chinese teachers feel that students who ask questions in class are rude.

Finally, *jiang hua*, like laughter, has a special evaluative meaning in China. In China one of the key definitions of someone with status is one who can convince others to listen to what he has to say and, ideally, persuade them to follow his ideas *(you haozhaoli)*. If an audience that is supposed to be listening to you speak chooses instead to *jiang hua*, this is a clear indication that it does not judge your merit, and your status, to be exceptional. If the audience *does* listen quietly to you, this is one of the most significant manifestations of the high esteem they accord you.

The evaluative nature of the classroom, and the fact that such evaluation is public and is an almost immediate reaction, gives a Chinese class session the character of a performance. I certainly felt like a performer the first time I stepped up to the podium to teach. As I entered the classroom, all the students turned and looked at me, and then started applauding. As I reached the lectern, students waited in great anticipation for the start of my performance, as excited students from other classes crowded around the outside of the classroom's windows, looking in.

As a kind of performance, class in China becomes a prime face-arena. There is a performer as well as a public audience that responds to his competence throughout his performance. These are all the conditions under which face can be lost. The fact that a key merit in Chinese society—academic ability—is what is on public display in the classroom makes the classroom that much more of an important evaluative domain and that much more of a domain in which participants are vulnerable to losing face.

Students and teachers frequently told me that both teacher and student are vulnerable to losing face during class. If the student displays an unexpectedly high level of incompetence, he will lose face. As mentioned before, he also loses face if criticized by the teacher. Teachers lose face for the same reasons—if they are incompetent or are criticized publicly by their students. Laughter or *jiang hua* from the audience communicates the audience's lowered esteem for the performer and thus are an important step in making him lose face, or in intensifying his feelings of humiliation.

Fear of losing face has a profound effect on the reactions of students during class. Junior middle school students (roughly, ages twelve to fifteen), who have little sense of face, are often very eager to answer the teacher's questions, and they raise their hands high in response to any question. But by senior middle school, students almost never voluntarily answer the teacher's questions because by that age (roughly, ages fifteen to eighteen) they have become sensitive to face and thus fear answering incorrectly. This phenomenon is most evident in English-language class, where the stakes are the highest, and where students are therefore the most vulnerable to losing face. Virtually every foreigner who teaches a foreign language in China finds that his students are very reluctant to be called on in class. My students would watch me carefully while I lectured, but the minute I raised a question, they would cast their eyes downward, hoping not to be called on. When I did call on someone, normally loud-voiced students would rise timidly and speak in a nearly inaudible voice. Virtually every student I called on during my first few weeks in China, probably numbering nearly 1,000 students (since I rotated through every class in the school), shook visibly when called on to speak. Many showed other signs of nervousness, such as head scratching and nervous laughter. Though somewhat less pronounced, students' reactions were similar when called on to speak in other classes. I even saw a number of students during class meetings, where the topic under discussion was not specifically academic, be so paralyzed with nervousness when called on to speak that they could not utter a single coherent Chinese sentence.

### Teachers and Discipline Problems

In many ways the discipline problems teachers encounter at Third Affiliated are similar to those encountered by teachers at similar American schools. Students do not always complete their homework and sometimes cheat on tests (and, even in college, frequently submit partly plagiarized papers, a practice that bothers foreign teachers a great deal but less so Chinese teachers, perhaps because Chinese educational practices have traditionally encouraged students to quote the words of great men to express their own ideas, and have given little support to students to put their thoughts in their own words). Students do not always pay attention in class, sometimes they talk back to the teacher, and sometimes students get into fights. In many of the classes I taught, students were often very noisy, talking with their friends and not paying attention. In junior middle school classes I sometimes spied a glimpse of wads of paper, or paper airplanes, flying through the air behind my back. As discussed above, some students did homework for other classes, read novels, or even played cards while I was trying to teach them. Some students whom I called on to speak were less than willing, and had a sullen and resentful expression on their faces (though other students were just the opposite, very eager to have a chance to speak English, albeit nervous when actually called on to do so). When Xu Laoshi called on one student to answer a question in a senior grade one English class, he swore at her (for no apparent reason) and sat down. If I had not been in the back of the classroom auditing, Xu Laoshi later told me, she would have made this student leave the classroom.

Despite having similar discipline problems Chinese teachers do not always define those problems the way American teachers might. Many of the American teachers I knew, all of whom were teaching university students (undergraduates and graduate students), felt, as I did, that *jiang hua* was a serious problem in the Chinese classroom. There were many times I had to shout in order to be heard. A few of these American teachers had to leave their classroom because there was so much talking that they could not conduct class. Even foreigners who taught English to middle school *teachers* (the teachers were enrolled in year-long professional development courses at various universities) found that the teachers often talked a great deal (in Chinese) to each other during the class period, making it very difficult for their foreign teachers to conduct class.

*Jiang hua* is not as much of a concern to Chinese teachers. The first few times I taught I was surprised that teachers, who were present during my class, did not stop my lecture in order to reprimand students who were talking and not listening. I asked many Chinese teachers how they felt about *jiang hua*. They said that teachers are concerned about *jiang hua* in primary school, and fairly concerned as well in junior middle school. But by senior middle school they consider it only a minor offense. This is partly because, as explained above, *jiang hua* is considered a legitimate reaction of students to a lecture they believe to be worthless. Another reason, though, is that by senior middle school teachers have a more serious phenomenon to worry about: romantic relationships between the opposite sexes. Chinese middle school students are not allowed to date, and if a boy and girl spend too much time together during the school day, teachers (who, as they often told me, are very astute observers of such things) will notice and will have a talk with the students involved. All the teachers with whom I spoke, even those whose views were, in general, progressive, believed that middle school students should not be allowed to date or to have romantic relationships *(tan lian ai,* literally, "talk love"), and they believed that it was the teachers' duty to prevent their students from having romances.

Another class of discipline problems not considered serious are actions by students to make their classmates laugh in class. Quite often students, especially males, will do or say something funny to make the class laugh. This is seen as somewhat disruptive and naughty *(tiaopi),* but students and teachers both told me that teachers like students whose naughtiness takes the form of making people laugh. This may be because the actions of such students provide comic relief from the pressures of face felt by students and teachers.

The teachers and administrators with whom I spoke seemed to hold high standards for school attendance and punctuality, even though I never received a consistent answer on what these standards are, or how Third Affiliated deals with attendance problems. Not only teachers but even the principal never seemed to know, when I asked, what time a given class period started. There was a bell at the start of each period, but the switch for the bell was activated manually, so the starting time for a given period would vary by a few minutes from day to day. In China it is teachers, rather than students, who move from classroom to classroom, so student tardiness never seemed to be a problem. There was a problem with students coming late for the first period (in which case students must ask permission from the teacher before they are allowed to enter the classroom). A group of students discussed this problem with an administrator, and the students suggested that the starting time for school be made a little later to make it easier for some students to get to school on time. (This suggestion was not put into effect.) Tardiness and attendance are supposed to be recorded by a student cadre, the assistant class monitor, but students told me the assistant class monitors rarely keep attendance records. If a teacher at Third Affiliated notices that a student is often late or absent, the teacher will usually have a talk with the student.

In many ways the domain of the teacher's control is larger in China than it is in America. Teachers often take responsibility for aspects of students' character, as well as in-class behavior. For example, being selfish is considered a very bad trait, and teachers will criticize students for selfish acts, even those outside the classroom. Teachers are also held responsible for the actions of students outside the school. If students get into fights off school grounds, a very serious matter, it is generally the school authorities who are expected to punish the offending students.

In general Third Affiliated, a key school, had fewer discipline problems than many other schools. Chinese educators remark that academically capable students, who often come from educated backgrounds, cause fewer serious problems than do students from uneducated worker or peasant backgrounds. I was told that at some non-key schools students wait in gangs near the school and beat up teachers as they leave the school. An informant from the countryside said that where he is from some parents will even beat up their child's teacher if they become unhappy with the teacher for some reason. Even at Third

Affiliated a few years ago (but not during the Cultural Revolution) a teacher suffered serious facial bruises when a student pushed him down a flight of stairs.

Despite the fact that Third Affiliated is a key school, the district government of the district of Northeast City in which Third Affiliated is located issued an edict that the junior middle school component of Third Affiliated has to start accepting any student, regardless of ability, who lives in the neighborhood of the school. In 1988 the first group of neighborhood students enrolled. School administrators told me that these students have created significant new discipline problems, which administrators explain as resulting in part from the students' uneducated family backgrounds. Fights have increased, and there are some groups of students who stand outside the school gate and threaten to beat up students who come through the gate unless they give up their money.

### Face and Disciplinary Methods

Traditionally, the main method of discipline in China was to hit and beat students, sometimes quite severely. After 1949, as new teacher/student relationships were being advocated, beating and its practitioners came under heavy criticism. Beating is thus no longer the primary means of disciplining students, and many other methods have been adopted. Nonetheless, some teachers still use physical punishment to discipline their students. A seven-year-old American child who spent a year in primary school in China told me that teachers hit students on the wrist with a rod when they misbehaved. Another American, who spent a year in senior middle school in China, told me that one of his teachers carried a rod that she used to strike students' desks when they did not do their homework. She also yelled at students until they were almost in tears. At Third Affiliated a middle-aged female teacher known for her ferocity would pull students' ears and call students down to her office, where she would yell at them and call them names such as "big potato."

At Third Affiliated the majority of teachers do not employ corporal punishment. Instead they rely on a variety of disciplinary methods that conform to a general principle, namely, that the teacher, in disciplining a student, must protect the face of the student, unless he has committed a serious offense. If the offense is serious, the teacher can publicly shame the student, making him lose face as a form of discipline and punishment. This disciplinary principle follows from the general obligation that the Chinese have to protect each other's faces in ordinary circumstances.

## Face and Theories of Discipline

Every student and teacher to whom I talked about disciplinary methods reiterated this general principle. One Third Affiliated student pointed out that this approach is the most effective one for controlling students. If a student is publicly humiliated for a small offense, he will feel intense animosity toward the teacher, and will become more disobedient, rather than less.

A teacher can protect a student's face by not disciplining or criticizing him in public, or by disciplining in such a way that he is not singled out. In the latter case, a teacher might, for example, say, "Some classmates are talking too much." A teacher can also protect a student's face by praising him first and only then, cautiously, pointing out his faults. This method is more applicable to moral or behavioral faults, but can also apply to academic faults, since a good teacher should also be sensitive to a student's face when correcting his academic mistakes in class.

These commonly accepted principles have been codified as an academic educational theory, *zhengmian jiji jiaoyu* (literally, "positive and active education"), which has been accepted by both educators and educational theorists. The guidebook for teachers used by Third Affiliated has a whole section discussing the theory of positive education and urging teachers to practice it. *Zhengmian jiji jiaoyu* is the use of positive measures—praise, awards, and heroes and models for students to emulate—to discipline students. The idea behind these positive measures is that by using noncoercive methods and by drawing on and emphasizing the students' strengths teachers can stimulate students' desire and ability to govern themselves and each other, and discourage them from relying on the teacher to tell them what to do.

Shu Laoshi gave me several examples of *zhengmian jiji jiaoyu* (not all of which may actually be feasible, but which at least help to illustrate the nature of the theory). If a teacher finds a student drawing in a book during class, the teacher should not call him a "petty hoodlum" *(xiao liumang)* but instead should recognize the student's artistic interests and form an after-school drawing class. Or if a student smokes, the teacher should not criticize him by name but organize a class meeting on the immorality of smoking, in order to educate all the students. If a student starts to become romantically involved with a member of the opposite sex, the teacher should try to reason with the student *(jiang daoli)*, telling him of the damage to his studies that can result from continuing the romantic relationship. Teachers should also have students set goals for what kind of person they would like to be at the end of the semester, at the end of three years, and in their lifetime.

Another important aspect to *zhengmian jiji jiaoyu* Shu Laoshi discussed is the use of models. For example, if a school has a student who has won a science or math competition, he should be asked to speak to the whole student body about his study methods. Photographs of good students might be put up on bulletin boards. Textbooks should talk about heroes.

### Face and the Practice of Discipline

While Chinese teachers do not always discipline students with respect for face as educational theory urges, much of the time they do. One manifestation of teachers' respect for face was their refraining from usual disciplinary measures whenever I was auditing a class, since a person's face is harmed all the more if a foreigner witnesses his failings being made public through discipline or criticism. Xu Laoshi, for example, did not force the student who swore at her to leave the room, something she would have done had I not been present. Also, if students were *jiang hua,* a minor offense, teachers never rebuked individual students by name, since such a rebuke of an individual during class is quite a serious punishment. (It is possible that public rebukes did occur while I was not auditing, but many teachers and students told me that, by and large, this does not happen.) Instead, they would call on the class as a whole to quit talking. I once saw Zhou Laoshi blow a whistle in order to get students to stop talking. Another teacher, who was having no success in quieting the class, called on the class monitor to get his classmates to pay attention to class. Teachers also stop lecturing if students *jiang hua;* sometimes the teacher will even leave the classroom.

In cases of disobedience that are still not serious, but perhaps more disruptive than occasional *jiang hua* (excessive first period tardiness, for example), the teacher may criticize the disobedient student. This is still done with respect to face, that is, in a private setting such as outside the classroom after class. As the example in Chapter 2 illustrates, this criticism can be quite severe, yet because it does not occur in front of the whole class, the threat to the student's face is small (which, however, is not to say that the criticism does not cause great emotional pain for the target of the criticism). Even when criticizing students in private a teacher is not supposed just to tell them what is right and wrong but rather to lead them to come to a conclusion of right or wrong on their own. Teachers should *jiang daoli,* literally "talk reason," or reason with students. To reason usually means to appeal to the student's desire for a successful future life; the teacher will try to lead the student to come to the conclusion that his disobedient behavior threatens his studies, which thereby threatens his future livelihood. Reasoning with students in private is used for many discipline problems, and it is the preferred method for dealing with students who have developed romantic relationships with the opposite sex. Although developing such relationships in middle school is considered a serious offense—one teacher even told me that the primary aim of discipline in senior middle school should be to prevent these relationships—teachers know that exposing a student's romantic interests to his peers is extremely embarrassing for the student. Therefore, teachers all told me that if they discovered a student who seemed to be starting a romantic relationship with another student, they would deal with this problem in private, in deference to the sense of self-respect of the two students involved. They said they would insist that the romance stop, but then would try to guide the students to decide on their own to do this, rather than using force.

Teachers do not always rely on private criticism of students to handle discipline problems. Sometimes, even if the student's offense is minor, the teacher criticizes him or her in class. Teachers are not supposed to do this, though, and if they do, they risk incurring the animosity of the target of criticism, as well as that of the whole class. (Below I will discuss how students can retaliate against a teacher who has criticized a student for a minor offense.) Some teachers criticize students in class, but they use humor in doing so, in order to protect the student's face. One student gave the following example: When the student's classmate was *jiang hua* in a loud voice, the teacher remarked, "Since your voice is so loud, you ought to join a cheerleading squad." Another means of discipline is for teachers to fine students. Students found carving on desks, for example, are fined five *yuan*, slightly more than a dollar, but more than half a day's wages. (One Third Affiliated student joked that schools institute fines in order to help resolve their financial problems.) Many teachers prefer not to handle discipline problems themselves. Instead, if there is a student who is causing problems, the teacher will tell the student's class teacher, since class teachers are really the ones charged with governing students. At Marketplace Middle School every period the teacher fills out a form rating the discipline of the class as a whole. Every day the class teacher checks the rating forms, and if they are not perfect, she asks the students who misbehaved to confess. If they confess, she keeps them after school to copy a passage from a magazine. If they do not confess, she asks the student cadres who was bad, and then makes the misbehaving students copy even larger passages than they would have had they voluntarily confessed. (This reflects the traditional Chinese judicial practice of being lenient to those who confess, and strict with those who do not.)

Then there is also *zhengmian jiji jiaoyu*, the use of positive measures in order to discipline students. While its ideals are not always carried out, many teachers did try to do so. In fact a very experienced class teacher at a large middle school in the countryside told me that even in the past teachers were expected to first point out a student's strengths, before moving on to criticize him. At Third Affiliated I saw several of the examples cited by Shu Laoshi when outlining the theory of positive education: outstanding students were called on to discuss their study methods; class meetings were held throughout the school if a particular discipline problem was becoming widespread. These discussions were led by students, often in the form of a debate (such as, for example, "Should middle school students be allowed to date?"), thereby, at least in theory, not forcing a particular viewpoint on students. Another method of discipline at Third Affiliated was to have students evaluate their own behavior annually. These evaluations, along with evaluations of each student made by the class teacher and by his classmates, are put in the student's file. The dictates of *zhengmian jiji jiaoyu* also influenced the classroom presence of teachers. A number of model teachers whose classes I audited, as well as some teachers on educational programs on Chinese television, taught with an almost exaggerated friendliness. This was especially true of some female teachers, who smiled throughout class, and talked in a high-pitched voice, as if to suppress any malevolence while accentuating their benevolence.

One of the prime examples of reliance on positives to control the behavior of students is the prevalence of awards students receive from the schools. At the end of every school year the schools give awards to students, among the most important of which is the award to *sanhao xuesheng,* literally "three-merit students," those who excel academically, morally, and physically. At Third Affiliated the student cadres in each class nominate students from the class who excel in all three categories. Academic excellence, the most important criterion, is judged on the basis of exam scores in the class. Moral excellence, means, above all, that the student has demonstrated a willingness to help his classmates. Physical excellence refers to athletic ability, and is judged on the basis of a moderately difficult athletic test that the students must take. Once nominated by student cadres, all the students in the class vote for the person they think should be a three-merit student. Only a few students are chosen, one of whom is usually the class monitor.

Awards are also given to classes as collective entities. On December 9, a patriotic holiday commemorating a 1935 student uprising, Third Affiliated convened an all-school assembly on the playing field outside to celebrate the holiday and give awards. As with most such assemblies the audience of students faced a long table at which school administrators sat. The assembly started with speeches about the glories of patriotism. Awards were then handed out to classes excelling in various categories. For example, an award was issued to classes (that is, *ban)* in each grade for being the most disciplined. This judgment had been made by a committee of student cadres from the whole grade, who would walk around the halls during the semester and score classes based on how attentive they were to the teacher. Interestingly, roughly half the classes in a given grade were given this award, and this same percentage held true for other awards. Other honors, also judged by student cadres, were awarded to the classes that held the best class meetings; wrote the best wall newspapers; sang best; were most informed about current events; or demonstrated correct ideological thinking *(sixiang).* During this ceremony the Communist Youth League advisor, who had organized the assembly, kept stressing to me the use of the collective to educate and discipline students. This theme of the collective and the theme of patriotism were meant to reinforce each other, since pride in one's class, a collective, is supposed to teach students pride in the national collective, the country as a whole.

### Discipline by Public Criticism

Not surprisingly, I did not see many instances of public criticism or public disciplining of individual students, since these methods are reserved for the worst offenses. Perhaps the best example is cited in Chapter 2, where I described an all-school criticism of students who had beaten up a classmate. I also heard about an all-school criticism of a boy in junior grade one who had "taken excessive liberties with a female student." The boy was criticized and expelled from Third Affiliated for one year. Sometimes, students are made to write self-criticisms and read them in class. These self-criticisms are posted in the hallways, where they will be seen and read by everyone. During class the teacher sometimes deliberately tries to cause misbehaving students to lose face by making them stand throughout class, in the classroom, as punishment. Zhou Laoshi once became very angry because many of her students in senior grade one had not done their homework. She made those students, about thirty in all, stand during class and do their homework while they were standing. She also refused to teach during that period. By making them lose face this way, she said, it would both punish them and persuade them to mend their ways. (However, Xiao Li, commenting on this method, said that a teacher who disciplines this way only makes himself lose face, because having to resort to such tactics shows that the teacher cannot get students to do what he wants them to do.) Students who must stand are visually separated from their classmates, a kind of physical metaphor for loss of face.

### Competition in Class

The heavy emphasis on evaluation—both in Chinese culture, as described in Chapter 2, and in the classroom, as described in this chapter—has as its corollary an enthusiasm among the Chinese for competition. Their competitiveness is manifested in many different contexts of daily interaction. Getting on the bus seemed to me a supremely competitive activity. As the bus pulls up to the bus stop, people race for the doors, and push and shove to try to be the first passenger to get on. This competitive aspect to boarding a bus was impressed on me especially when one of my students, who had seen me yielding to other people at the bus stop, remarked that American men clearly do not have the same ability as Chinese men for getting on crowded buses. For my student, being able to win the competitive struggle to be the first one on the bus was a real virtue.

In almost every endeavor, the Chinese, males and females alike, compete with one another to try to win the most exalted of all positions in China: first place. The Chinese compete for first place both for themselves, as individuals, and for the collectivities to which they belong. There is a great desire in China for the country to be number one, especially in economic terms, and many of the people I met want to do whatever they can to help ensure that their country captures the top position. My students said that being competitive is something that comes naturally to people. However, competitive virtues are also socialized into children by their parents and teachers. Being competitive and not yielding to others gives one face. But even more important, it gives one's superiors face, if one is successful—which is a major reason that parents and teachers push their children to compete.

The Chinese are not only competitive and willing to compete, but also interested in watching any activity that is competitive. Shortly after arriving in China, I asked my students what they cared about the most. Several students said that they cared most about the Olympic games (the summer Olympics were on at that time), since they wanted to see how many medals the Chinese athletes would win. Students watched as much of the Olympic coverage as they could, and talked about the Olympics with great excitement. One student described in her diary in English how she felt when a Chinese diver won a gold medal: "We should remember the exciting moment. Xu Yanmei won the first gold medal for our motherland in the diving . . . contest. . . . When our national flag was rising slowly, I couldn't help holding my breath. Congratulations!"

Because of this predilection for being competitive, competitions are very prevalent in China. Competitions are especially congruent with Chinese culture in that they help resolve the conflicts the Chinese feel about showing off. Many Chinese want to show off their merits, but they cannot do so voluntarily or else they will be seen as arrogant and disrespectful of norms for modesty. Competitions overcome this conflict by providing a structure in which one can legitimately show off, since the structure of competition inherently compels one to display one's merits.

At Third Affiliated competitions are a frequent occurrence not limited to athletics. In the afternoon, after school, the school periodically assembles all the students in a given grade to watch selected students from that grade compete. A panel of teachers determines a winner, and scores for all contestants are announced after they perform. I saw quite a wide variety of such competitive performances: story-telling contests, singing contests, debates, English-language dramatic contests (to see which group of students could write and perform the best English-language play), and so on. The school also has athletic competitions in which all the classes in one grade compete against each other to see which class is the best at a given sport. Sometimes there are all-school sports meets in which students compete individually in a variety of sports. All individual scores for students in a given class are added up, and classes' composite scores are compared and ranked.

It must be said that student reaction to such competitions is not always uniformly enthusiastic. At the all-school sports meet, the thirty students watching the long jump reacted very little to the proceedings, not seeming very interested, while a large crowd of students at a nearby running race cheered wildly for the contestants. Also, as the junior middle school story telling wore on for over an hour, students in the audience started to become restless and *jiang hua*. However, in general students are very interested in competitions. In Chapter 2 I described how students crowded around me when I was judging an English-language play contest, to see how I was ranking the various performances. Before an all-school singing contest, to which attendance was necessarily limited, students tried to squeeze past ticket-takers without having tickets. I even saw one boy begging a student cadre, by putting his arm around the cadre and appealing on the basis of their long-term friendship, to give him one of the extra tickets the cadre still held. (After about ten minutes of begging, the student cadre relented.)

Third Affiliated teachers and administrators recognize this high level of interest in competitions, and try to make an activity competitive whenever possible, in order to keep the students' attention. Above I described how competitions between classes are used to discipline students. In fall of 1989, following government orders to stimulate newfound patriotism in students, school administrators staged singing contests in which students and teachers competed at singing patriotic songs. Also, when I first started teaching oral English, teachers advised me to play games with the students in order to hold their attention. When I did so, students came up to me to tell me they had really enjoyed the class, and they asked me to continue to have them play games in future classes.

Chinese teachers often use competitive games in their own classes. One history teacher begins her competition by having her students divide into four groups of about fifteen students each (a convenient and often-used division in Chinese classrooms since students are seated in four row groups—*xiao zu*—each of which is comprised of two rows paired together). Each student then picks a story from ancient Chinese history, often a story about a particular historical personage, and tells it to his group. The best student in each group is selected and then tells the story to the whole class. Finally, selected students tell their stories before the whole grade in contests similar to the story-telling contest mentioned above.

One Marketplace Middle School Chinese language and literature *(yuwen)* teacher whose junior grade two class I observed had students divide into small teams of about five students each. Each team sent one of its members to the blackboard for the competition. Each of the competitors was required to write five words exemplifying certain structural characteristics, and the first competitor to do so won that round for his team. Students were clearly engaged by this competition. When the competition began, the contestants ran to the blackboard excitedly, and the members of the various teams in the audience rooted enthusiastically for their respective team-member-contestants.

Another junior grade two language and literature teacher whose class I observed at Third Affiliated used a similar approach. Her approach was a competitive question-and-answer game. Each of the classroom's four row groups *(xiao zu)* made up a team; two teams competed against each other at a time, with one asking questions about the text the students were studying, and the second team responding to these questions.

The reaction of the students was quite lively. Each time a student asked a question or gave an answer, his classmates would laugh or cheer in unison, and this often set them off discussing with each other the merits of the various questions and answers. I had a chance to talk at length with the teacher of this class. She felt that her approach was very successful in stimulating students' interest, which she attributed to its competitive nature. Her approach was based on a method she had seen used by an education professor, a method she had modified so that it was competitive and resembled the competitive knowledge quiz shows that are common on Chinese television. She felt that by making classroom exercises competitive she could stimulate the students to participate in class more actively and willingly.

### The Teacher/Student Relationship

Whenever I talked to teachers about the teacher/student relationship, they inevitably compared the relationships of the past with those of the present. Teachers told me that in traditional China (pre-1949) the teacher was the absolute ruler, much like the emperor, and students were his subjects. Or, as another teacher said, teachers were the cats and students were the mice. Whenever a student disobeyed the teacher's commands, he would beat the students as punishment.

To a large extent, the image they portrayed of the past was accurate. Teachers were supposed to beat their students and were considered good if they did so. A traditional saying reflects the assumed function of beating: "If you don't get beaten, you won't grow up; you must be beaten all the way up until you become an official" *(bu da bu cheng ren, dadao zuo guanren)* (Guo 1979 [1928]: 31). Parents believed that students could progress only under the guidance of a strict teacher, and they wanted the teachers to be as tyrannical as possible. One Chinese author recalled that in his family it was the custom for parents to wrap a rod in red paper and give it to their child's teacher to use on the child (Tong and Li 1979: 14; Chiang 1946: 81). Students were hit by the teacher with rods on the head, palms, and buttocks, commonly resulting in bruises and broken skin (Guo 1979 [1928]: 31; Tong and Li 1979: 14). As a result, students lived in great fear of their teachers, and hated them (Tong and Li 1979: 14).

Supporting the absolute authority of the teacher was an ideology according the teacher a position among the five dominating components of Chinese society and cosmology. These components, in the traditional view, were heaven, earth, the emperor, one's father, and one's teacher *(tian di jun qin shi)*. Ancestral shrines displayed golden characters representing these five absolutes (Chiang 1946: 79). The teacher was viewed as a father figure. There were many traditional sayings reflecting this view, such as: "One day as your teacher makes someone your father for life" *(yiri wei shi zhongsheng wei fu)*.

The traditional association between father and teacher meant that the twentieth-century attack on lineage, patriarchy, and the traditional authoritarian father/son relationship entailed an attack on the traditional teacher/student relationship as well. A handbook for primary school teachers published in 1950 (henceforth cited as "Handbook"), the year after the founding of the People's Republic of China, makes this conclusion explicit by saying that the efforts to create a "new teaching method" were linked with the larger struggle between old family relations and new family relations (He 1950: 121). So, as new ideologies and practices arose to supplant the absolutism of patriarchy, many began advocating the democratization of the teacher/student relationship.

The history of the view that the teacher/student relationship ought to be democratic is complex. In some ways, Chinese culture had always ensured, at least in principle, some balancing of the power held by the teacher and the powers of the students. Also, an experienced countryside class teacher told me (as did Shu Laoshi) that really good teachers had always been respectful of students' faces and emphasized praise over criticism. But the revolutionary changes in Chinese society in the twentieth century brought about new educational views and the codification of an ideology rejecting the traditional authoritarian teacher/student relationship. Shortly after the founding of the Chinese Communist Party Mao helped found the Self-Study University. The university's manifesto criticized the despotism of traditional schools and their dull teaching practices (Cleverley 1985: 89).

Many educational documents and articles following this set forth their conceptions of democratic teacher/student relationships and repudiated the despotism of the past. The Handbook is a good example of such a document. It rejected the negative, authoritarian discipline of the traditional classroom, "negative commands," in favor of "positive hints" (He 1950: 124). Its author wrote: "The old style schools always used negative means to punish children. This kind of punishment is useless, since everyone likes to hear words of praise, and no one likes to be yelled at. Therefore, we need to use the method of encouragement to control children's behavior and to get them to study" (author's translation, He 1950: 124). In addition, many newspaper articles criticized the practice of corporal punishment. Teachers who taught at

Third Affiliated during the 1950s remember that anyone who beat or hit a student was criticized by his fellow teachers during political study, and might also have been criticized by the principal.

Not only was the absolutism of teachers in the disciplinary sphere renounced, but the view of the teacher as bearer of absolute knowledge was challenged. Educational policymakers urged students to correct mistakes in teachers' lectures, and they called on teachers to accept such criticism. The Handbook described a primary school that exemplified the new practices; at that school, the Handbook claimed, "Occasionally, students correct some mistakes of their teachers, and teachers immediately accept the correction with an open mind" (He 1950: 121). As an example, the Handbook describes how a teacher at that school attributed the colonial status of Africa to the laziness of its people. The students did not believe this, and went to the teacher to proclaim his answer incorrect. The teacher admitted that his view was incorrect, a product of capitalist thinking (He 1950: 121).

As education was expanded to include more people who had not previously had a chance to go to school, curricula and teachers alike were required to become more responsive to the life experiences of these new students, many of whom were from poor, uneducated peasant families. Many educators, such as Tao Xingzhi, a student of John Dewey, created textbooks with stories drawing on familiar situations from everyday life. Tao changed Dewey's concept "education is life" to "life is education," and he urged that teaching not be limited to book knowledge but include knowledge drawn from experiences external to schools. Educational policymakers advocated teaching students by drawing on students' own experiences, and actively involving them and their knowledge in the learning process. These policymakers rejected the old passive role of students. The contrast between the old and new views was articulated in the Handbook. In the old view, "The teacher is the starting point, and students are passive"; the new teaching method, however, stresses "arousing students to seek understanding themselves" (He 1950: 121). Teachers and students, furthermore, were encouraged to learn together (1950: 122).

The view that teachers should not hold absolute power over students, and that the teacher was not the repository of absolute unchallengeable knowledge, was taken to its extreme by Mao before, and during, the Cultural Revolution. At that time, Mao believed that teachers had little to teach students at all, and that teachers should be learning from students rather than students from teachers (Cleverley 1985: 154–55). He also, as described in Chapter 3, called on students to take power away from their revisionist superiors, including teachers.

Mao's Cultural Revolution view did not prevail, but an ideology renouncing the absolutism of teachers remains. Whenever I asked teachers or students what kind of relationship teachers and students should have, I always heard similar answers. Informants said that teachers and students should be equals; their relationship should be one of friendship, rather than one between the older generation and the younger generation. Teachers and students should learn from each other. If the teacher makes a mistake, students can correct him. As in any friendship, teachers and students should help one another whenever either of them encounters difficulties. The teacher should have emotional feelings *(ganqing)* for his students, should try to understand how his students feel, and should get to know what they think. Only occasionally was the inequality of the relationship hinted at, as when informants said that the teacher should care for/love his students *(ai, aihu)* and students, in turn, should respect *(zunjing)* their teachers.

Toward the end of my stay in China I asked a group of thirty students if this image of the teacher/student relationship, in fact, accords with reality. Most of the students answered in the negative. They pointed out the physical difference between teacher and student in the classroom. It is the teacher who is at the front standing, while students sit facing the teacher. The teacher has the power to make you do things, the power to make you do homework and take tests, and the power to tell you that you have failed. Students' image of their teachers also emerged whenever they wrote plays in which there was a classroom scene. I saw several groups of students perform plays in English class that they had written, in which they portrayed their teachers as angry, scolding despots. A number of students and teachers admitted to me that teacher/student relationships are not good at all. Xiao Zhang is one who holds this view. He said that the relationship between teachers and students is not good from primary school through graduate school, citing a newspaper article describing how one graduate student went unrecognized by his own advisor when the two met on the street one day. Third Affiliated teachers even recognize the problems in the teacher/student relationship. The school once had all classes convene a class meeting to discuss relations between teachers and students. In the class discussion I observed, the class monitor began by explaining that many teachers are concerned that they do not know what their students are thinking and feeling, and perceive a gap between them and their students—the reason the school had set the teacher/student relationship as that week's topic. During the discussion students asked if I would answer some of their questions about America. Many of their questions reflected the tensions between teachers and students in China. One student wanted to know if American students argue with their teachers. Another asked if Americans have to write self-criticisms. When I said that we do not they laughed and remarked, with obvious resentment, that their teachers compel them to do so.

As the above suggests, the teacher/student relationship is not one of equality despite government claims to the contrary, and this can often cause conflict. Teachers in China are charged with controlling almost every aspect of students' lives: their studies, their political views and activities, and their romantic lives. (This in no way contradicts the previously discussed powers of students to criticize teachers and challenge their authority. In fact, I believe one reason teachers and others in positions of authority cultivate so many different ways in which they can exercise power over their subordinates is precisely because of the ever-present potential for rebellion by subordinates.) Throughout their education Chinese students are kept in groups of around fifty students (sometimes more) who study and, at college, live together. (Even middle-aged teachers who spend a year of professional enrichment training at the university study and live in such groups.) Each group constitutes a class *(ban)* and for each class there is an advisor (the class teacher in middle school) who is responsible for all aspects of the lives of the students. In college the focus becomes controlling students' political views and activities. Especially after the 1989 student uprising, college advisors have the power to determine where a student will be assigned to work after graduation based in part on his political views. I even heard that poor political attitudes could get one expelled from the university, and that a middle school student with bad political views will not be admitted to college (it is not clear if the latter policy, reminiscent of Mao's era, has actually been put into effect.) In addition middle school teachers are responsible for keeping students from developing romantic relationships. (College students are allowed to date, although they are not allowed to have premarital sexual intercourse.)

As for studies, the true authoritarianism of teachers really became evident to me in a discussion with teachers at Marketplace Middle School. They asked me how American teachers handle students who do not want to study. I said that if students do not study and do not do their homework, their grades may suffer. The Marketplace teachers pressed on. "What if students still don't study? How can you *make* them study?" This made me realize that these teachers, as many of the teachers I knew in China, believe that students should not be allowed, in the final analysis, the choice of whether or not to study. Teachers must get their students to study; the only question is whether they will use force or persuasion to do this.

But there is another side to the reality of the teacher/student relationship. The ideology about this relationship, as discussed above, holds that teachers should care for and love their students. I did, in fact, sense that some teachers did have strong caring feelings for their students. Since teachers are collectively responsible for such a wide range of aspects of their students' lives, their care for students seemed deeper and more emotional than the caring that American teachers have for their students. Many students and teachers said that the teacher should be like an older brother or sister, or a mother or father, to their students. Many times this seemed to be true. (Such familial relationships between student and teacher can be found in both the city and the countryside, but they are especially evident at rural schools, where the majority of students live at the school, often quite a distance from their homes.) Like parents, teachers are concerned about the social and emotional well-being of their students, in addition to their intellectual development, a role teachers must play since there are no psychologists or social workers in the schools in China. Zhou Laoshi, for example, learned that a boy who had been her student two years earlier was virtually unable to function because he was overwhelmed with anxiety about taking the college entrance exam. Although he was no longer her student, Zhou Laoshi spent a great deal of time talking to him, trying to allay his fears. In the end, he passed the entrance exam and was accepted into college.

Many teachers are also concerned about the material and physical well-being of their students. One student told me that she was often invited into her teacher's home for breakfast. (Sometimes teachers even take troubled students into their homes to live with them.) One boy did not have enough clothes to wear during the winter, so his teacher gave him some clothes. Another student told of his vivid memories of the time he was accompanied to the hospital by his teacher after being injured at school. This latter is a common story. The Chinese place a great deal of emphasis on mutual help given in times of crisis (such as injury or sickness) between people who have a close relationship—friends, parents and children, teachers and students. Descriptions of a teacher who helps a sick student in some way, or a student who helps his sick teacher, were among the most common stories I heard told by school administrators whenever I visited schools. A primary school textbook currently being used contains a story about a teacher who visits a student, only to find that the child's mother is sick. The teacher immediately goes to the stove and cooks some (Chinese) medicine for the child's mother (n.a. 1987a: 72–74).

In practice, then, teachers are both strict and controlling, and loving toward their students. This may appear to be a contradiction, but it in fact is not. In China strictness and concern are often linked together, since the reason for being strict is supposed to be concern for the future welfare of a child or student. In a thick guidebook for teachers issued to all Third Affiliated teachers, and to many teachers at other schools in the province, there are several pages discussing the "combined principles of making strict demands of students while also respectfully trusting them." In this section is the following passage:

> The foundation for respecting and trusting students is to love them with great warmth. . . . This love is both deeply sincere and provides long-lasting support. . . . This love is not the kind of one-sided love of only obedient students, or students good at their studies, but is love for the entire body of students. . . . With this lofty love the teacher will not overlook the student's faults, or leave him alone, or show favoritism to some students, or dislike others. (Author's translation, Li 1986: 118)

In many ways the teacher/student relationship is still like the parent/child relationship envisaged by traditional ideology. The combination of strictness and love described above is often found in the way a Chinese parent relates to his child. Mutual help in times of crisis is expected between parent and child, just as it often occurs between teacher and student. Parents expect in particular that when they are old, their children will take care of them. Such care sets up a reciprocity between the generations. Many students said that they wanted to reciprocate the energy their parents had put into raising them both by having great accomplishments and by caring for their elderly parents. Students also said that they felt they should reciprocate the energy their teachers put into instructing them by achieving great things. Such accomplishments are reciprocation because, as discussed in Chapter 4, students' achievements bring fame and face to both parents and teachers, another parallel between parents and teachers.

### Teachers Students Fear, Teachers Student Like

When I talked with students about how they felt about their teachers, they often mentioned the same, particular emotion: fear *(pa)*. This was borne out by my own observation of students in the presence of teachers. Once I was talking with Xiao Liu on the campus of Third Affiliated, and as one of his teachers approached he hid behind me, even though he is a good student and had done nothing in particular that might require concealing himself. Xiao Liu merely explained that this particular teacher is very strict, so he fears him.

When students say they fear their teachers, their use of the word "*pa*" is close to, but much broader in meaning than, the English word "fear." *Pa* can have a variety of meanings. It can be used, as "fear" is in English, to refer to one's reaction to the danger posed when encountering a potential mugger in the street. One can also use it to indicate shame or embarrassment. If your friend is about to give a performance and feels nervous, for example, you can say, *"Bie pa,"* which means, "Don't feel nervous and embarrassed." *Pa* can also be used to mean that you do not want to associate with someone. It can also be used to mean that you should be careful in someone's presence. Men will sometimes say that they *pa* their wives, meaning that they must watch their behavior around their wives in order to avoid being scolded by them. Finally, *pa* can be used to describe a physical aversion to something. For example, you can say that you *pa* the cold, or that you *pa* eating hot peppers. Both have a feeling of aversion as well as a feeling of timidity. Many of my Chinese friends, noting that I did not wear as many layers of sweaters in cold weather as they do, said that I do not *pa* cold, and their admiring tone of voice was similar to the way they would have spoken had I done some brave deed.

If all these meanings of *pa* have something in common, it is, as several informants told me, their signification of the aversion that one feels when confronted with something dangerous. *Pa* means that something makes you vulnerable, and makes you desire to escape from it, and to recoil from it. This explains why students said that they fear their teachers. As many students explained to me, students fear their teachers because teachers can harm students: they have the power to criticize and shame them, and make them lose face. Because of this, students must be careful and controlled in the presence of a teacher; they even feel an emotion similar to stage fright. By contrast, in the company of their peers, who do not have nearly as much power to criticize one another as the teacher has, students can be much more carefree. Not only is this difference actually evident in the sense of abandon displayed by students when they are together without a teacher present—their loud talking and laughter—but there is also a physical manifestation. Students quite literally shrink back when a teacher whom they fear approaches. (I observed a similar reaction on the street to those of us who were foreigners in China.) They are recoiling from the dangers such a person genuinely presents to them.

Students' fear of a particular teacher does not necessarily entail dislike for that teacher. Zhou Laoshi, for example, was universally liked by students and teachers and is one of Third Affiliated's most popular teachers. The first time someone said students are afraid of many teachers, and mentioned Zhou Laoshi as an example, I could not believe it. Zhou Laoshi is a kind, soft-spoken, almost angelic woman, and I could not imagine anyone fearing her. Other students subsequently confirmed this reaction, explaining that they fear her because she holds them to very high standards and never misses a chance to rebuke them for their failings. Usually, however, she only criticizes students privately or in small groups. Sometimes when I was talking to a student, she would come up to us and matter-of-factly tell me that the student is lazy, or only an average student.

Zhou Laoshi is popular despite being feared because students know that she always tries to be fair in her criticisms. Furthermore, she is sometimes critical and strict with students because she cares about them, and they know this. She is also popular, she told me, because she is sometimes humorous in class and lets students laugh. A good sense of humor was the trait students mentioned the most when I asked them what qualities make a teacher popular and well-liked. This is because humor offsets and balances the feeling that students have of being vulnerable to the teacher's criticisms. Because the classroom is such an evaluative face-arena, students are always under a great deal of pressure to perform. A teacher who can make students laugh from time to time helps them relax and makes them less embarrassed and less likely to lose face if they are criticized.

Many of the other qualities students like in teachers also relate to face and criticism. Students hate teachers who criticize unfairly, those who criticize students for something that is not really blameworthy, and those who criticize some students more than others. Treating all students equally, and not exhibiting favoritism, is another key trait of a well-liked teacher in China.

### *Students Challenge Their Teacher*

Students also criticize their teachers. Previous chapters have explained the cultural principles underlying such criticism. What follows is drawn from a class I observed and was permitted to tape record. In this class students argued against their teacher, and at one point criticized him and got him to admit his mistakes. What is especially surprising about this is that the class was a politics class held in the autumn of 1989, at the height of the government crackdown on "bourgeois liberalism." It was generally believed at the time that the government was going to reinstitute a policy of admitting or rejecting students from college in part based on their political credentials. To argue openly for Western, democratic values, and to argue against one's politics teacher, was risky for these senior grade three students. Nonetheless, many of these students took this risk.

The class was structured as a discussion of the issue posed at the start of the class by the teacher: "Which is better, Western democracy or Chinese democracy?" The teacher, a young man, prefaced the discussion by saying that the students could say anything they wanted to say and did not have to come to the same conclusion as their textbook. (Such a preface is common in such situations, even when the person issuing it, as in this case, does not mean it.) After a short pause, one student stood to speak, and his classmates applauded (presumably because of his bravery at being the first to volunteer). But he changed his mind, said, "I'm not going to speak," and sat down, to a disappointed moan from the class. Then there was more clapping as another student stood, smiled impishly, and said quickly, "Western democracy is better."

His classmates laughed and applauded loudly. The laughter here is interesting yet typical. I often noticed that when someone refutes someone else's views (here the student refutes what he knows are the Chinese government's views), the audience laughs.

Before citing specific exchanges I will describe the general trajectory of the class session. Students stood one after the other to proclaim Western democracy better than Chinese democracy. About eight or nine students (out of a class of about forty-five) spoke, and all but one of these were males. Not one student held that Chinese democracy is better than Western democracy, though one student did say that he believes it will surpass Western democracy after it develops to its fullest potential. Students who did not speak clearly supported the views of those who did, often applauding once a speaker had made clear his belief in the superiority of Western democracy. The tone of the class was fairly relaxed. Several students smiled impishly as they made their statements, and the teacher also smiled from time to time and seemed to respond to students without sounding angry. Every time a student made a statement, the teacher, however, tried to refute the student's point. The teacher's refutations were usually longer than the statements made by the students. His arguments were ones commonly found in Chinese politics books. He said that China is more democratic because the vast majority of people in China, the workers, are the masters of the country. The West is ruled by minority capitalists, who divide power among each other, but never allow a worker or poor person to take control. When a student complained that unlike in the West the Chinese do not have freedom of speech or freedom of the press, the teacher replied that the American press is controlled by capitalists and therefore would not allow a pro-Communist article to be published. He admitted that China's press is also controlled but concluded that no country allows publications that threaten the ruling class. He argued that in China this ruling class is the majority, the workers, while in the West it is minority capitalists who rule.

Following is a passage illustrating how students challenge their teacher. The teacher and students are talking about communication between the people and their leaders, especially meetings between students and government officials. (Because of rather unfavorable recording conditions in Chinese classrooms, the tape of this politics class was difficult to transcribe even with help from two native informants.

Therefore, occasional sentences in this and following passages are not exact transcriptions. However, many sentences were transcribed word for word and, in any case, the tape was audible enough for my informants and me to feel that the nature and meaning of the dialogue is well represented by the following transcription):

Teacher: In our country, students can meet with every head of a department under the party Central Committee to have a dialogue, and this can be broadcast on television. Isn't this public [that is, making communication public, rather than private or secret]? *(Students talk among themselves in response to this, and moan loudly, obviously disagreeing.)* In America presidential candidates have to pay for television advertising of their views. In China there are public news reports and television broadcasts. How isn't this public? *(Students continue to talk among themselves, commenting negatively on what the teacher is saying. In Chinese this is called* yilun.*)*

First Student : You have to look at the circumstances at the time. If the students hadn't protested [the student is referring to the protests against the government that occurred in the spring of 1989], would there still have been dialogue [public dialogue between students and government officials]? Now the protests are finished. Is there still dialogue? *(The student asks his questions with a complaining tone of voice.)*

Teacher: You're wrong. You don't understand the situation. *(Students all laugh.)* Since 1985 leaders have held dialogues with the students every year. *(Students all moan loudly, in disagreement.)* Since 1985 every year in Shanghai Jiang Zemin [the general secretary of the Communist Party] has held dialogues with college students. You can see this in the papers. *(Students* yilun.*)*

Second Student: (who does not stand, but comments loudly and in a disparaging tone of voice from the back of the classroom): How can *that* be called dialogue?

Teacher: How isn't that dialogue? Jiang Zemin went onto campus and talked with students. How is that not dialogue? *(Students* yilun.*)* You shouldn't think leaders' and students' dialogue is forced by the [1989] unrest. Dialogues had been going on before. But during the unrest student demands were too harsh. Everyone saw the situation on television, but it's not that before they didn't have such meetings. Before martial law several department leaders held dialogues with students, but it wasn't broadcast on television. You shouldn't think the dialogues were forced by the student movement. Maybe they were forced, but previously they weren't. Leaders and students held discussions as equals.

Third Student: You [meaning the teacher] said before that speeches of U.S. candidates were useless and were just form without any substance, isn't that right? (Students laugh.) Then in our country why don't we permit that form, even if it has no use?

Teacher: China also [like America] has the form of openness. (Students yilun throughout this response.) Newspapers can raise different opinions. If you say we don't have the form of openness, this shows that your understanding is insufficient. If you don't believe me, I can find a newspaper to show you. (Here, the teacher's tone has become somewhat angry.)

Third Student: If socialism is better than capitalism, then it should be advanced in all aspects. But in fact why is China more underdeveloped?

In this passage students openly disagree with the teacher, and the class as a whole expresses its disagreement by moaning and making negative comments to each other in response to the teacher's statements. While the tone of voice of students who speak is fairly challenging, they temper their challenge by making their statements in the form of questions that they know the teacher cannot fully answer. This is a good example of how asking questions is a form of challenge, as described earlier in this chapter.

In the passage below a student criticizes the teacher more openly and forces him to admit his mistakes:

Student: Hu Laoshi (their teacher's name; used instead of saying "you") always compares from his own perspective and never from others' perspectives. You shouldn't always take your [that is, China's] strengths and compare them against others' failings.

Teacher (somewhat angry): Then you can't compare the weakness of socialism with the strengths of capitalism. *(As he says this, students moan loudly.)*

Student: Hu Laoshi compares the ideal form of socialist democracy with the already existing form of capitalist democracy. This comparative method is *(he pauses)* not fair. *(Students applaud).*

Teacher (seeming sincerely contrite): This comparative method of mine perhaps is not right. *(Students laugh.)* On this issue my method has not been used well, I admit. But no one has used it well. You [meaning the students] use strengths and compare to weaknesses and so do I. What other methods are there?

It is hard to convey in print how much of a moral critique, rather than merely an academic dispute, the student was making against his teacher in this exchange. This sense of a moral critique was very evident to me while I was auditing the class because of the way the student spoke. Here, rather than speaking as a defiant and angry inferior, the student adopted the calm but insistent tone of voice used by parents and teachers when they lecture their children about their wrongdoings. For a moment, the student was acting as though the teacher's moral failings had lowered his status and raised the student to a position above his teacher.

The above passages demonstrate how an inferior can stand up to a superior, and even get his superior to admit his mistakes. What is interesting about these passages is the support students give to each other in such challenges. Although many students did not stand to speak against the teacher, through their laughter, moans, and applause they signaled unanimous opposition to the teacher's views and consistent support for their peers. This banding together of inferiors to oppose a superior is a familiar pattern in China, recalling the 1907 classroom incident, described in Chapter 3, in which seven students criticized their teacher while a group of their classmates watching from outside joined the protest by chanting anti-teacher slogans. That incident progressed in a manner similar to the class portrayed in the dialogue above, as the students watching from outside and the seven students inside banded together in a joint moral critique of the teacher, eventually forcing his retreat.

## The Politics of Criticism and Disobedience

### *Reciprocal Disrespect*

Chapter 4 described how face is maintained in China by a principle of mutual respect, which obligates all adult Chinese to honor their own and each other's faces. The converse of this principle is a principle of reciprocal disrespect, in which if someone does not respect you, then you are entitled to disrespect him. According to this principle once someone fails in his societal obligations to face by unnecessarily injuring yours, then you may injure his. In fact, retaliating against him by trying to make him lose face is one way that you can restore your own face.

This principle, which I will call the principle of reciprocal disrespect, operates in the classroom and accounts for many of the examples of classroom criticism that occur. A number of informants articulated this principle for me as it applies in school. They explained that if a teacher unjustifiably criticizes a student in public, the student will most likely seek revenge by criticizing the teacher in public. Likewise, if a student criticizes the teacher in public, the teacher may also retaliate by publicly criticizing the student.

I personally experienced this principle in operation a number of times while I was in China. The first was when I was coaching a group of about fifteen young English teachers at Third Affiliated in spoken English. I naturally called on the teachers individually to answer some simple questions, but they clearly resisted. They answered in short sentences, many with an obviously sullen or irritated expression. Also, those who were not answering a particular question would *jiang hua* with each other. Finally, a few teachers told me they were unhappy with the way I was teaching (they were particularly unhappy that I was calling on people to speak, rather than lecturing for the whole time period) and, eventually, they stopped coming to the class.

Puzzled by this, I talked with a professor and friend at Northeast University about the teachers' reactions. He laughed and said this was a very familiar reaction. Young English teachers, who have had the benefit (which older teachers have not) of organized instruction in English during their college years, are expected to be able to speak English well. By calling on these teachers in front of their peers, I was unknowingly putting them on the spot, making them perform a skill in public at which they were expected to succeed. In such a situation, if they did not succeed, as occasionally did happen, then they would lose face. Without knowing it, I had made these teachers lose face. Their response to this was to criticize me and, ultimately, make me lose face by refusing to come to my class.

Interestingly, the principle of reciprocal disrespect even helps explain some of the criticism that took place during the Cultural Revolution; not all the criticism during that time period was the result of national class and political struggles. One informant told me that during the Cultural Revolution one of his teachers called those students in his class who could not answer his questions names, such as "stupid egg." Since this was a form of public humiliation of his students, one student in the class sought revenge by writing a big character poster attacking the teacher, and other students in the class signed it.

### Criticism as a Means to Challenge One's Rivals

Criticism is also a means of attacking rivals. Since the public recognition of your merit is one of the key factors to secure your status, by criticizing you publicly, and thereby challenging the public's judgment of your merit, someone can lower your social standing and/or raise his own.

I saw a fascinating example of this at Third Affiliated, involving two rival teachers. One was Xu Laoshi, who had been demoted from teaching English in senior middle school to teaching it in junior middle school. The other teacher, who replaced her, was an older woman (Xu is a younger teacher) who had recently used her connections to come to Third Affiliated. As with most older teachers, this one was considered an excellent teacher by most teachers and administrators at Third Affiliated, even though no one had been allowed to audit her class. Xu, never one to be swayed by public opinion, doubted that her replacement could be very good. Angry about being demoted and angry at the teacher who took her place, Xu decided to strike back.

Her plan began to materialize one day when she asked me if I would request to audit a class taught by her rival, whom I will call Zhao Laoshi, and if I would let Xu accompany me during my audit. I was truly puzzled at Xu's request. She then explained the situation described above. Xu further expained that if she, herself, requested to audit Zhao's class, Zhao would refuse, but if I made the request, it would most likely be granted. Xu's reason for wanting to audit the class was to destroy Zhao's reputation as a good teacher. Xu wanted to audit the class and then write an article for Third Affiliated's journal for teachers, in which she would expose the incompetent teaching methods of her colleague, Zhao. Xu hoped that doing this would swing public sentiment at Third Affiliated against Zhao, and possibly lead to Zhao's demotion and Xu's promotion back to her old teaching position.

As it turned out, I was not able to request to audit Zhao's class because my stay in China was nearly over by that point, and my time was limited. However, Xu got Zhao to permit her to audit the class by herself. After the audit Xu told me that, just as she had thought, Zhao's methods in class were horrible. As I left China in 1989 Xu was preparing to write her exposé.

### Inciting Inferiors to Criticize One's Antagonists

Criticism can also be a weapon for superiors to use against their inferiors. Interestingly, superiors will often use the criticism weapon indirectly. This is because superiors must respect their juniors' faces (except in extraordinary circumstances), so they are not able to criticize juniors freely themselves. Instead, to contend with problematic junior X, a superior may find a person of even lower status than junior X and have him, the person who is an inferior to junior X, criticize junior X. That is, the superior incites someone of low status to criticize a person of middle status who is threatening to the high-status superior. At schools, for example, administrators may encourage students to criticize teachers. Wu Laoshi told me that this is what she believed was the real motivation behind a meeting called by Third Affiliated leaders to allow students to air their grievances about their teachers (see Chapter 2). Wu said the Third Affiliated leaders wanted to collect information on the incompetence and improprieties of Third Affiliated teachers in case any of them were to cause problems for the Third Affiliated leadership in the future; the leaders could then deal with such a teacher by confronting him with students' criticism of his immorality and/or incompetence. This pattern—high-status leaders inciting low-level inferiors to criticize those middle- (and sometimes high-) status individuals who are the leaders' antagonists—is familiar in Chinese society, and was especially characteristic of the Cultural Revolution, when high-level leaders fostered the Red Guards' criticisms of, and attacks against, the leaders' opponents.

## *Evaluation, Disobedience, and the Politics of Age and Gender*

One of the patterns I began to notice in student challenges—both criticism of teachers and disobedience—is that younger teachers are far more likely to be the targets of such challenges than are older teachers. As described previously, students like to test the knowledge of teachers by giving them a difficult question to answer *(kao)*. Younger teachers are frequently subjected to these tests by students, but older teachers rarely are. Furthermore, students will complain about a younger teacher's teaching ability, both behind the teacher's back and to school administrators, much more often than they will complain about an older teacher. It is common in China for students, especially good students, to complain to a teacher, or to the principal, about the teacher's teaching practices and ability, often asking the principal for a new teacher. I heard of a number of examples of such complaints by students and in each case the teachers about whom students were complaining were young (under thirty five years old). Finally, whenever anyone told me that a student had publicly criticized a teacher, or that a certain teacher's class was very unruly, I always made a point of asking the teacher's age. In every case the teacher was young; often the target was also female.

One example of disobedience to a younger teacher at Third Affiliated involved a first-year English teacher in her early twenties, whom I will call Jiang Laoshi. I had a chance to talk with Jiang and found her English reasonably good, far better than that of most of the older teachers at Third Affiliated (who had learned Russian in school and only later taught themselves English). Nonetheless, students and teachers alike were merciless in their criticism of her. (Only one boy said he felt that she had feelings just like everyone else and so it was wrong for students to treat her the way they did.) Students told me that she did not know English well and could not teach. They disobeyed her in and out of class. For instance, when she was the teacher responsible for helping organize an extracurricular oral English activity, and had just finished suggesting to me how it might be organized, a girl participating in the activity came over to me and, in a loud voice that Jiang could probably hear, said, "I think our teacher's suggestion is a bad one, and you should not follow it."

In class students were equally disobedient. Students often laughed at Jiang when she made mistakes. Virtually all of Jiang's students would *jiang hua* throughout her class. Many times she was forced to leave the classroom because the noise prevented her from teaching. Students eventually asked Third Affiliated administrators for a different teacher. Rather than sympathize with her, Jiang's colleagues at Third Affiliated also attacked her. They said that the fact that she was driven out of her classroom by students talking showed what a bad teacher she was. They remarked that she was clearly inexperienced. Jiang even told me that teachers made fun of her, joking about her hairstyle and her countryside-style clothes. (Jiang had grown up in the countryside.)

The behavior of students toward older teachers could not have been more different. If an older teacher did something very immoral, or criticized a student too harshly in public, students might rebel against this teacher, but otherwise, by and large, students protected the faces of older teachers by, for example, not criticizing them and not complaining about their teaching methods. I neither heard of nor saw an older teacher have the kind of discipline problems faced by Jiang Laoshi; students paid attention in classes taught by older teachers. In addition, students idealized older teachers and their ability. One older teacher read me a few cards sent by his students. One student wrote: "When we're apart, I thank you from the bottom of my heart. Your teaching, encouragement, and humorous words will live in our hearts. I wish a rainbow will come into your heart. I wish you more students who love you." Another: "Anything I've achieved contains your blood and sweat." A third: "To the hard-working gardener: [The teacher-as-gardener is a common metaphor in China.] You bring up our generation with your blood and sweat. We shall remember your teachings, even if we move to a far corner of the world."

It is true that the above teacher was a very nice man, but the contrast between the reactions of his students and those of Jiang's students suggests a far greater contrast between those two teachers' actual abilities and dispositions than actually existed. The one way in which they did differ was age (and, of course, gender, an issue explored below), and this explains the contrast in the students' reactions to them. Students respect older teachers but tend to look down on *(qiaobuqi)* younger teachers because they generally believe that older teachers are much better at teaching than are younger teachers, since older teachers have more "experience" and more "knowledge." This is one reason why younger teachers have more discipline problems in their classes. Students sometimes believe that younger teachers do not have much of value to say in their lectures, so students will *jiang hua* during younger teacher's lectures, as they did during Jiang's class.

Of course, not all younger teachers are disliked by their students. Students even told me that they like *(xihuan)* younger teachers better than older teachers. They said that younger teachers' views on different subjects, politics for example, are more similar to their own views, so they feel closer to many of their younger teachers than to older teachers, whom students are more likely to fear. But "like" is contrasted with "respect" *(zunjing)*: Students generally say they have more respect for older teachers. As this like/respect dichotomy suggests, the fact that students like younger teachers better does not mean that they believe they are better teachers. After all, students also like their peers, but would not listen to a classmate if he took over as teacher. It is older teachers who win students' respect, and it is they who can best hold the attention of students during class.

Students' views on younger and older teachers were shared by teachers and administrators and, in fact, by most others in Chinese society. Older teachers (those above about fifty fall in this category, while those between, roughly, thirty-five and fifty are middle-aged), because of their age and "experience," are considered to be better than younger teachers. Whenever I visited a school in China administrators always called in an older teacher to talk with me. They referred to such a teacher with profound pride as an "experienced teacher." Experience is thought almost automatically to make a person meritorious. Even those who became teachers later in life (as sometimes happened, as a result of the disruptions of the Cultural Revolution) are still considered to have more experience, in the form of life experience, than younger teachers, and this is thought to make them better teachers. There were a number of times when I felt strongly that certain younger teachers were better than their older colleagues. As discussed in Chapter 2 this was especially evident among English teachers, since younger teachers had years of formal training in English, while older teachers did not. Nonetheless, people invariably gave highest esteem to older teachers because it was assumed that, despite the deficiency of their training, age and experience still made them better. As this example suggests, then, the Chinese in large part accord status and reputation based on age, but justify this status based on a presumption of superiority in merit.

I found the same pattern with respect to sex discrimination. One informant told me that women are equal to men in China. When I challenged him by citing the inequality in the occupations they hold, he explained, with absolute certitude, that this discrimination is justified, because women are quite clearly less capable than men. This view of women is manifested in the classroom. While being older seems to override gender (so that students tend to respect an older female teacher as much as an older male teacher), among younger teachers it is females, such as Jiang Laoshi, who are more likely to face disobedient students.

The existence in China of an ideology that maintains that older people are more accomplished than their younger counterparts guarantees that the elderly will possess many powers denied the young. Wu Laoshi, a younger teacher, often talked about this power differential and, although she could not do much about it, complained about it bitterly. One example she cited is that older teachers have the right to critique younger teachers' teaching methods openly but younger teachers cannot critique the teaching of older teachers (though some younger teachers, such as Xu Laoshi, certainly set out to challenge this general assumption, as described above). At Third Affiliated every semester any teacher aged thirty-five or younger is required to give an open class, which all teachers teaching the same subject as the teacher of the open class are allowed to attend. After the class the older teachers take turns evaluating the teacher of the open class. They comment on such issues as classroom presence, gestures and expressions, teaching method, quality and clarity of explanation, and so on. This evaluative process is by no means merely a mechanical exercise. The Chinese place a great deal of importance on the evaluation of teachers, a fact that became clear when older teachers asking me about American education showed great interest in how American teachers are evaluated. But Wu and many other younger teachers bitterly resented having to give open classes, since they saw this requirement as underscoring their subordination to older teachers. (They had resented their previous subordination even more. In the past younger teachers were required to attend older teachers' classes, to watch them teach and to learn from their methods. Younger teachers protested against this requirement, and the practice of having younger teachers give open classes was adopted as a substitute.)

Perhaps the larger significance of these open classes is to demonstrate that teachers, in this case younger teachers, are both evaluators in their own classes and evaluatees as well. Thus, in China, there is no strict dichotomy of evaluator/evaluatee based on status or age as there is in other societies. In China anyone who evaluates is also subject to being evaluated himself.

### Playful Debate and Criticism

Criticism is not always used in China to challenge someone's status and/or to assert superiority over another person. Criticizing someone, or debating against him and his views, can be done playfully, so as to ratify a relationship of equality and friendship with that person. Challenging a person playfully while you are in a relaxed and friendly environment communicates how close you feel your relationship to be, just as does the flirtatious joking between lovers with which Westerners are more familiar. This is because only friends whose relationship is solid and close can playfully challenge each other without being held back by the fear that their challenges will be misinterpreted as serious or hostile.

The examples of playful criticism and debate that I witnessed in China were like serious challenges except that the smiles and laughter of the person challenging, and/or the person being challenged, as well as the fact that the challenge usually occurred in an informal, friendly setting, showed that the challenge was not to be taken seriously. Also, playful challenges, in contrast to serious challenges, only occurred between people who had a close relationship, and such challenges only seemed to strengthen the bond between the challenger and his target, as evidenced by the bursts of conversation, smiles, and laughter that inevitably followed a playful challenge. For example, Shu Shizhe (see Chapter 1), who seemed to have a secret crush on her class monitor, Wang Jianjun, often said things in his presence like, "Our monitor is a fool!" Following her criticism, she would always laugh heartily. (This laughter had a different quality from that meant to make someone lose face. Laughter that occurs in a relaxed, unperformative environment, in conjunction with smiling, is good-natured and generally not face-threatening. The laughter in all the examples cited in this paragraph is of this type.) For instance, I once waited with Zhou Laoshi and Wu Laoshi at a bus stop for another teacher, a male teacher with whom they are friends and who is about the same age as they are. When he showed up late, Zhou and Wu took him to task, all the time smiling and laughing to show that their irritation was not really genuine. He, too, smiled and laughed.

I often saw students playfully debate each other. Whenever I would talk with them informally, in a relaxed setting, it was very common for one student to say one thing about China and for another student to smile as he called his classmate's views "nonsense" and offered an alternate view.

Teachers and students who have a good relationship also engage in playful criticism and debate. Students, for example, liked to teasingly disagree with Zhou Laoshi. In class she once said something about the students' sports meet that was not true, and the students, in mock defiance, immediately chanted out the correct statement in unison. Wang Jianjun's class teacher once said before me and an other teacher that Wang is not a conscientious student. Wang, an excellent student, knew that this was a joke and smiled. One teacher who is well liked by students often laughingly calls students stupid or foolish during class. Wu Laoshi even told me that students like that teacher primarily because he teases them in this way. Students often tease such teachers back. Such playful teasing between students and teachers helps create a more relaxed atmosphere and bridges the gap that often exists between teachers and students.

Criticism and debate thus have two significances. The first is serious and seeks to challenge relationships. The second is playful and aims to confirm a relationship. When the Chinese laugh and smile in criticizing or disagreeing with each other, as in the examples cited above, they signal that their challenge is not a serious one. As a result, all the political intentions of a serious challenge—retaliation, rivalry, and so on—are denied while their opposites—friendship and equality—are confirmed.

**Chapter Summary**

This chapter describes the fundamental role played by evaluation and by face in the classroom. The chapter begins with a discussion of the ways in which the classroom is made into an evaluative domain. Students have a broad repertoire of ways in which they respond to, and evaluate, their teacher's lectures and their classmates' contributions in class. These responses include laughter, engaging in private conversations with friends, or rapt attention. By varying their responses according to the quality of individual episodes during a given class period, students become like an audience, and create a performative atmosphere in class. Because it is a type of public performance, class also becomes a prime arena in which face, both the teacher's and the students', can be lost. This vulnerability to loss of face in the classroom helps explain why students in China are so nervous about participating in class.

Since students are so vulnerable to losing face during class, teachers must discipline with respect to face: protecting students' faces when disciplining them for minor offenses, but attacking the faces of student-offenders when their violations are more serious. Teachers, for example, will rarely publicly criticize individual students for talking during class, since this is considered to be a relatively minor offense. The educational practice of *zhengmian jiji jiaoyu*, in which teachers use praise and persuasion to discipline students, is another important example.

The next section considers how the evaluative nature of the class-room and of Chinese society more generally shapes the teaching methods teachers use. Students are very competitive and interested in competitions. As a result, teachers stage numerous competitions both in and out of the classroom in order to arouse the interest of their students.

The complexities of the teacher/student relationship are then discussed. Traditionally, this relationship was an authoritarian one, with one's teacher being associated with one's father. Revolutionary changes in Chinese society entailed a reformulation of the teacher/student relationship, and an ideology for the democratization of this relationship was codified. While teachers still exercise authoritarian power over a wide range of facets of a student's life, including intellectual, social, and emotional facets, the responsibility for the student's total well-being often leads a teacher to feel deep concern and love for his students. This is one way in which teachers remain, as in the past, like parents. Teachers, like many parents, are both strict and controlling and caring and loving of their youngsters.

One particular aspect of the teacher/student relationship is the fear that students often feel toward their teachers. This fear is a genuine reaction to a dangerous situation: the vulnerability of the student to losing face because of being criticized by the teacher. Teachers liked by students often used various means, such as humor, to allay or temper the fears of their students.

The next section of this chapter presents an example of a politics class where students openly disagreed with, and criticized, their teacher. The topic of discussion was the relative merits of Western versus Chinese democracy. Students all asserted that Western democracy is better, and they disputed the teacher's rationale for claiming the superiority of the Chinese system.

Finally, the chapter analyzes the politics of evaluation and disobedience in the classroom, and what students and teachers can get out of such challenges. One reason for making such a challenge is revenge. If someone makes you lose face, you can gain it back by making them lose face. Another reason is rivalry. Since status is supported by a reputation for merit, if you publicly criticize a rival, you have a chance to lower his status and possibly raise yours. A third reason is that criticism may be a means for a superior to deal with his antagonists. In such cases, superiors will often not do the criticizing themselves but will incite those of low status to criticize the antagonist. Fourth, challenges often reflect and reinforce age and gender hierarchies in China. Students are often more disobedient toward, and critical of, younger teachers, especially younger female teachers, while lauding older teachers.

This chapter ends with a discussion of how the Chinese can smile and laugh while they criticize in order to make their criticism playful. While serious criticism is used as a weapon against an enemy or rival, playful criticism is used to signal the strength of a relationship with friends.

# 6

## Socialization in the Family

Socialization at schools is complemented by socialization in families, and in this chapter I turn to a description and analysis of what I observed in Chinese homes. Before beginning this discussion, it is important to describe how these observations were carried out. In many ways I found it considerably more difficult in China to learn about what family life is like than to learn about what school life is like. It was easy to become a daily presence at Third Affiliated, but I could not be in someone's home every day without actually living there, a situation that is very difficult to arrange in China. Thus my view of family life was more restricted than that of school life, which was all the more true given that my intentional research focus was the school and not the household.

However, I found myself in several circumstances that allowed observation of everyday family interaction. Wu Laoshi invited me to her house for lunch or dinner about twice each week during the first seven months of my stay in China. Wu's husband also invited me to come once a week in the evening to talk with him about Chinese and American affairs. Wu and her husband are young and consider themselves progressive, so they did not treat me with the stilted formality Chinese traditionally employ toward their guests. Rather, they were relaxed and friendly, allowing me to see them behave in a normal manner. What was most fortuitous for my purposes was that Wu and her husband have a son, about five years old, who was always around whenever I visited. This gave me an excellent opportunity to see how one young Chinese couple raise their child, whom I will call Xiao Wu. Much of the discussion in this chapter is based on what I learned from my visits with Wu and her family.

During my last five months in China I went to the same restaurant every day for lunch and dinner, which gave me the opportunity to observe a second family. The restaurant, a very small establishment, was managed and owned by a couple in their early twenties, who had a three-year-old son named Yingying. My Western eating partners and I became good friends with the restaurant's owners, and even with Yingying. Yingying was in the restaurant with his mother and father almost every day, so I was able to see how his parents socialized him. This was an important complement to my observations of Wu and her son, since Yingying's parents are uneducated and, as petty entrepreneurs, of low status (although their restaurant had made them fairly well off financially), whereas Wu and her professor husband are intellectuals. Of course, both Yingying and Xiao Wu are boys, so the majority of my observations were of male socialization. Also, all my observations were carried out in the city, so my descriptions are of socialization among urbanites.

Other situations supplemented my observations of Yingying and Xiao Wu, including several meals with Zhou Laoshi, her husband, their six-year-old son, and Zhou's brother and sister-in-law and their five-year-old daughter. I also spent several days during Spring Festival with Xiao Yang's family, and his siblings had several young children. I had dinner a number of times with families with adolescent children. Finally, I interviewed many of my students about their family lives. Some of the following discussion is based on the results of these interviews.

## The Historical Background of the
## Parent/Child Relationship

Whenever I asked informants what the parent/child relationship is like in contemporary China, conversation often turned, as with discussions of the teacher/student relationship, to the past. Informants contrasted contemporary family relations with those existing in traditional China. They stressed the fundamental inequality of the traditional parent/child relationship, and the obligation of children, especially sons, to obey their parents and serve them as they aged. Informants told me that parents, especially fathers, held great power over their children and would beat them if they did not obey parental commands.

While undoubtedly exaggerated, as images of the past can often be, this view of the authoritarianism of traditional Chinese parents is, nonetheless, an approximation of the truth. Many authors, both Chinese and Western, have described Chinese patriarchy and the subordination of children to their fathers and mothers (C.K. Yang 1959: 10–11, 93; Liu 1959: 48; Potter and Potter 1990: 18). This subordination was most clearly evident, for sons, in the dictates of filial piety. Sons were required by the norms of filial piety to obey their parents dutifully and to cater to their parents' welfare, even if at their own expense (C.K. Yang 1959: 89; Baker 1979: 102–3; Liu 1959: 48–60). (However, filial piety did not prevent children from rebuking their parents. As pointed out in Chapter 3, Confucius declared that filial piety actually required sons to rebuke parents if the latter acted unjustly or unwisely—Hucker 1959: 195.) Many works of literature, everything from nursery tales to novels, idealized legendary filial sons who made extraordinary sacrifices for the sake of their parents (C.K. Yang 1959: 89; F. Hsu 1981: 81–83). Families' reputations for virtue were in large measure based on having filial sons (M. Yang 1945: 52). So were individuals' reputations, since being a good, filial son was one of the main marks of the virtuous man (F. Hsu 1967: 146–47). The state sponsored lectures on the virtues of filial piety and recognized such virtues where practiced by awarding an arch or a tablet, an indication of the strong state support given for filial behavior (Baker 1979: 118–21). The state, and lineages, required filiality in their codes of laws and rules and meted out severe punishments for those who were unfilial (C.K. Yang 1959: 89, 93; Liu 1959: 48–60). All these factors worked to guarantee that sons in traditional China would be compelled to obey and serve their parents, as filial piety required.

One of the most salient characteristics of the filial obligations of Chinese sons toward their parents is that these obligations were permanent, in force not only while the son was a child, but after he grew up, and continuing even after the death of his parents. In his youth, a boy would be cared for by his parents. When his parents reached old age and infirmity, he was obligated to care for them as repayment for the care they had given him (Baker 1979: 71; Liu 1959: 50–54; C.K. Yang 1959: 90; F. Hsu 1981: 81, 114–15). After their deaths, he was expected to remember them through ancestor worship, and a major part of that worship involved continuing to care for the material and emotional needs of deceased parents symbolically (Baker 1979: 72–74; Liu 1959: 51–54; F. Hsu 1967: 167–99, 243–44). Thus the mutual dependence and mutual obligations of parents and sons ensured the continuity of their relationship. And continuity of parent/son relationships was consistent with, and reinforced, the Chinese patrilineal social structure, in which the permanence and continuity of the generations through the male line was the most important aspect of social relations.

Not surprisingly, then, marriage, the creation of an intragenerational relationship with an outsider, was a threat to parental and patrilineal control, so parents sought control over their children's marital affairs. In traditional China parents arranged their children's marriages. The importance of the husband/wife bond was downplayed, and the purpose of marriage was seen as acquiring a daughter-in-law, and her labor and reproductive capacity, for the man's parents (F. Hsu 1967: 57, 241; M. Yang 1945: 54–55, 67; Potter and Potter 1990: 18, 21; Baker 1979: 32–35; Liu 1959: 77–84; C.K. Yang 1959: 22–24; F. Hsu 1981: 50). The married couple lived near or with the husband's family (Baker 1979: 2, 22; Potter and Potter 1990: 19–20), and the young woman, upon marriage, entered into a new relationship of obligations to her husband's parents. The severity with which the mother-in-law commanded her daughter-in-law is legendary in Chinese culture (Baker 1979: 42–47; Potter and Potter 1990: 20–21).

Arranged marriage first came under attack during the Taiping Rebellion, when the Taipings advocated that marriage be based on personal choice and arranged marriage abolished (Baker 1979: 176). Subsequent Chinese revolutionaries, both Communist and non-Communist, recognized that since arranged marriage and filial piety were key sources of power of the traditional family, attacking them was necessary if the power of the family and lineage was to be curtailed and substituted with the power of the state (C.K. Yang 1959: 19; Baker 1979: 179–80, 199–200, 211, 214). (This substitution of the state and society for the family is still recognized. One parent told me that her old, outdated way of thinking—her belief that her children belong to her—had given way to the realization that her children belong to society.) The Marriage Law of 1950 was a major initiative in this direction. It outlawed arranged marriage, thus terminating, at least in principle, a major source of parental power in traditional China (Baker 1979: 183–84; C.K. Yang 1959: 31–36, 39–44). The Marriage Law also contained stipulations regarding parents' responsibilities toward their children, a change from the traditional ideology of filial piety, which was concerned only with the duties required of children toward their parents (C.K. Yang 1959: 101–2). The creation of a system of old-age pensions for workers in the state system (Whyte and Parish 1984: 71, 73) further undermined traditional parent/child relationships since many parents would no longer need to rely on their children for support in old age. Finally, filial piety, once supported by the state, was challenged by the Communists as being feudal and exploitative (C.K. Yang 1959: 90–91). This was part of a larger challenge to the traditional, authoritarian parent/child relationship.

## Parent/Child Relations in Contemporary Chinese Ideology and Practice

This challenge continues, at least in ideology. I found that an ideology calling for the rejection of authoritarian parenting and its substitution with more egalitarian parent/child relationships is quite prevalent in contemporary China. Many of my informants said that parents and their children should be like friends, equal in status and willing to help each other. They should talk openly with each other and understand each other's feelings. Parents should try to set a good example for their children and should reason with them, rather than giving them commands to follow. Children should not feel compelled always to obey their parents. If parents are "right," then children ought to heed their parents' wishes; if not, children should be allowed to criticize their parents' mistaken views.

In reality the parent/child relationship in China is far from equal. It is commonly accepted that parents should control aspects of their children's lives ranging from their studies to their sexuality.

### How Chinese Parents Control Their Children

According to the ideology of the new parent/child relationship, parents are not supposed to hit or beat *(da)* their children as a form of punishment. In practice even parents who consider themselves progressive continue to *da* (from now on I will often use this Chinese word, which is broader and more inclusive in meaning than such English words as "hit" or "beat") their children. Parents often slap their children's palms or spank them. One teacher somewhat proudly told me that she hits her son's buttocks with a stick until the skin turns red. Parents also use the threat of beating their children as a means of discipline, even if they do not actually *da* the child. Wu Laoshi often warned disobedient Xiao

Wu repeatedly that she was going to *da* him, though I rarely saw her carry out these threats. While it is more common for parents to *da* preadolescent children, parents also *da* their teenage children, especially the males, who are more likely to get into serious trouble.

To *da* children is accepted and is often seen as a necessity. Xiao Li said that he must *da* his three-year-old daughter whenever she will not do what he tells her to do. Whenever she persists in standing on the couch, or sitting on a dirty floor (floors in Chinese homes are uncarpeted and are often dirty), two examples Xiao Li cited, he will *da* her. The teacher who spanks her son with a stick said that if she did not do this, she would not be able to control him when he grew up. Wu Laoshi told me that one of her colleagues at Third Affiliated walks with a limp. Because of this, he cannot run after his son and *da* him, and as a result the son has turned into a juvenile delinquent. The Chinese actor who had been to America (mentioned in Chapter 5) drew a burst of laughter from his student audience at Third Affiliated when he told them that children in the United States call the police to report their parents as criminals if their parents *da* them. (While the actor's observation was undoubtedly a reference to the reporting of child abuse to the police, his use of the word *da*—which can mean anything from a slap to a severe beating—obscured any implication of child abuse, and made it sound as though American children call the police whenever their parents spank them.) This seemed humorous to to the audience because, as the actor remarked, parents routinely *da* children in China.

In general even progressive Chinese who reject the use of force to compel obedience from children still believe that good parents must use persuasion or other means to get their children to act as they believe the children should act. There is a general feeling that children will not naturally do what is best for them but should, and must, be made to do what is in their best interests. In intellectuals' households, for example, parents (as described in more detail below) feel that it is their duty to expend as much effort as necessary to make sure that their children study hard. As is the case with teachers, being a progressive parent in China does not usually refer to one who allows children wide latitude in making their own choices. Rather, a progressive Chinese parent is one who relies on methods that are not directly coercive in order to, nonetheless, ensure that the children do what their parents and society want them to do. The Chinese place high value on family education *(jiating jiaoyu)*, teaching children how to behave, and they feel that parents who closely supervise their children *(guan)* are the best kind of parents. A number of Chinese attitudes reflect the value attached to family education. Many people, for example, told me that the biggest problem with divorce is that it leaves a child with the inadequate supervision of a single parent. Also, the Chinese say that juvenile delinquency results when children are not watched closely enough by their mother and father. The inevitability of parental supervision for the typical (nondelinquent) Chinese child is best summarized by one student at Third Affiliated who, hearing her classmate say that his parents do not supervise him and let him make his own choices, remarked with calm objectivity, "That's not possible."

### *Parental Control of Academic and Sexual Behavior*

The authoritarianism of many Chinese parents is perhaps most clearly manifested by their control over their children's studies. Chinese parents, of course, want to see their children succeed, a desire reflected in the traditional saying that parents "hope their sons become dragons" *(wang zi cheng long)* (the dragon is a sign of good fortune). The success of one's children is especially significant to Chinese parents, as discussed in Chapter 4, because one gains honor and face through one's children's success. Also, parents traditionally relied on their sons for financial support in old age. While, at least in urban areas, this is much less common today than in the past, parents still seek the comfort and security that come from having a successful child who can help out his elderly parents if they run into difficulties. For these reasons, raising a successful child is a high priority for most Chinese parents. Since academic achievement, especially success on the college entrance exam, is one of the main prerequisites to the attainment of high social status, parents feel that it is extremely important to push their children to excel in school.

I observed many instances of parents pressuring their children to study and succeed academically. One mother, who had just finished telling me that she had renounced the coercive methods that are so common among Chinese parents, then went on to say what she did to guarantee that her son would succeed in school. She encouraged her son, even when he was a preadolescent, to stay inside and read rather than going out to play (which, she told me, was necessary in order to prevent his talent from being wasted). She would not let him read children's books and, instead, bought him math books, which she made sure he read. Her son did win an international math award, proof enough to most people that her methods must be good. Third Affiliated established a class for parents on parenting—specifically devoted to how parents can raise a "talent"—and she was invited to give lectures to the class.

Such parental supervision of children's studies is common. Many of my students at Third Affiliated told me that when they were in primary school, their parents would sit next to them as they did their homework, and inspect it upon completion. Most of my middle school students were not allowed to watch television except on Saturday evening (Sunday is the one day off from school), and some parents would not even watch television themselves, so as to set a good example for their children. Many parents actively guide their children's studies. Once when I was invited for dinner at Shu Laoshi's home, one of the other guests, spotting me on his arrival, proclaimed that it was a "golden opportunity" to have encountered a native English speaker. He rushed home and brought back his middle-school-age daughter, whom he attempted to persuade—much to her absolute embarrassment—to speak English with me. A Third Affiliated teacher once told me that she took her daughter, who is in college, on a summer trip to Guilin, a favorite destination for tourists because of its beautiful scenery. This mother did not make the very long journey to Guilin to show her daughter the city's scenery, however. Rather, she brought her daughter there in the hope of giving her an opportunity to practice English with some of the many foreign tourists who go there. Such parental involvement in the studies of older children is not unusual. The first time I met Xiao Li, my conversation partner, his father was with him. Although Xiao Li is twenty-eight, and has a wife and a daughter, his father wanted to supervise the arrangements we were making for our conversation practice (English for Xiao Li, Chinese for me), and Xiao Li's father made a number of comments on how we might best carry out our conversations.

Of course, it is important to point out that Xiao Li's father, as is true of the majority of people I met in China, is an intellectual. While uneducated parents also want their children to be successful, and realize the importance of school, their lack of education often prevents them from taking as direct a role as educated parents take in supervising the education of their children. As a result, the few young Chinese I met whose parents had, in fact, given them a certain degree of freedom, and allowed them to make many of their own choices, came from uneducated backgrounds. (These families were not necessarily typical uneducated families, however, and the average uneducated parent is by no means less authoritarian than his educated counterpart. In some ways, just the opposite is true. Uneducated parents, for example, are more likely to *da* their children.) One woman graduate student told me that her father, a worker who had received less than two years of formal schooling, would rarely scold her and her two brothers. Her father never forced the children to study, and in fact would tell them to be mindful of their health if they were studying too much. He was rarely critical of his children and, instead, praised them a great deal. (Interestingly, when all three of his children got into college, a big accomplishment for any family in China, this man's friends all came to him to ask him how he had made his children so successful.)

Complementing parental control over children's academic activities is the control over their romantic lives. Every parent I knew was adamant about the necessity of forbidding their children from developing romantic relationships before graduation from senior middle school. Many people (and teachers too) said that if young people were allowed to date, their studies would suffer, and their future livelihoods would, most likely, be compromised. (I also suspect that Chinese parents feel the converse to be true: If teenagers feel enough academic pressure, they will not think about sex. This, undoubtedly, provides some of the unspoken motivation for parents to push their teenage children to study.) Thus parents forbid their children to date and threaten to *da* them if it is ever revealed that they have violated this proscription.

Xiao Yang told me what happened when the parents of his girlfriend, whom I will call Xiao Deng, found out about their daughter's relationship with Xiao Yang. While in college Xiao Yang fell in love with Xiao Deng. She was an eighteen-year-old woman who had graduated from middle school, had passed the college entrance exam, and was ready to start college in the fall. Even though she had passed the college entrance exam, her father forbade her to date until she began attending college. After entering college she started to spend time with Xiao Yang. One day, however, her father saw the couple walking in a park. That night Xiao Deng's father and mother confronted Xiao Deng about this. Xiao Deng's father slapped his daughter on the face. Xiao Deng's mother told Xiao Deng angrily that her body (Xiao Deng's) belonged to her (Xiao Deng's *mother*), and she insisted that Xiao Deng break up at once or be disowned. When Xiao Deng refused, her mother demanded that Xiao Deng return all of her possessions to her parents. Xiao Deng's mother even asked Xiao Deng to give up her eyeglasses, whereupon Xiao Deng took her glasses off, smashed them on the floor, and fled to her college dorm. Her father then talked to the head of the department in which she and Xiao Yang were students. The department head in turn talked to Xiao Yang, told him his relationship with Xiao Deng had ruined the harmony of her family, and warned Xiao Yang that if he did not stop dating Xiao Deng, he would be expelled from college. Needless to say, that brought the couple's relationship to an end.

### The Consequences of Chinese Parental Control

While the above example may represent the extreme in Chinese parents' attempts to supervise their children, it illustrates how far parents will go to assert control over their children, a control that extends, as Xiao Deng's mother said, even to their children's bodies. This example also shows how parental authoritarianism can lead to conflicts, sometimes severe ones, between Chinese parents and their children. A number of times I saw children of around six or seven, both male and female, hit their parents; this seemed to be a precursor to future conflicts that would arise as those children entered adolescence. Many Third Affiliated students described to me the tensions between them and their families. They said that their parents do not try to understand them, unfairly insist that they study all the time, and often treat them like young children. Some students told me that a generation gap *(daigou)* exists between many young Chinese and their parents. According to Third Affiliated's guidebook for teachers, Chinese teenagers do not want to be seen in public with their parents, and they are reluctant to share their thoughts with their mother and father, "closing up" and "locking" their inner thoughts from their parents (Li 1986: 58, 60). I even heard stories of teenagers who were not on speaking terms with their parents. One girl told me that there are some students who tell their feelings to their parents but, she commented, "We don't like such people. They will have no friends and when they grow up they will be very lonely." Quite a few students said that they fear *(pa)* their parents. They are especially afraid that they will do something to cause their parents to *da* them. Fear of parents is often manifested in the same ways at that of teachers. In my few visits to homes with teenagers, the teens talked infrequently and with restraint compared to the loud, talkative manner with which they interacted when together without adults present. Also, teens try to limit their contact with their parents. As the Third Affiliated guidebook suggests, many Chinese teens are reluctant to be seen in public with their parents, and one rarely finds teens and parents together in public settings. In general, then, despite the new ideology that parents and children should be friends, the majority of Chinese youngsters, even those on good terms with their parents, avoid having the kind of contact with their parents that they seek to have with their peers.

### Parent/Child Mutual Dependence

The general restraint on casual contact between parents and children in contemporary China is in many ways consistent with, rather than a transformation of, traditional parent/child relations. In traditional China the relative formality of parent/child interaction was one facet of a relationship in which parent and child were bound to each other not by an emotional, peerlike bond, but by mutual, transgenerational obligations to provide for each other's welfare.

In revolutionary China the traditional parent/child relationship was attacked and this entailed an attack as well on filial piety. I found, however, that both the ideology and the practice of mutual dependence between children and parents survive though in diminished form and alongside certain new values for parent/child independence. Most of what follows is drawn from my observations and interviews at Third Affiliated and in Northeast City, and this describes urban ideology and practice. Informants and friends, some of whom grew up in the countryside, confirmed that the parent/child relationship in the countryside remains much closer to the traditional ideal.

When I first met students at Third Affiliated, one of their most common questions about life in America concerned parent/child relations. Many of the students had heard that Americans are much more independent of their parents than Chinese youth, and they wondered if this was true. They asked about part-time jobs in America, and how this makes teenagers less dependent on parental financial resources.

Many students also asked me if it was true, as they had heard, that Americans become totally self-sufficient at age eighteen and receive no more financial support from their parents after that age. (They had not heard about the dependence of many American youth on their parents for tuition money.) I sensed a certain admiration for the financial independence of American youth, so I asked informants how they felt about what they believed were American practices. Xiao Li confirmed for me that the Chinese do admire the financial self-sufficiency that they believe characterizes American youngsters. He said that many young Chinese, especially intellectuals, would like to be financially independent of their parents. For example, while workers do not mind the huge sums of money that their parents (especially the parents of the groom) must pay when they marry (and may, Xiao Li said, even enjoy being the recipients of parental largesse), many intellectuals are embarrassed about having to rely on their parents for such large sums.

Urban Chinese also seek to live independently from their parents. Sometimes this is not possible because of the shortage of housing in Chinese cities, leading young adults to live with their parents for a few years, even after they get married. Nonetheless, such young adults still usually want to live apart and they will do so if given the chance. Most of the students I spoke with said they expect to live apart from their parents, and most of the adults I knew lived this way. This is often necessary because of job assignments in cities distant from one's parents. In such cases children may see their parents only once a year. (I was surprised to find, however, that adult children who lived in the same city as their parents still did not visit their mother and father very often. For example, one man I knew who was in his thirties goes to see his parents only once or twice a year, despite living only a short distance from them.)

While seeking independent living arrangements, urban Chinese nonetheless expect, as in the past, that once their mother and father reach infirmity, it will be their duty to take care of them *(yang)*. As in the past, the most common justification informants gave for this obligation is the requirement of intergenerational reciprocity: Since their parents cared for them in childhood, they must repay their parents by caring for them when they reach old age. (Interestingly, the requirements of intergenerational reciprocity hold as well between teachers and students, since students often told me that they felt they should make great achievements as adults in order to repay the efforts their teachers expended on them when they were students.) In some cases such care includes financial support. I knew a number of middle-aged adults who sent money to their own elderly parents. One teacher I knew sent about 15 percent of his monthly salary to his parents. This practice is less common than in the past, however, because of China's establishment of a social security system covering a large percentage of the urban elderly. What is still important is that children, both sons *and* daughters, help their parents to do things that the elderly can normally do themselves only with difficulty. This includes helping them move heavy objects, running errands for them, making meals for them when they are in the hospital (Chinese hospitals rarely provide meals for patients), and so on. Sometimes adults have their elderly parents move in with them. The elderly parent(s) take care of their grandchild and, in return, they receive assistance with their daily affairs from their children. In other cases children live near their elderly parents in order to care for them. After graduation from college, Xiao Li intentionally took a job assignment in Northeast City (where his parents live), so that he would be able to care for his parents when they reach old age. Helping aged parents with their daily affairs means much more to the Chinese than it may seem to a Westerner. Helping others to do things they cannot do alone, even mundane things, has great significance for the Chinese, as it is a primary means of expressing friendship and love. Thus the elderly like to be helped with their daily affairs by their children since this lets them know they are loved.

As in the past, taking care of elderly parents is not only the practice but also the ideal; it is how a good person is expected to behave. Good sons and daughters are expected to care for their elderly parents. (Informants told me that, in cities, women are better at such care-taking.) The Chinese have great contempt for children who do not care for their elderly parents. Many articles in the Chinese press describe the abandonment of the elderly in the United States. Some articles have even described Chinese who abuse their elderly parents, and elderly abuse is a recognized problem.

Since the obligation of adult children to take care of their elderly parents remains of great value in China, various socialization practices are aimed at teaching young children this value, or values related to it. On two separate occasions mothers told me that they actually encourage their children to share a portion of their meal, or candy, with their parents, thus teaching children to recognize and yield to parental needs. Xiao Li said he repeatedly tells his three-year-old daughter a traditional Chinese story to teach her filial values. The story, *Kong Rong Rang Li* (Kong Rong Gives Up the Pears), is about a boy whose father bought pears from the market and gave them to Kong Rong, aged four, to distribute to the family. Kong Rong gave most of the pears to his parents, the second largest quantity to his older siblings, and kept the smallest amount for himself. Kong Rong's actions are regarded by the Chinese as very praiseworthy.

## The Socialization of Cultural Values

### Socialization for Self-Sacrifice and Socialization for Self-Interest

Having been told by informants of the importance of teaching children to sacrifice their own interests for parental welfare, I was especially surprised when I also observed parents indulging many of their children's wishes, yielding to their demands, and generally supporting children's self-interested behavior. In fact the parents who insisted that their children yield to them were also the ones I observed indulging their children's desires. Wu Laoshi was one of those who told me that she forced her son, Xiao Wu, to give her part of any candy she bought for him. In general Wu Laoshi often seemed to be socializing Xiao Wu to conform to his parents' wishes. Whenever Xiao Wu disturbed the tranquillity of his household, by screaming or messing up his parents' papers and books (which I am sure he did deliberately, in order to provoke a reaction from his parents; Xiao Wu often laughed mischievously as he did these things) Wu Laoshi quickly and forcefully reprimanded the child, saying, "I don't like you," or "I'll die of irritation [because of you]," or "How foolish you are!" or "Uncle Marty will laugh at you." She often threatened to *da* him. During an evening's visit I heard her issue countless rebukes and threats. Like other parents I observed with children around Xiao Wu's age, she seemed to act as if it were inevitable that her son's behavior would conflict with the way she wanted him to act; she clearly communicated to Xiao Wu that he could not behave as he wanted and must yield to his parents' wishes. However, during meals Xiao Wu made his own forceful demands known and Wu Laoshi always gave in. For example, if we were drinking wine, Xiao Wu would insist on being given a full glass to drink too, and Wu Laoshi always relented. (In other families, I saw two different cases in which a young child of about four or five was given wine to drink.) Surprisingly, Xiao Wu was given any food or drink he demanded.

The apparent tension in Wu Laoshi between socializing obedience to parental prerogative and allowing and even encouraging her son's pursuit of self-interest was manifested in many families. As in Wu's family, this tension was most evident during meals. The following description of parent/child interaction during meals is an accurate portrayal of how young children and their parents interacted in each of the several families I observed.

Typically, the child would eat with his hands, reach across the table to grab food, spill his drink, move around a lot, or otherwise act in a manner disruptive to others eating the meal. Whether accidental or intentional (the latter was often the case), parents responded to each of these disruptions by sharply rebuking their child. Even otherwise mild-mannered parents frequently and harshly criticized their children throughout the course of the meal for such disruptions. However, such insistent parental control had its complement. Children would often demand a certain dish or a certain drink. Their demands were very insistent, repeated continuously and in ever-increasing volume or accompanied by whining, pouting, or crying. While an American parent might have said "Stop your crying" and refused the request, all the Chinese parents I observed said, "Okay, okay," and fulfilled whatever demands their child made of them, almost embarrassed at being confronted by an angry child. If this parental reaction sounds familiar, it should. Parents confronted with an insistent child acted in a manner strikingly similar to the way any status superior acts when confronted with an indignant and demanding inferior, as described in Chapter 4. In their families the Chinese learn that if they are forceful and indignant in making their demands, any superior will avoid lowering himself into the embarrassing position of a direct confrontation and instead will usually calmly acquiesce to the inferior's request.

Avoiding confrontation is just one reason why parents often yield to their children's demands. Parents also yield to their children's demands in order to balance, and reciprocate, the demands that parents make of children. Even in traditional China the son's obligations to his parents were never one-sided and unbalanced. Parents and sons were seen as having reciprocal obligations to each other and, in fact, a parent's fulfillment of his duty to his son was what obligated the son to serve his elderly parents (C.K. Yang 1959: 90; Liu 1959: 50–54; Baker 1979: 71). This is still true today, since, as described above, the Chinese often say that they must care for an elderly parent as a way of reciprocating the energy he expended caring for them when they were just children. Thus parents will submit to some of their child's demands as a way of obligating the child to cater to *their* current or future needs. As one father told me, Chinese parents try to fulfill the material needs of their children, and they expect their children in turn to study hard, and make great achievements to bring fame to the whole family. The fact that any fame is shared by the family as a whole also helps explain seemingly contradictory socialization practices. Parents may want to teach their children to make personal sacrifices to benefit their parents, yet parents must also encourage a certain degree of self-interest in their children, since they want their children to pursue the fame and wealth that benefit not only themselves but the parent as well.

### Socialization and Face

One of the prominent characteristics of the dynamics of face is the dependence on two opposing emotions. In order to be able to lose face, a person must have a sense of shame—a vulnerability to shame—without which he would not be able to feel the embarrassment that leads to loss of face. Yet, in order to be able to lose face, a person must also have a sense of honor—pride in himself and a desire to display his merits and virtues to others and conceal his shortcomings—because without it he would have no face to lose. Face depends on both a sense of honor and a sense of shame, and children must be taught both if they are to learn sensitivity to face successfully. (As discussed in Chapter 4, a sense of honor and self-respect—in Chinese, *zizunxin* or *lianchi*—is different from honor/glory itself—*guangrong, guangcai*. To avoid confusion below I will refer to a "sense of honor" or "pride," both of which, in this context, can be taken as synonymous.)

Parents teach these seemingly contradictory emotions by dealing with children of different ages very differently. Except for very young children (approximately, those below age six), who are not really held responsible for their behavior, parents are almost universally highly and openly critical of their preadolescent children. As mentioned above, Wu Laoshi and other parents of young children criticized their children almost continuously during meals. In general, almost anything young children do is cause for parental rebukes and criticism, and I never saw anything a child did elicit parental praise. Once, for example, Wu Laoshi was sorting through pictures drawn by children at Xiao Wu's nursery school. Unable to find Xiao Wu's creation, she asked him, "Where's your bad picture?" Such criticism of preteenage children's accomplishments and behavior teaches them an awareness of their own fallibility and lays the foundation for a later sense of shame.

As children enter adolescence, their parents' approach to them changes radically. My informants universally told me that as they became adolescents, their parents stopped criticizing them for everyday mistakes because, "As adolescents we are no longer children, and so parents must be sensitive to our faces." By no longer criticizing children for everyday mistakes, parents encourage their children to develop a sense of honor and a sense of shame. The development of a sense of honor occurs because adolescents realize, and are often told, that parents, teachers, and other authority figures are no longer criticizing them for everyday mistakes because they, as adolescents, are developing a sense of honor. Adolescents thus learn that they *should* feel a sense of honor, and they come to view having a sense of honor as a mark of maturity. Yet adolescents also develop a vulnerability to shame, since if they are criticized, this will signal to them that whatever they have done is serious enough to warrant temporarily treating them like a child once again. Such treatment is infantilizing and engenders strong feelings of shame. Having acquired a culturally sanctioned sense of honor, yet vulnerable to the shame caused by criticism, adolescents develop sensitivity to face.

### Socialization and Gender

The first time Wu Laoshi mentioned to me that she had a son, she commented, "My son is very naughty" *(tiaopi)*. I replied, "Oh, I'm sure that's not true. I'm sure he's a good child." But Wu insisted that her son truly is naughty. Her tone of voice, however, was not one of resignation, but one of hidden pride. Following this discussion with Wu, I met other parents who were secretly proud of their naughty sons. One parent actually said that boys *should* be mischief-makers and they should not be too obedient *(ting hua)*. Countless people said that naughty individuals are often very *congming*, a word that means "smart" and especially refers to innate, unschooled intelligence. I was also frequently told that while girls sometimes make better students, boys are more *congming*. One person even told me that being naughty helps make boys *congming*, implying that mischief leads to a kind of street smarts. Thus there is covert encouragement for boys to be naughty; intelligence, a highly valued trait in China, is associated with naughtiness and is seen as deriving from it in part. I observed this phenomenon in the way Wu Laoshi socialized her son: While Wu always reprimanded her son whenever he got into mischief, I sometimes suspected that she was secretly condoning his actions. This might help explain why Xiao Wu deliberately got into mischief, and why he also laughed mischievously as he carried out his pranks.

My Chinese friends often told me that because of China's population policy permitting families to have only one child, parents have become extremely protective of that one, precious child. While I saw signs of such protectiveness—parents escort younger primary school children to and from school, for example—I also saw many instances in which parents did not interfere when their children encountered dangerous situations. Boys, in particular, seemed to be allowed such encounters. Xiao Wu went outside as he pleased to play in the area near his parents' apartment building and even was allowed to go out during the several hours of darkness preceding his bedtime. Yingying, only three years old at the time, frequently crossed the busy street in front of his parents' restaurant by himself. Many trucks and buses drove on that street at speeds around thirty-five miles per hour, but this did not seem to worry Yingying's parents, who let their son come and go as he pleased. They were equally nonchalant when my Western eating companions and I spotted Yingying playing with a cigarette lighter. Xiao Wu's parents also were unconcerned about the possible dangers when they let Xiao Wu play with a medical syringe, with a needle still attached. Bravery is a trait that Chinese men are supposed to have, and parents socialize this value into their sons by allowing them freedom of movement and action, even if this brings the boys into contact with danger.

One aspect of gender socialization that I had difficulty investigating was the pressure to study. Traditionally, school was for boys and educating girls was seen as a waste of time and money. Parents felt that the time and money invested in schooling a daughter would only be lost, since women moved away from their natal villages upon marriage. When I asked informants if the traditional view still holds, they insisted that today parents in urban areas put equal pressure on their sons and daughters to study. They explained that this is especially true given that parents in cities now have only one child. Since I did not live with a family, I cannot confirm or deny what informants told me. However, the persistence of the tendency for higher education to increase a man's chances for marriage but actually decrease a woman's marital prospects leads me to doubt informants' claims that parents have equal academic expectations of boys and girls. Parents want their children to marry and have children, and the more education a woman receives, the less likely it is that she will be able to find a man to marry her. In addition, Xiao Li once admitted to me that his father, a fairly progressive man, had nonetheless put most of his efforts at guiding his children's educations into Xiao Li, rather than into Xiao Li's two sisters.

One final aspect of gender and socialization that deserves comment is the respective functions of fathers and mothers in raising children. There is a very strong belief that fathers and mothers should both play a significant role in raising children. Indeed, one can often see men on the street carrying or transporting on their bicycles infants or very young children. Men seemed very comfortable escorting their young children in public, and I often saw great warmth in fathers' eyes as they interacted with their children, especially those aged about four or five and younger. Other observers of Chinese socialization have noted that when children reach the "age of reason," about six years old, their fathers change from being very warm toward them to being strict and aloof (Wolf 1970: 40–41; D. Ho 1986: 3–4). My observations confirmed this. Wu Laoshi interacted with her son, who was just about at the "age of reason," a great deal (even though her interaction often consisted of criticism), while Wu's husband maintained a dignified reserve. Informants explained to me that it is the mother who usually takes care of the child's everyday needs—food, clothing—while it is the father who is primarily responsible for supervising the child's education, making sure, for example, that he does all his homework.

## School–Family Linkages and the Socialization of Children

The primary vehicle of communication between the school and parents is the class teacher *(ban zhuren)*. As explained in previous chapters, a given student's class teacher is the person who bears ultimate responsibility for the thoughts and actions of that student. If there is a problem that the school cannot solve alone, it is the class teacher (rather than the principal) who contacts the child's parents. At many Chinese schools the class teacher visits the child's parents to discuss the problem. However, many Third Affiliated students' families live a considerable distance from the school, making home visits difficult. Instead, Third Affiliated class teachers ask a student who has caused serious problems to have his parents come to the school. Asking a child's parents to come to school is considered very serious, and is reserved for serious offenses. One such offense students and teachers often mentioned to me is when a student who is forging a romantic relationship with a member of the opposite sex refuses to heed a discreet advisory, usually issued by the class teacher in private, to end the relationship. The class teacher might then request that the student's parents come to the school. Parents are usually very embarrassed to have to meet with a class teacher about their child's offenses, and will often *da* their child as a punishment after a meeting with the class teacher. Students really fear being beaten by their parents, so they try to avoid committing the kinds of serious offenses that lead class teachers to request such a meeting.

Class teachers also meet with parents of non-misbehaving students. Every semester, following midterm examinations, each class teacher convenes a meeting at the school for all the parents of the students in the class he supervises. This meeting is a group meeting in which the class teacher reviews the performance of the class as a whole on their midterms and urges parents to increase the pressure on their children if the class's midterm scores, when compared with other classes' scores, are low.

In addition to group meetings with all parents, the class teacher meets separately with those parents whose children have done especially poorly on the midterm exams. I was able to observe two such meetings, both of them group meetings. The first was attended by five parents and the second by twelve. Mothers and fathers were both present, though no child was represented by both parents; mothers outnumbered fathers two to one.

The meetings were held in small meeting rooms at Third Affiliated during the afternoon, and lasted for several hours. Parents and class teacher were seated at a table, and they remained seated as they spoke. The hour of each meeting I observed consisted of parents speaking individually to the group, each for about ten to fifteen minutes, about their children and their children's study habits. Since these were students who were not doing well in school, parents were critical of their children's poor study habits. Many parents played out dialogues that they seemed to have actually had with their children, telling what they had said and how their children had responded. The parents' tone in these dialogues was forceful and angry. They told of the many arguments they had had with their children about studying harder, yet they also complained that their children persisted in their poor study habits nevertheless. This caused them to worry about whether their children would be able to pass the college entrance exam.

Examples of parents' complaints are numerous. Many parents objected that their children watched too much television, at the expense of study time. One mother said her child listens to the radio while doing homework. One father said his daughter stays up too late and so has difficulty getting up in the morning. He also said she spends too much time jogging. Parents also spoke of their efforts to help their children improve their study habits. One mother recounted her suggestion to her son that he make a short summary every Sunday of what he had learned in each class during the week. A father said his daughter complained that whenever she asked her chemistry teacher questions after class, he answered abruptly and confusingly and then left the room. This girl's father advised her to persist in asking questions, despite her teachers' reactions. He related that he had told her forcefully: "The only way is to ask questions, isn't that right?"

Parents also leveled criticism at some of their children's teachers. One mother reported that her daughter had said her math teacher criticized her in front of the whole class. Another parent said his child is afraid to ask questions because he fears his teacher will say, "What kind of a question is that?" Yet another complaint was that English class takes too much time to prepare because students have to memorize passages and recite them in class. Xu Laoshi, who had accompanied me to this parents' meeting, responded defensively and angrily that even though students hate to memorize and recite, there is no alternative for learning a language. Xu later told me that parents often attack teachers, especially the class teacher, during these meetings. She said that when she was a class teacher, she would deflect such attacks by striking first, telling parents in a parents meeting that their children were all very lazy.

As is not uncommon in Chinese meetings, while a given individual was addressing the group as a whole, other parents in the group carried on their own conversations on the side with each other. The class teachers, however, listened to each parent's comments and complaints carefully, making no responses of their own, and not directing the flow of conversation from one person to the next. After all the parents had finished speaking, and had vented their frustrations (which seemed to be the aim of the meeting), the class teachers made their own statements. There is a general feeling in China that one mark of an intellectual is the ability to explain the causes for a phenomenon, even if such explanation requires simplification (as often happens) or speculation. The class teachers, as educated people, responded appropriately and typically by calmly analyzing *(fenxi)* the underlying causes for the students' poor study habits. One explanation was that noise from construction at Third Affiliated made it difficult for students to concentrate. Another explanation, one I often heard, was that the high earnings of uneducated, street vendors were a powerful disincentive for students to study. After the class teachers' short analyses, the meetings ended with parents formulaically thanking the class teachers and asking that they continue their careful supervision of the parents' children.

### Some New Developments in Linkages among Schools, Government, and Parents

Over the last ten years or so there has been a proliferation of new linkages among schools, government, and parents. In particular local-, provincial-, and national-level governments as well as the schools themselves have developed various strategies for teaching parents to do a better job raising their children. As several scholars explained to me, since parents are now allowed to have only one child, they feel that they are less likely to raise a "talent," the goal of all of the Chinese parents with whom I spoke. Therefore, parents are anxious to learn how to improve their parenting skills, and numerous institutions have arisen to respond to these needs. I visited two such institutions involved in research and teaching devoted to improving parenting methods, a parenting institute that, among other activities, publishes a newspaper for parents, and a program at a junior middle school to teach parenting.

The parenting institute, which is funded by the Northeast City municipal government, was founded in 1981; one of its main accomplishments has been the publication since 1984 of a weekly newspaper for parents. The editor told me that the newspaper is written for, and primarily distributed among, less-educated residents of Northeast City (though the editor said those in other provinces also read it), since their parenting skills are not considered to be as well developed as those of educated parents. The sample copy of the newspaper I was given is four pages long and has such headlines as, "How I Learned to Be a Good Father," "Does Your Child Dread School?" and, for children rather than parents, an advice column (which I will discuss further in Chapter 7) entitled "One Should Make a Positive Response to Parents' Loving Concern."

The article by the father is typical of stories that parents often tell when they are speaking or writing in a public setting. (Indeed, at the junior middle school parents' program described below I heard each of several parents tell virtually identical stories.) The story is of the father's radical transformation from bad parent to good. He writes:

> In the past I was autocratic and rough toward my kids, always thinking that they were immature and disobedient. Often all it would take was for my kids to not do things the way I wanted them done, the way I instructed, and I would always loudly upbraid them, and even use a club on them.

The father says that he then read the parenting institute's newspaper and "thoroughly transformed my undesirable, irritable, and rough temperament, so now my children and I are always equals, and very amiable" (author's translations, Sun 1989).

Two things are especially interesting about this father's story. First, it exemplifies the kind of story of transformation and rectification that the Chinese have been taught to tell. Second, it articulates the ideal, though seldom achieved, parent/child relationship: amiable and equal.

The article on fear of school briefly describes the fear children often feel when first starting school, and it offers some suggestions on how parents can help their children overcome such fear. It recommends that parents patiently explain the importance of school to their children, and suggests that they cultivate their children's independence by urging them to practice relating with age-peers. Parents should point out to a child those of his acquaintances who also go to school and encourage the child to go to school with his companions (n.a. 1989a).

The second institution I visited was a junior middle school that runs a parenting program for parents of the school's incoming, junior grade one students. Participation in the program is voluntary but encouraged, and is tuition-free, but parents must buy the textbook. The school principal told me that 95 percent of incoming students' parents enroll in the program, making for a total of over 200 enrollees. He explained that the enthusiasm of parents results from their desire to learn how to make their children become "talents" *(rencai)*. The program has eight teachers, all of whom are also teachers in the junior middle school. Each one takes a turn lecturing on an area of parenting skills in which he or she has some expertise. Lectures and program activities are held once a month, for several hours in the evening. The whole program lasts for the entire academic year and is repeated every year.

The Northeast City municipal government issued a document calling on all schools in the city to establish parenting programs, but few have. One reason the school I visited has one is that it is a third-class school *(sanlei xuexiao)*, a non-key school for difficult students, and the school has a very high percentage of students who are disobedient and/or unwilling to study. A major cause of students' misbehavior, the principal explained to me, is that students' parents are mostly uneducated workers and street vendors, so they are not good at raising their kids. Parents of the school's students are "unscientific" *(bu kexue)* and "feudal" *(fengjian)* in dealing with their children. Some beat their children in order to control them, and some do not supervise them at all, both of which are parenting approaches the principal feels are inadequate. In addition since most of the parents are uneducated, they are not able to be their child's "home teacher," as is expected of parents in China. The principal said that in order to rectify such poor parenting and, ultimately, to make students more obedient and more studious, his school had decided to establish a parenting program.

I had the opportunity to audit forty-five minutes of the monthly meeting of the parenting program. There were over a hundred parents in attendance that night. They were seated at desks in a large classroom. The portion of class I observed was devoted to a lecture by the school's party secretary about teaching children morals in the home. The lecture was abstract and theoretical, which is very typical of much Chinese academic discourse but surprising given that the parents in attendance were largely uneducated. They seemed to listen quite carefully, however, and many took notes. Much of the lecture dealt with the importance of family education *(jiating jiaoyu)*. The lecturer began by saying that family education is a prerequisite to effective socialism and civilization. She said that whether one family does a good job raising their child affects the entire country. She also told parents that schools can be successful only when assisted by families and by family education that is coordinated with school education. She ended her lecture by telling the parents that they must do a good job teaching morality to their children in order to prevent China from raising more youngsters such as one of the central leaders of the 1989 student movement in Beijing, Wuer Kaixi.

## Chapter Summary

This chapter describes the socialization of Chinese children based on my observations in several Chinese homes, supplemented by interviews with informants and friends. In ideology, the traditional views of the parent/child relationship—which stressed the inequality of parent and child and commanded obedience to parents and service to them as they aged—have been rejected. Informants said that parents and children should be like friends, willing to help each other, equal in status, and entitled to disagree with each other.

In practice, Chinese parents still exercise a great deal of authority over their children. The use of physical punishment is accepted by many parents. Some parents prefer persuasion, yet nevertheless insist that their children yield to their wishes. This is particularly true with children's schoolwork. Parents benefit from students who are scholastically successful, so they put a great deal of pressure on their children to study. Romance, which is viewed as an interference to one's studies, is forbidden until after senior middle school, and even then parents often cannot tolerate their children developing romantic ties. The pressure to study and the restrictions on romance lead many Chinese adolescents to conflict with their parents, and references to a Chinese generation gap are common.

The traditional obligations of mutual dependence between the generations have been diminished, yet nevertheless still exist. Many informants seek to live apart from their parents, yet nonetheless expect to help their elderly parents with their daily affairs. Parents welcome such assistance and encourage it by socializing their children to sacrifice their own interests for the benefit of parents.

Many parents, however, encourage both self-sacrifice and self-indulgence. They criticize their children harshly yet yield fully to many of their wishes. This seeming contradiction is partially explained by the fact that parents give things to their children in order to obligate them to reciprocate in later years.

Teaching face, too, presents certain contradictions, since parents must teach children to develop both a sense of shame and a sense of honor. They do this by criticizing young children harshly, while refraining from everyday criticism of adolescents. This leads teenage children to feel the pride their parents' behavior implies they should feel, while leaving them vulnerable to feeling shame when they are criticized.

The chapter next discusses gender and socialization. Boys are covertly encouraged to be naughty, and they are allowed encounters with dangerous situations. As for the role of parents, mothers and fathers maintain close relationships with their children until about age six, after which fathers become more removed, and mothers handle the child's daily needs.

The chapter ends with a discussion of the linkages between families and schools. The class teacher plays a key role in linking schools and families, by meeting with parents of disobedient students as needed, and meeting every semester with the parents of all students. Meetings between the class teacher and parents whose children were not doing well academically are described.

New links between schools and families have developed in the last decade as institutions respond to parents' increased desire to know how to raise an only child. Two such institutions are described: an institute that publishes a newspaper on parenting, and a junior middle school that holds lectures to teach parents how to do a better job raising their children.

# 7

## The Topography of Emotion

### Face and Emotion

Given the centrality of face in Chinese social relations, it is not surprising that face and emotions related to it are prominent in the emotional topography of the Chinese. One emotion commonly experienced among the Chinese I knew is anxiety. As discussed in previous chapters, it is public recognition of one's merit that the Chinese most strive for, which means that performances, or situations resembling performances, are very significant for the Chinese. For a performer it is, above all, in a performance that his merit or lack thereof is displayed, resulting, respectively, in the preservation or loss of his face. With such psychic and social consequences at stake, performers feel a great deal of anxiety about the quality of their performance. Since any situation in which one's merits are performed before virtually anyone but family can lead to loss of face, the anxiety associated with performance is prevalent. I described in Chapter 5 how every student I called on to speak in oral English class shook with nervousness. Anxiety over academic performance reaches its peak over results on the college entrance exam, since that exam determines college attendance and hence is extremely important to one's future career and status. Many students I knew endured months of anxiety and sleeplessness before taking the exam. In a number of cases, the afflicted individuals were so incapacitated by their nervousness that they had to refrain from preparing for the exam for anywhere from several months to a year in order to recover their mental stability. The effects of anxiety are compounded, I believe, by the positive value the Chinese place on being active *(huoyue)* and energetic. Combined with anxiety, the high energy level of many Chinese makes them quite nervous and leaves them vulnerable to bouts of insomnia, a very common affliction among my Chinese friends and acquaintances.

Feelings of shame and embarrassment, and the enduring feeling of one's own inferiority *(zibei)*, are other face-related feelings common among the Chinese. Those who publicly fail to perform in accordance with expectations, or those whose moral failings are made public, feel embarrassment, shame, and possibly lost face. A feeling of inadequacy can result from such things as an uneducated family background or, in males, short physical stature. Xiao Zhang told me that many intellectuals in China *zibei*, which he thought might be because their pay and status is low. The failure to become famous and attain the success for which so many Chinese strive can also result in a feeling of shame and/or a sense of inferiority. Cui Jian, a famous Chinese rock singer who says that the purpose of rock music is to "get rid of people's sense of shame," expresses in one of his songs the feelings of those who fail to achieve a reputation. His song entitled "Nothing to My Name" laments: "The land beneath my feet is passing. The water by my side is flowing. But you're always laughing at me that I've got nothing to my name" (n.a. 1989b). One informant told me that all Chinese have at least some feelings of inadequacy, and the stronger your sense of pride and self-respect *(zizunxin)*, the more likely you are to feel inadequate, since your strong self-respect causes you to have high expectations of yourself that, in reality, you cannot realize. This psychological dynamic helps explain the seemingly contradictory personalities of so many Chinese, who are both proud, and even arrogant, and yet also insecure about their abilities.

Many scholars of China have described the negative sanctioning in Chinese culture of open hostility, and Xiao Li remarked to me one day that the Chinese are "the best people in the world" because they repress aggression. Such antiaggression ideals are contradicted, however, by the high frequency of aggression seen in China. I took the bus daily, and every day or two I would see an argument or a fight between strangers on the street or on the bus. As pointed out in Chapter 4, males, the educated, and other higher-status people would yield in such fights, while the true aggressors were those of lower status. This suggests that there are overt antiaggression norms to which those of higher status, in particular, respond, while aggression is tolerated, and perhaps even covertly sanctioned, among those of lower status.

There is also a certain context in which aggression is expected and, in some sense, encouraged. One response allowed to the Chinese in reaction to the humiliation of losing face is to become angry and to attack the source of their humiliation. If a teacher criticizes a student, making him lose face, that student may seek revenge against the teacher by trying to make the teacher lose face. If the student can succeed in making the teacher lose face, and/or delegitimate the teacher's original criticism by arguing that it was unfair and/or insensitive to the student's face, then the student recovers some of his own lost face.

*Other Prominent Emotions*

Whenever I asked about relations between students, the response was frequently, "We're all equals. We're all friends." Indeed, there is a very strong emphasis on friendship and on the equality among friends. However, the majority of Third Affiliated students sought recognition for the merits that the Chinese so value, and thus were very competitive with their classmates. Some students quietly admitted to me that they were secretly trying to achieve higher test scores than certain of their classmates. Also, those who did well, or those who received special attention and favors from teachers, often aroused the jealousy of their classmates. One informant, who has lived for years in America, stressed to me the outstanding capacity of the Chinese to feel jealousy.

Jealousy and competitiveness in China tend to undercut some friendships. In addition, during political movements such as the one after the spring 1989 protests the government intentionally tried to weaken its student-adversaries by getting students to turn against each other and inform on each other's "counterrevolutionary" activities. While the government's strategy did not seem to work in 1989, its strategy, along with jealousy and competitiveness, presents a challenge for building and maintaining truly close friendships in China. Despite their overt friendliness, many of the young people I knew seemed lonely, and a few of my friends admitted that they felt this way. Some Chinese, too, seek solitude. Cui Jian, the popular Chinese rock star, who is in his late twenties, said in an article about him: "I don't have a girlfriend—that would be exhausting and at the moment I'm just too tired. Sometimes I think I will hide away and become a hermit" (quoted in n.a. 1989b).

As for positive emotions, the Chinese tend to distinguish a kind of momentary happiness from lifetime happiness and prosperity. *Gaoxing* means "happy," but in use is often closer to "high-spirited," since people will describe a lively discussion among close friends and say that everyone was very *gaoxing. (Yukuai* is often used the same way.) *Xingfu* refers both to happiness and to well-being and prosperity, which shows the extent to which the Chinese see a happy life as synonymous with a secure, prosperous one. This view of happiness as deriving from prosperity is often encouraged by teachers and especially by parents, whose own happiness and peace of mind in old age are secured by the prosperity and success of their children.

One of the emotions I found to be especially widespread among the Chinese is hope *(xiwang).* There is a general tendency among the Chinese to anticipate the distant future, and to expect, or hope, that it will be much better than the present. The Chinese I knew thought about, and planned for, the future quite often. Many of my friends who wanted to come to America knew that it would be years before that dream might become a reality, yet they continued to study English and plan for the realization of their dream. Third Affiliated teachers often talked to their students about the kind of life the students might lead in decades to come. If a student did poorly on a test, his teacher or friends would console him by saying that he should not give up hope since there was still a good chance for him to become a success in the future. The almost moralistic tone with which teachers would talk of students' bright futures led me to suspect that attention to the future might somehow be related to the Chinese attentiveness to the elderly. One politically moralizing text in a magazine for youths that I came across confirmed my suspicion. An article in that magazine said: "Respecting the elderly shows that we [the Chinese] are full of confidence about our future and our own old age"(Yu 1984: 55). This quote nicely connects respect for the elderly and the Chinese faith in the future. Chinese youth are encouraged to regard their own distant futures as bright in order to persuade them to have high regard for their own future old age, and for old age and the elderly in general.

Many Chinese youth are also very idealistic. This is perhaps related to the prominence of hope. It may also be related to the reverence for, and faith in, those people and things who rank number one, since such reverence encourages the Chinese to believe that what is perfect and infallible can, in fact, be achieved. One of the most common images of a perfect world in which contemporary Chinese youth have faith is also the society that they consider (economically) number one: America. Many of my friends and acquaintances idealized America, and they became disappointed or inattentive if I mentioned some of its imperfections. One friend told of his fantasies of America. With almost boundless enthusiasm he exclaimed: "I dream I will go to America. I can see in my dream what it's like. The streets are sparkling clean. The streets are filled with bright lights, and with many cars and buses driving by. You wave your hand and a taxi pulls up."

Idealism's almost inevitable complement is disillusionment, and this is also common among many Chinese youth. Several informants told me that youth in China have no faith any more in any organized political or social value system, and this leads them to feel bitter. Many are guided only by a desire to make money, and lack any broad ideals. Many of my friends admitted to feeling existential dilemmas, and one told me that it is quite common for Chinese youth to experience such dilemmas. Common questions pondered are, "Who am I? Why am I here?" Another common emotional reaction results from the gap between the ideal and the real. In Third Affiliated's guidebook for teachers is the following passage:

> Middle school students' needs of all kinds are constantly increasing [compared with childhood], yet they still lack the ability to determine whether or not their needs are reasonable, which results in a contradiction between subjective wishes and objective reality. This constantly intensifying contradiction is a social factor accounting for middle school students experiencing confused, vacillating, and intense emotions. (Author's translation, Li 1986: 52)

One informant reported that the pain from the gap between the ideal and the real led two young Northeast City residents he knew to kill themselves.

The tension between a faith in ideals and a sober realization that one should not expect too much is expressed in a poem written by a female student at Third Affiliated, entitled "Fantasy." (The translation is mine.)

> I have a feeling I'm about to see you on the boundless snow
> In the midst of darkest night I imagine this scene, as peacefully I
>    enter a dream world

Early morning I look to the dewy sky, searching for you, eyes
  sunken in
To start a new life
I'm fantasy's madman
You really don't exist
But still I go on imagining, imagining
Since you can give me what I hope for
Respectfully I listen to the cry of cicadas after a rain
This is the sound of the unhappy person getting a new life
My spirit sings along with this song
Stands on the green wave-crest
Light breeze's comforting stroke announces the end of suffering
Remaining rain dripping into my eyes turns into soundless crying
I feel a yearning for my voice
Yet I dare not expect too much from the future
Nor look back on what has already passed

**Emotions in the Chinese Voice**

In the following sections I portray various types of emotional experiences of individual Chinese I knew in China. A few words are necessary about the sources on which this portrayal is based. There is a great
interest among Chinese adults, particularly parents and teachers, in
finding out what their youth are thinking and feeling. This interest is in
part politically motivated, since some teachers and administrators want
to make sure that students have the "correct" attitudes about their
government and nation. But the interest also is fueled by their desire to
know what youth really think about them. While Chinese strive for the
public accolades of fame, that public acclaim can be rendered shallow
by gossip and by private and/or secret sentiments of envy and hatred
among supposed admirers. Many Chinese are therefore very concerned
to find out what their juniors *really* think of them.

Not surprisingly, their juniors are very reluctant to tell them, fearing
reprisals if they admit contempt for superiors. Only if the relationship
between a subordinate and superior is very close and trusting will true
feelings be admitted (hence making such disclosures is one of the true
signs of emotional closeness between people). In most cases the Chinese are guarded about revealing their feelings, and adolescents, in
particular, are unwilling to make revelations to adults and teachers.
Third Affiliated administrators recognized this when they had *ban* con-

vene meetings on the teacher/student relationship, in which it was explained that teachers wanted these meetings because they did not know what students were really thinking.

While the phenomenon described in the preceding paragraphs pertains primarily to the privacy of emotions toward others, I think this privacy extends as well to emotions generally. Many of my Third Affiliated informants said that they do not reveal their inner thoughts and feelings to anyone. I found this to be true, since even quite friendly Third Affiliated informants told me very little about their inner lives. (Close, male friends my own age, however, did reveal their own feelings to me.) Since I was interested in students' feelings, I tried another approach and asked to see some of their writings, especially their diaries (which are less private than in Western countries). Some students agreed to let me see their writings and to use them as "material" for my study. Most of what follows is drawn from these sources. (The majority of these sources were in Chinese and I have translated them into English, checking my translations with native informants where necessary. Some of the sources were in English. In such cases I have corrected minor grammatical mistakes. Unless otherwise indicated, a given source below was originally written in Chinese.)

Because these sources were not as numerous as I would have liked, the following is not a full documentation of students' inner lives but rather a selective one. Selection has also occurred with regard to the types of emotions manifested in the passages I excerpt. In students' writings positive emotions are often expressed in order to convince the teacher or parent who might read the writings (even diaries are read by parents and teachers) that the author is a person of good character. The author will describe his feelings in a way that displays his adherence to political and social ideals. (A number of authors, for example, described their euphoria at giving up a seat on a bus to an elderly person, something I never witnessed despite riding the bus daily.) Since this section is intended to portray what Chinese youth actually feel, not included are what were obviously politically motivated descriptions of feelings. Much of the following, therefore, describes what might be considered negative emotions. One other bias concerns gender. Females are much more frequent diary writers than males, and so most of the sources I was able to obtain at Third Affiliated were written by females. The few quotes from males are identified as such.

## *Competitiveness and the Pressure to Study*

In Chapter 5 I described the competitiveness of the Chinese, and of the Chinese students at Third Affiliated. The coveted position of being number one motivates the Chinese to compete with each other. In schools such competition for the top position is further intensified by the connection between academic performance and the quality of one's future life. Middle school graduates who pass the college entrance exam are assured of a job when they graduate from university, whereas middle school graduates who fail the college entrance exam quite often face unemployment. Thus students are under a great deal of pressure to study hard in preparation for the college entrance exam. At elite schools such as Third Affiliated the pressure to study and the accompanying competitiveness are especially intense.

How do students feel about competition and pressure to study? I raised this question with a group of Third Affiliated students. Most of them said they believe competition is desirable because it stimulates them to work harder in school. However, a few students described adverse emotional consequences to competition. One girl, who is a very good student, said her teachers make her work very hard to prepare for scholastic competitions, even insisting that she study on Sundays. During the competitions she gets very nervous and, despite her preparations, often loses. This makes her feel sad and disappointed. In such cases she believes competition is undesirable. Another student described the pain of losing. She said she always wants to be the best, and is especially sensitive to people's opinions and feels hurt when they do not regard her as best. In such situations she lays in bed at night, with tears streaming down her face.

For many students, competition, and the pressure to study, make school unbearable. One student described his time in school as a "nightmare." Another student wrote of the pressures she feels, and her strong desire for liberation from those pressures:

> Going outside my room, a night sky ornamented with millions of stars rules over everything. I want to put down the heavy burden of my heart, and in a free world breathe freely. But my responsibilities won't allow me to snatch a moment of leisure. A night-flight airplane twinkles red and green lights in the distant sky above. My heart is recklessly teased by it. No, my heart is not that calm. My heart is a never-calm sea, which

surges big waves intermittently. However, whenever I am this way—conflicted, agitated, and pacing without knowing where to go—it's only then that I feel I am me. It's not that sober and reasonable, secular-spirited me. I want to loudly, piercingly, shout, making my voice prick a hole in the night sky. Listening to a shout so full of vitality is one road to fulfillment.

Interestingly, many teachers at Third Affiliated recognize the intense pressures felt by students, and some of them even advocate curriculum changes designed to reduce the pressure. One older teacher at Third Affiliated who leads a group of teachers exploring possible curriculum reforms told me he believes that Chinese middle school students are under too much pressure. He admires the American system, which he characterized as allowing students in middle school to balance studies with recreation, and he would like to see such a system adopted in China.

Students are able to temporarily escape the pressures they feel by *war*. *War*, a term used very often in Chinese, is hard to translate into English but is perhaps best captured by the words "play" and "socialize." Unlike the English word "play" however, *war* can be used to describe the amusements of children or of adults, since it primarily refers to any fun social interaction among friends. To *war* is to temporarily put aside all of the usual constraints of social interaction and their usual serious consequences. A group of Chinese who are at play will all talk at once, laugh frequently, and playfully argue with each other. They will not need to monitor what they say and do, since when at play among friends, in contrast to most other social interaction, they feel the threat of being evaluated and seriously criticized by others is minimal.

Many Chinese have a real tendency to occasionally "let loose" and play, and such playful occasions are remembered with great fondness. When I asked students to depict their most vivid memory, almost all of them described an occasion when they were at play with their friends, with "everyone equal, unrestrained, and having a great time." One male student happily recalled his junior middle school *ban*, and his classmates' playfulness and naughtiness. (As pointed out in Chapter 5, this behavior is tolerated and sometimes even condoned by teachers.) He told me:

> I really remember my junior middle school *ban* with great fondness. The relations between my classmates were very good. We were often

together in activities, so happy. . . . It left a deep impression. . . . [Our *ban* was] the most naughty. During class we were so active. Students would all rush to answer the teacher's questions. Class seemed quite wild! [He laughs.] Quite animated! [He laughs again.] All the teachers thought our *ban* was naughty. After class we would play, in all kinds of ways. There was a bit of everything, not at all like obeying school rules. Really wild.

### Students' Relationships with Parents and Teachers

Pressure to study comes not only from the students themselves but even more so from parents and teachers, since they earn face by the achievements of their children and students. Sometimes, the study pressure exerted by teachers and, especially, parents is intense and conflicts with many youths' desires to relax and socialize with their friends. This conflict can lead many students to feel animosity toward their parents and teachers, seeing them as the enforcers of the drudgery of having to study.

One student described in her diary her general feelings of animosity toward certain teachers:

My personality's a bit eccentric. In primary school you're supposed to give New Year's presents. But I didn't give a present to Class Teacher X. . . . Now it's New Year's again. . . . My eccentric temperament has returned. I didn't give Class Teacher Y a present. My psyche has sprouted a detest-the-teacher anger. . . . Sigh! My eccentric character! Others can't figure it out. Neither can I.

At the opposite extreme students sometimes manifest genuine sympathy for their teachers. Once when many students in Zhou Laoshi's class failed to do their homework, Zhou, a normally serene woman, got very angry. She mentioned this unhappy event to me, and one of her students wrote about it in her English diary, commenting: "Today isn't a fine day, and my heart is also unhappy. Mrs. Zhou got angry in class. I've never seen that."

In an English diary entry one student described her view of some of the antagonisms found in Chinese families:

This play [which she had seen and is describing] was an American play. . . . It showed us one family in the United States. . . . All of [the family members] got along well with one another and everyone had a kind heart. Once, in time of trouble, the mother helped her children out as a friend would do. Mother and children were like close friends. The children were free to do what they wanted.

After watching this play, I began to worry about the fate of China's families. Chinese parents always force their children to do all kinds of things. "Don't go out. Don't go swimming. Don't read novels. Don't watch T.V. Don't write letters." Chinese parents order their children around like officers. Their children don't take their fate lying down so there are gulfs between parents and children. Every day I hear the cries of children. What pity I feel for them!

Another student wrote of her animosity toward her mother:

I now feel I increasingly detest my parents. If I have my own arrangements, first watch a bit of T.V., within ten minutes it starts: Mother begins to shout, "In the interest of your studies you must set aside a bit of time [for studying]." I want to do things my way. Mother persists in opposing me. She says, "Make keeping up with your studies your first priority." Study, study, everything is study! Can it be life only consists of study? It really makes one consumed with irritation.

If I write a letter or write in my diary, I always have to take precautions to prevent mother from reading it. . . . [Mother]: "I would never read your things." In reality whenever she sees a letter, or my diary, she always has to read it in great detail. Parents always do that. That's totally rotten.

Whenever I hear mother's tone of voice, I feel ill at ease. Her voice has that "My daughter got into Third Affiliated, so I'm quite terrific" tone to it. I totally detest this. . . . Mother's absolutely mentally deranged.

A couple of aspects of this passage deserve commentary. The mother's words sound fairly well intentioned in English, but the Chinese phrases (such as *ba ni xuexi ganshang qu wei zhong)* sound like slogans (and in fact parallel many political slogans), thus clearly communicating the girl's perception of her mother's alienating condescension toward her. Also, most of the adjectives the student uses to describe her mother are preceded by intensifying adverbs. This is common in Chinese rhetoric and it has been a frequent strategy in political tracts describing China's internal or external enemies. The above passage's similarity to such political rhetoric further strengthens the student's portrayal of her mother as her antagonist/enemy.

Another student's English diary shows support for her mother while condemning her father for, apparently, hitting her mother:

> Poor mother! My heart is crying, for my dear mother, for me. I want to die sometimes. "Go to another world," I often say to myself. But I can't. I must live on! Study hard, work hard! I must trust mother softly. When I grow up, I won't marry any boy! I hate them! I won't leave mother until she is dead. Mother! Mother! I do not know what on earth my father is. He is a man who knows much learning, but he is a selfish man, too! If he did love my mother, he wouldn't hit her! . . . I'll go back to school tomorrow. Other classmates may be very happy. But I? Sadly? Oh, I don't want to know!

In a second passage she writes:

> Janet's [Janet is the English name of her good friend] mother is too strict with Janet. Sometimes she's too conservative. Janet is afraid of her. But they all say that my mother is so kindly that they all love her. I think they're right. I love her dearly. Wherever I go, I won't forget her. I have learned a lot of things from her. When I was a little girl, she taught me how to walk, speak, and sing. It was she who taught me that our motherland is the People's Republic of China. I always think she is beautiful. I like to watch her quietly. And I like the way she holds me in her arms. My dear mother.

### The Pains and Pleasures of Teaching

Whenever I was alone with a group of teachers, they launched into a description of their unhappy lives as teachers. The majority of them said that they had not wanted to become teachers but had been sent to teacher training universities after graduation from middle school, leaving them essentially no occupational alternatives. Foremost among their complaints were the low pay and low status of Chinese teachers, compounded by what they felt were long working hours. One teacher explained that whereas in other fields fame is earned through one's own actions, a teacher earns fame through his students, if and when they become successful. Thus teachers must wait years before their merits are recognized and their efforts bear fruit. They put in a great deal of effort yet receive little, at least little immediate, satisfaction and compensation. Teachers recited two sayings to express this situation:

"Teachers are like chalk. They crush themselves in giving others knowledge"; and "Teachers are like a candle. They light others and burn themselves out."

Many teachers also complained about disrespectful students and students' lack of interest in their studies, a disinterest teachers often attributed to the fact that China's economic reforms have made it possible for a petty entrepreneur to earn several times more than can a college graduate. Zhou Laoshi, though one who generally enjoyed teaching, lamented the disinterest of many students and their irresponsible attitude toward their studies. She told me that sometimes she gets so angry when her students do not do their homework that she feels a tightness and pain in her chest. Teachers also complained about their students criticizing them. While the public posture required of teachers was that they accept and encourage their students' criticisms and complaints, Wu Laoshi told me in private that she cannot stand it when her students criticize her.

Teaching can also bring great pleasure to Chinese teachers. One older teacher named Ma Laoshi told me that one of the most memorable days of his life was his twenty-fifth reunion with a class of former junior middle school students for whom he had been the class teacher in 1964. (Such reunions are uncommon, Ma said.) The reunion was organized and paid for by the class's former class monitor, who had grown up to become a wealthy owner of his own company. The reunion was held at one of Northeast City's large parks. Ma and his students (but not their spouses, since the reunion organizer had stipulated that spouses and children should not be brought along) ate dinner there, and then danced outside to music played on a cassette deck. At dinner all the students drank to the health of their former teacher and Ma could barely hold back his tears. Especially emotional were the apologies from a few students to Ma. When the Cultural Revolution broke out, those students had criticized Ma. Now they asked for his forgiveness.

## Helping Youth with Emotional Concerns

As elsewhere, in China young people sometimes experience emotional difficulties that they cannot resolve by themselves. Schools in China, unlike schools in such countries as the United States, do not have on-staff full-time psychological counselors (nor, for that matter, did I ever hear of any professional, full-time psychologists in Northeast City. This is changing slowly, however, since within the last few years a few universities have established counseling services, as has one branch of the Beijing municipal government. See Sui 1988 and Wang 1989). The class teacher is supposed to be someone with whom students can talk about their problems, but most of the students I asked said they do not discuss their personal feelings with their class teachers. Students sometimes turn to a trusted teacher for advice, as described in Chapter 5. Other students turn to their friends for comfort. Yet another method is for young people to write to newspaper advice columnists. Many newspapers and magazines print letters from distressed youths and supply brief replies. In some cases advisors receive the letters from youths and answer them directly, rather than publishing the letters and responses in the newspaper. One such advisor, whom I met and got to know quite well (described at greater length below), is even visited at his house by youths who travel great distances to seek his counsel.

Following are some examples from magazines and newspapers of letters from youths and the corresponding replies from the newspapers and magazines' advice columnists.

The first example comes from a regular column in a magazine called *Family (Jiating)*. The letter writer is a disabled twenty-five-year-old male. He first relates how, despite his handicap, he has had many accomplishments in athletics, academics, work, photography, stamp collecting, and so on. Recently someone introduced him to a potential mate, a woman whom he, however, felt was undesirable. He says his friends thought that because of his handicap he should not be so choosy about selecting a mate. This hurt him, and he has resolved that "I don't want to add family unhappiness [that is, an undesirable wife] to my already very bitter life" (author's translation, n.a. 1987b: 30).

*Family*'s advice columnist responds:

> You carry with you a wounded heart, and you have used handicapped feet to walk a life of twenty-five years, and have also had many accomplishments in work and study, and cultivated all kinds of interests. This is not at all easy! I think the reason you can do this is because you are strong-willed, and have a sound mind, which is the most important thing of all.
>
> You don't look down on yourself, don't just drift along, and you use

your intellect to govern your life. Also, in the choices of love you don't randomly improvise. This is not simple to do. People often say life has its strong people. These "strong people of life" usually doesn't mean those with developed muscles, or those who can eat twenty steamed buns at one meal. Rather it means those people who dare to look reality in the face, those who don't let themselves be overpowered by cruel realities, those having the will to surpass others, with firm conviction. I think you are precisely this kind of person. (N.a. 1987b: 30)

The advice columnist then goes on to tell how he recently met a disabled professor who had, through persistent efforts, secured his dream of becoming a medical specialist and professor. This professor also found a beautiful, intelligent, and virtuous wife. The columnist concludes:

So, you absolutely shouldn't feel depressed and pessimistic. All you have to do is diligently enrich yourself, elevate yourself, make great contributions to society and the nation, and you certainly can establish a prosperous and happy household. In our society, there are a fair number of young women who haven't at all accepted common prejudices, and who most value a person's fine soul. (N.a. 1987b: 30)

The columnist ends by cautioning the writer against excessively high expectations; he then compliments the correspondent on a well-written letter, encourages him to keep up his studies, and reiterates his judgment that one's mind is more important than one's limbs (n.a. 1987b: 30).

This is a fairly typical letter and response, which illustrate several features common in Chinese endeavors to aid someone in emotional distress. The first is the emphasis on hope. The columnist cites a concrete example of another disabled person he knows personally and describes how that person has succeeded both in his career and in finding a desirable spouse. The columnist then follows this by telling the letter writer that there is hope for him to be similarly successful. However, he also cautions the letter writer not to have hopes that are too high, since he says these could lead to increased "vexations" *(kunao)* (n.a. 1987b: 30). While instilling realistic hope may be a common characteristic of any good therapeutic technique, it is also an especially common technique of most Chinese therapy. Consistent with what is described above as the prominence of hope in the Chinese emotional topography, counselors and friends of people with emotional concerns almost always remind the troubled person that "there is still hope."

A second feature is the exhortation to persist with one's studies. Often when someone is in a position to give advice in China, especially advice to a person with romantic troubles, the advice includes such an exhortation, further support for my contention in Chapter 6 that study is encouraged in part to keep youth from putting too much emphasis on love and sex.

Third, there is the advice columnist's praise of the letter writer. Praise, like criticism, plays an important social and psychological role in China, and the Chinese are very aware of its value. It is quite common for Chinese to say, "Everyone likes to have others praise him." When the Chinese want to cement a friendship or relationship with someone, they often will praise him. When they want to request something from someone, they often will praise him. (I knew when someone was about to make a request of me whenever they started praising me.) Teachers sometimes use praise to motivate students who are having academic difficulties, and the values of praise are codified in the theories of *zhengmian jiji jiaoyu* (see Chapter 5). And when the Chinese want to soothe someone, they will praise him. This is a cultural pattern to which the columnist above was undoubtedly responding.

Advice columnists do not always affirm everything about their letter writers. Many times columnists urge their writers and readers to reform their behavior to be consistent with various Chinese values, such as harmony between husband and wife or between children and their parents. The following example illustrates this.

This passage comes from the newspaper for parents that was discussed in Chapter 6 *(Jiazhang Bao)*. It too has a regular advice column, and in one such column two teenagers wrote in to describe problems with their parents and ask for advice on dealing with them. The first letter writer relates that as soon as his parents find out that he has not done well on a test, they make him copy characters or copy a page of English. This makes him feel emotional pain as well as pent-up anger (Lao Wang 1989: 3). The second letter in this column is from a seventeen-year-old female from the countryside whose studies consumed increasing amounts of time, to the detriment of the amount of time she spent doing her household chores. Her parents reacted by beating her and scolding her, and even told her to "Get out" *(gun)* because "We're unable to raise you" (Lao Wang 1989: 3).

The columnist responds to both letter writers in one response. Part of his response contains the following advice:

> [You] must change the negative into the positive, change the passive into the active. . . . [You ought to] impel the good relationship between both sides [both parents and child] to constantly develop. . . . This so-called require the passive to turn active, this is not just to require those who are children to not one-sidedly demand their parents' care and concern, but also to take the initiative to care for parents' life and work situations, and even their interests and mood. Do your best [this is still directed to children] to make your own words and deeds bring happiness and satisfaction to your mother and father. (Lao Wang 1989: 3)

This is very traditional advice. Both letter writers wrote in with complaints about parents who are uncaring and/or too controlling. The columnist advises them both to try to accommodate their parents' needs and wishes. Such advice is the essence of the traditional dictates of filial piety.

### A Counselor to Youth

At Northeast University I had the opportunity to meet and talk at length with a middle-aged education professor who, in his spare time and for no pay, is a counselor to youth. Youth throughout the country know about this professor, whom I will call Lu Laoshi, because of several magazine articles written about him. Troubled young people, usually in their teens or twenties, write to Lu seeking his counsel. Lu said that he receives between three and ten letters every day from young people from all over the country. The majority of these, perhaps 80 percent, come from women, which Lu believes is because young women are more secretive about their personal lives with people they know than are young men, and thus they prefer to turn to a non-acquaintance, such as Lu, for help. Lu spends time daily answering the letters he receives. He responds to each letter writer directly with his advice, rather than publishing the letters and advice in a newspaper or magazine. Sometimes troubled individuals will travel to Northeast City and visit Lu at his house. On some occasions Lu has fed and housed such individuals for several days, while counseling them about their problems. He has kept in touch with some clients for several years and visits them when he goes to other parts of the country for meetings. He considers his clients to be his friends. They often treat him like a father, and address him as such in their letters.

Lu's technique has several prominent characteristics. Lu says that he tries to be nonjudgmental in his approach to his clients and their problems. He does not treat psychological problems as moral problems, and does not criticize or rebuke his clients. He also feels that it is important not to be surprised or shocked when clients express their problems. In treating them, he said his role is just to "give the key to open the door" or to "show the way." As with the first advice columnist cited above, a central component of Lu's advice is the expression of hope and praise for his clients. The emphasis on both hope and praise is captured in the following quotation by Lu in an article about him.

> There was one young woman [one of Lu's clients] who compared herself to a gold-rimmed bowl, a bowl that had fallen on the ground and smashed. Even if you pick it up, and try to tack it together, it's still a broken bowl, and cannot be restored. In my letter I told her, "You are a jewel. It's just that you've been covered with a layer of dust. I'll help you wipe away the dust. You still are a jewel that can give off a radiance to dazzle the eyes. Whatever good fortune young women of your generation can obtain, you also should for sure be able to obtain." (Zhou 1989: 14)

Another characteristic of Lu's advice is that he often includes an exhortation to his clients to study, as was the case with the advice columnist described above. The evidence he offered me of the success of his method was not some proof of his clients' recovered emotional well-being but rather statistics on how many of them had been accepted to college and/or secured a good job.

Lu's clients suffer from a variety of problems. Following are some examples.

One letter he received was from a teenager in the countryside who had been raped when she was nine years old. (Lu said he has received quite a few letters from young women who had been sexually violated in their youth.) Her letter ended with a veiled suicide threat, in which she said that she would "enter hell" if he did not respond within twenty days. Lu wrote back to her that being raped was not her fault, that she was just the same as all other women, and could marry in spite of the rape. She wrote again that she was afraid the rape might have given her a disease that would make her sterile. Lu responded by making an appointment for the young woman with a doctor in Northeast City. Lu invited her to his house, and when she arrived, he fed her and treated her like a guest. He bought her tickets for a famous singer's concert in Northeast City that night, and he introduced her to several college students who accompanied her to the concert. The next day Lu took the young woman to the doctor, who concluded that she was healthy and free of disease. She spent a couple of days at Lu's house and finally went home. As she was leaving, Lu praised her and said he believed that she could become a college student. Lu said that she has kept in touch with him ever since and, three years after he first met her, she visits him during vacations. Lu proudly told me that this young woman did, in fact, enter a key university.

In another case a woman who was a student at a very prestigious university engaged in sexual relations with her boyfriend. He subsequently ended their relationship. (This is a very serious matter for a woman because Chinese men do not want to marry women who have lost their virginity, and many of them will divorce a new bride if they find out she is not a virgin. Therefore, when a man ends his relationship with his girlfriend after they have had sexual relations, she faces the prospect that she may never find someone to marry.) The female student wrote to tell Lu that she was going to kill herself on her birthday, and gave the date. Lu wrote back immediately, mailing the letter by express mail. She replied that she still planned to kill herself. Lu then sent back a highly emotional letter, which prompted her to reply, saying that her critical period had passed.

A common romantic problem encountered by Lu's clients is unrequited love. A male college student once went to Lu's house and told him his tale of unrequited love. He had written a love letter to a young woman, and had been refused. He could not sleep or eat. Lu pointed out that the young man was tall, successful in his studies, and of good moral character. This, Lu told him, meant that his marital prospects were very good. However, Lu also told him that if he did not get his mind off the young woman, his studies would suffer. Lu sent him off with a book on unrequited love. Later, the client returned and said that he still was suffering emotionally. Lu then gave him a letter he had received from another young man also experiencing unrequited love.

This made Lu's client laugh in recognition that others were afflicted with problems similar to his own.

The final example, drawn from the magazine article about Lu, illustrates another feature of Lu's approach. Lu acts as a surrogate father to his clients, specifically, by taking care of the full range of their needs—their material needs, health needs, and emotional needs. This parental approach is common in China. In Chapter 5 I described how teachers sometimes take responsibility for the full range of the needs of their students. More generally, authority figures in China take responsibility for a wide range of the aspects of the lives of those under their authority, in pseudoparental fashion. This means that authority figures have extensive methods by which they can control their subordinates. Working unit leaders, for example, have authority over their employees' housing and even over their employees' marriages, and they can use this authority to reward or punish employees. But such extensive authority has as its complement that the Chinese expect leaders and authority figures to take care of a wide range of their needs, and they laud authority figures who do so while condemning those who fail to do so. This is evident in the section of the magazine article on Lu that I paraphrase below. That section not only describes Lu's fatherlike approach but affirms it.

The text begins: "Young people take [Lu] to be their father precisely because he has fatherly love for them." What follows is an account of an apparently psychotic (jingshenbing) young woman and Lu's approach to her. The woman was a college student who slept while her classmates went to class and made noise while others slept. One day she threw a stool from a second-floor window, and bit those who tried to control her. Her university department wanted her to go to the hospital, but she refused. Lu was called in to help. Since she was an English major, Lu greeted her in English, in order to establish a rapport with her. He told her that he would treat her "as my own daughter." She giggled at this, but he continued to "patiently comfort" her. After Lu accompanied the woman to the hospital for a checkup, the woman said she was hungry, so Lu took her to a restaurant. There Lu had the chef prepare a dish that was the speciality of the province in which the woman had grown up. She said it felt like a holiday, and Lu then extracted a promise from her to enter the hospital the next day. From then on, Lu earned her trust and she became a frequent guest at his house. Eventually, she recovered and with "relatively good grades finished college." The article's author concludes: "[Lu must have been moved by fatherly love for the woman since] if it hadn't been for fatherly love [Lu] would not have poured his heart out for a psychotic person whom he didn't know" (Zhou 1989: 15–16). It is, in fact, true that Lu's actions and attitude toward the young woman—his general concern and patiently caring manner and especially his taking her to a restaurant to feed her—were clear signs of his desire to be a surrogate father to her. This kind of patient, parentlike care that the Chinese often expect from a person in a position of responsibility earns such a person praise and respect.

**Chapter Summary**

This chapter describes the experiences and emotions of individual Chinese and relates these to cultural characteristics previously described. The chapter begins with a consideration of the emotions that are especially prominent among the Chinese. Because of the centrality of face, emotions related to it—anxiety, shame, embarrassment, and feelings of inferiority—are quite common. Among students, this is most clearly manifest in anxiety over their performance in class and on the college entrance exam. Face also accounts for some instances of aggression in China. One response to losing face is to become angry and attack the source of one's humiliation. If such an attack is successful, the attacker may recover his face.

Another prominent emotion is jealousy among peers. Jealousy and competitiveness can make true friendships difficult, and this sometimes leads to loneliness. Among positive emotions, hope is especially strong. The Chinese are future-oriented and anticipate the future as a time that will be better than the present. This orientation toward and faith in the future may be related to esteem for the elderly, since regard for one's own future old age can entail respect for old age in general. This section ends with a discussion of the idealism of Chinese youth and their occasional disillusionment.

The second part of the chapter uses quotations from Chinese people to illustrate aspects of their emotional lives. One such aspect was competitiveness. Because of the pressure to be number one, and to pass the college entrance exam, many students at schools such as Third Affiliated feel enormous pressure to study, a pressure from which they often want to escape. This pressure is also externally imposed. Parents and teachers push their youngsters to study, and as a result many youths feel animosity toward their parents and teachers. Teachers complained about the low pay and low status of the teaching profession. Disrespectful and disinterested students was another common complaint. Some teachers, however, also described the pleasures of teaching.

The last part of the chapter considers how the Chinese aid youth who are in emotional distress. Two methods discussed were the magazine and newspaper advice columnist and its corollary, the person who advises youth through letters or during their visits to his house. Several cultural characteristics arose from the examples presented. One is the emphasis on praising the client. The client is not only praised but is encouraged to feel hope, consistent with the Chinese emphasis on hope. Another characteristic is the advisor's fatherly approach to clients, that is, his concern for all aspects of their well-being. Finally, the measure of the success of the advisor's or advice columnist's efforts is often external: the client's entrance into college, graduation from college, and/or attainment of a good job.

# 8

## Conclusion: The Paradox of Power

This study has presented a description of life at one Chinese middle school, Third Affiliated Middle School, and the cultural context in which it is set. I have shown how the cultural constructs of face, criticism, praise, and evaluation influence teacher/student relations as well as the nature of the educational process more generally. I have also discussed the ways these constructs affect family life, and their effects on individuals' emotional experiences.

Even if Third Affiliated were totally idiosyncratic, a description of its culture would still contribute to the larger anthropological enterprise, the knowledge of how one human community operates, based on intensive and long-term ethnographic research among its members. But Third Affiliated is not totally unique, and much of what I found there exemplifies characteristics of Chinese culture generally, and even characteristics of cultures similar to China's. This chapter concludes the study with a consideration of its significance for an understanding of China and Chinese culture, and its relevance for an understanding of other cultures.

### Representativeness of Third Affiliated

An important question to ask is: How representative is Third Affiliated of schools in China in general? Obviously, Third Affiliated is atypical in many ways. Above all, it is a key school and hence has select students from privileged backgrounds. Also, it is an urban school with urban students, in a country where 80 percent of the population still lives in the countryside. Third Affiliated is located in one region of China, and it would be fair to question whether what I observed there is true of other regions. Finally, would the cultural characteristics found at a school hold in other, noneducational sectors of Chinese society?

I cannot definitively answer any of these questions, since I did not spend an extensive amount of time in the countryside, in other parts of China, or at non-key, average schools. However, I did conduct interviews with people who went to both urban and rural, key and non-key middle schools located in a variety of provinces. I also talked informally with my friends, many of whom had grown up in diverse parts of China. At least half my formal and informal discussions were with people who had attended school in the countryside or in town schools drawing students from the surrounding countryside. These discussions were supplemented by a visit to a rural school and to several urban non-key schools. In Chapter 1 I mentioned my contact with Marketplace Middle School, a non-key school in Northeast City. The countryside school I visited was a key middle school in a medium-size town of about 50,000 people. Two-thirds of the students at that school came from the town, while the remaining one-third were children of peasants from the countryside surrounding the town. Unfortunately, the events in China in June 1989, the time of my visit to that school, necessitated cutting short my visit, but I did spend three days at the school teaching English and talking with teachers and a few students. Finally, living in China for thirteen months gave me exposure to other sectors of Chinese society in addition to the schools.

My findings from the sources and contexts described above are fairly uniform. Below I review some of these findings, briefly comparing them with what I found at Third Affiliated.

First, the evaluativeness of the Chinese, described in Chapter 2, seems quite uniform throughout China. Whenever I talked with workers I met in the street or in restaurants in Northeast City, they too were very concerned with discussing what is good, bad, and the best. They would, for example, become very animated in discussing superlative characteristics of the United States. Many of my friends who had grown up in the countryside and in various regions of China acted the same way. I felt in familiar territory at the countryside school I visited when, after seeing several groups of students perform plays in English, one boy asked me which group's play I thought was best.

Second, not surprisingly, students at non-key schools are generally not as competitive as students at key schools. Nonetheless, teachers still use competitive methods to stimulate students' interest in class. In

Chapter 5 I described auditing a class in which a Marketplace Chinese language and literature teacher used competitive methods to motivate her students. From the cheering of students for their classmates and the excited reactions of contestants, students seemed to be animated by a strong desire to compete. In the countryside those students who feel they are academically elite and have a chance to pass the college entrance exams are more hard-working and competitive than are their urban counterparts. This is because college, with the possibility of an urban job assignment upon graduation, is one of the only ways a rural inhabitant can move to the city, a popular goal. During one class meeting at Third Affiliated a student asked his teacher why anyone expected him and his classmates to study hard since, he remarked, they are already urban residents and so have nothing more to gain from studying hard. However, for rural residents of only average academic ability, the probability of passing the college entrance exam is very small. For them, in contrast to outstanding students, there is little to be gained, so these students are quite apathetic about academic endeavors. Mosher found, during a month of teaching and observing at a village middle school (apparently non-key), that students were concerned little with academic achievement and believed, as did adult villagers, that studying is useless (Mosher 1983: 105–30).

Third, notions of face and the possibility of lost face can be found in diverse parts of China, and the figurative meaning of face as representing one's publicly recognized esteem can be traced back to the fourth century B.C. (H.C. Hu 1944: 45–46). Face is clearly central in Chinese culture.

Fourth, the practice of criticism, and the existence of positive sanctions for inferiors to criticize superiors in certain contexts, varies somewhat throughout China. Some areas of China are especially well known for having people who are easily aroused to criticize others. One informant told me that those from northern China tend to be more critical than those from other parts of China. It is also sometimes thought that rural Chinese are more obedient to superiors than are urban Chinese. This may mean that students in the countryside are, under normal circumstances, less likely to criticize or be critical of their teachers, and more likely to be deferential to them. At the same time, however, during my three-day visit to a middle school in a town in the countryside, many teachers described conflicts with their students, and two male peasant students told me about serious arguments they had with their teachers. They were good students academically, and it may be that in the countryside, as in urban China, those of inferior status (such as students) who are highly ranked among their peers are somewhat more entitled to criticize their superiors than are less-accomplished peers. An informant from Taiwan articulated this principle best: She said that students in Taiwan also occasionally criticize their teachers, even doing so in public during class; an academically superior student criticizing a mediocre or poor teacher would be considered brave by his classmates and would be regarded as a "hero" *(yingxiong)*. An academically inferior student criticizing a well-liked, well-respected teacher, by contrast, might be seen as a fool. These are sentiments quite similar to those I found in mainland China (see Chapter 4). Furthermore, my informants told me that while any student is entitled to criticize an incompetent or immoral teacher, the student who is academically and morally outstanding is more entitled to do so than his less-perfect peers. This suggests that students at schools with academically superior students, such as Third Affiliated, would be more likely to criticize their teachers, while students at non-key schools would more often conflict with their teachers by misbehaving or cursing and abusing them. This distinction, while subtle, is one that I believe does hold between key and non-key schools.

## Relevance of This Study for Understanding Other Cultures

Since a primary focus of my study has been on face, criticism, and evaluation, this section compares my findings about China with those of other anthropologists working in societies where face and shame are also important in social life. This comparison must, of necessity, rely on the publications of other anthropologists, since I have not conducted fieldwork in other face or shame cultures. Thus, I offer the following less as a definitive formulation than as suggestive of issues for further research.

Ruth Benedict (1974) gave the classic formulation of shame cultures, defining shame cultures such as Japan by distinguishing them from such guilt cultures as America:

> True shame cultures rely on external sanctions for good behavior, not, as true guilt cultures do, on an internalized conviction of sin. Shame is a reaction to other people's criticism. A man is shamed either by being openly ridiculed and rejected or by fantasying to himself that he has

been made ridiculous. In either case it is a potent sanction. But it requires an audience or at least a man's fantasy of an audience. Guilt does not. In a nation where honor means living up to one's own picture of oneself, a man may suffer from guilt though no man knows of his misdeed and a man's feeling of guilt may actually be relieved by confessing his sin. (1974: 223)

In contrast to Benedict, others studying Japan, such as De Vos (1973: Chapter 5) and Lebra (1983), have pointed to the strong presence of guilt in Japanese culture. Lebra also describes the strong presence of shame in Japan, arguing that guilt and shame are not mutually exclusive, contrasting constructs but, in the case of Japan, mutually coexisting. She even contends that the Japanese emphasis on shame intensifies an orientation to guilt. Other scholars (for example, Goodenough 1963: 353–54; Piers and Singer 1953: 78–79; Creighton 1990: 290–92) have pointed out more generally that all cultures use both shame and guilt, and both internal and external sanctions, for social control, though in varying contexts and to different degrees. Even Benedict, as Creighton (1990) argues, recognized that the shame culture/guilt culture distinction was not absolute.

The revelant distinction to be made, then, may not be whether a society appeals to shame or to guilt, but rather, the extent to which, and the way in which, it appeals to shame. Therefore, in the following discussion I will not use the terms "shame culture" and "guilt culture," but instead "shame-socialized" and "non–shame-socialized" cultures. (The reasons for this terminology will become clear below.) Shame is defined here as the feeling that results from awareness of failure, an awareness generated either from within the individual himself or deriving from the reactions, real or imagined, of others. Defined this way, shame is also characterized by the fear of losing the respect granted by others, and fear of abandonment and rejection by them.

From my research in China and my reading of the literature on other societies where shame is important I suggest the following as characteristics distinguishing shame-socialized cultures from non–shame-socialized cultures.

What seems most distinctive about some cultures is not just that their members are sensitive to shame. Rather, what is most important and distinctive is that their members are *expected* to feel sensitive to shame and to the opinions of others and society more generally. In

China, as mentioned in Chapter 4, to say that someone lacks sensitivity to shame is one of the gravest insults that can be made. (See also H.C. Hu 1944: 52.) Catalonian villagers likewise use lack of shame as an expression of moral condemnation (Asano-Tamanoi 1987: 108). In Bali the necessity of shame is captured in the saying "Shame is the measure of a man" (Wikan 1987: 361). In southern Spain honesty and shame are paired together and the dishonest, unethical man is seen as shameless (Gilmore 1987a: 94). In Japan virtue, honor, and sensitivity to shame are virtually synonymous (Benedict 1974: 224). Therefore, some cultures are characterized by an expectation that all of the culture's members should feel sensitive to shame; shame is essential to personhood. These are the cultures I call shame-socialized.

Since shame-socialized cultures equate sensitivity to shame with virtue and hold in strong contempt those who lack such sensitivity, individuals in such cultures are strongly socialized to be aware of what others think of them, and are encouraged to act so as to maximize the positive esteem they are granted from others while trying to avoid incurring their disapproval. (This socialization for sensitivity to shame is why I call such cultures "shame-socialized" cultures.) Such cultures' individuals are also socialized so that, if and when they violate societal standards, they will feel psychological and social injury to themselves due to others' condemnation of their offenses, or due to their fantasies that others, and society, condemn them. This is shame, and loss of face. While these are emotions that those in non–shame-socialized cultures also feel, those in shame-socialized cultures tend to feel them more strongly because they have been explicitly socialized to be sensitive to shame. Also, the disapproval of others has greater social consequences for an individual in a shame-socialized culture than for a person in a non–shame-socialized culture. This is because in many shame-socialized cultures status is closely tied to, and often based on, the esteem one is granted by others. Thus, in a shame-socialized culture, one who violates social codes temporarily loses social status as well as the esteem of others. In the most extreme cases shame is characterized by the individual's rejection and abandonment by the group (Piers and Singer 1953: 16).

Since shame in shame-socialized cultures does more damage to an offender than is the case in non–shame-socialized cultures—both wounding his psychological well-being and depressing his social status and even his membership in the group—shame-socialized cultures are more likely than nonshame-socialized cultures to utilize shame (either the threat or the actual use by way of gossip or public condemnation) to control the actions of individuals and ensure their compliance with social norms and expectations. In studies of shame-socialized cultures the use of shame for purposes of control has often been noted (Brandes 1987: 131–32).

Creighton provides a useful example of how a culture's individuals are taught to respond to shame and are controlled by it. Her article (1990) discusses how the Japanese encourage individuals to value dependence on others and on the group. This emphasis on the importance of belonging lays the foundation for the dynamics of shame, since shame is characterized by rejection from the group. Japanese mothers activate the dynamics of shame in their children whenever the latter misbehave. When children misbehave, their mothers tease them and/or ignore them, thereby teaching children that negative acts will lead to rejection and abandonment by others, painful punishment for Japanese, who value a sense of belonging. The Japanese shaming techniques contrast with the methods of American mothers, who, as Creighton points out, are more likely to punish children by controlling and containing them—sending them to their rooms, for example (1990: 294–96, 298–301).

There has been much debate with regard to whether honor is a salient characteristic of shame-socialized cultures and, if so, how it relates to shame. Peristiany and contributors to his edited collection (Peristiany 1966a) portrayed the peoples of the Mediterranean as united by complementary codes of honor and shame, but more recent scholars of the Mediterranean have challenged Peristiany's portrayal (Wikan 1984; Gilmore 1987a). Wikan (1984) notes that while Mediterranean peoples do not speak of each other's honor in everyday conversations, they do frequently talk about shame. Therefore, she argues that honor may exist as a Mediterranean cultural code but that it is far less salient in social life than shame.

It would be hard to argue the same about China. It is true that, especially in the domain of moral evaluation (less so in the domain of judgments about talent and merit), shame is probably more salient than glory *(guangcai* or *guangrong),* yet the difference in salience is minimal. The Chinese, in contrast to Mediterranean peoples, do engage in everyday discourse about glory, especially glory earned through the recognition of an individual's or collective's outstanding talent and achievements. The desire for glory is thus nearly as important in the animation of ordinary social life as is the desire to avoid shame and loss of face. In that sense glory—the Chinese equivalent to honor—and shame form a complementary pair.

### Social Interaction as Performance

Shame-socialized cultures legitimize the judgments made by their members about each other since such judgments are a central means by which such cultures exercise social control. Moreover, certain kinds of judgments are socially privileged. In particular, shame-socialized cultures seem to be united in their tendency to use negative judgments about an individual's actions—rather than about the individual himself or his status or the sum of his actions—to urge individuals to act well and appropriately. The individual who, in a given situation, acts poorly is shamed. The result of granting legitimacy to the judgments of members of society about the actions of an individual is to turn most public social interaction into a kind of a performance, where one is watched, judged, and negatively evaluated if one's actions are found faulty.

Chinese constructs of face give interaction in China, both inside and outside the classroom, the character of a performance. Researchers of other shame-socialized cultures have made similar observations about the performative nature of social life. Lebra (1983) writes that the Japanese divide social occasions into those that are "on-stage," in which the goal is to strive for perfection of speech and bodily gestures and avoid actions leading to shame, and those that are "off-stage," in which the Japanese can relax and be uninhibited without fear of shame. Since the attention of others can have such extreme social consequences, often negative ones, the Japanese, like the Chinese, are extremely sensitive to attention and gaze directed at them. In its extreme form this sensitivity manifests itself as a neurotic disorder in which individuals fear any self-exposing actions, such as saliva swallowing, body odor, eye-to-eye contact, and so on (Lebra 1983: 198). What is interesting is that the Japanese not only feel vulnerable when they are stared at, but they also, unlike the Chinese, fear staring at other people. In addition, they feel embarrassed not just by public ridicule but also by public praise. Lebra describes this as the "exposure sensitivity of the outer self," the embarrassment felt by Japanese as a result of any kind of personal exposure (1983: 194, 198). Such sensitivity to personal exposure characterizes many shame-socialized cultures since the exposed individual is one who is especially vulnerable to shame—vulnerable to negative judgments by others in society about his actions.

In the Mediterranean the importance of shame leads to an emphasis in folklore on the eyes and ocularity. In folklore the eyes are both eroticized and connected to evil. These powers of the ocular sense derive from the important role of the eyes in shame, since shame occurs when one's faulty actions are seen by others (Gilmore 1982: 197–98). This connection between gaze and shame is felt as well in the Micronesian society studied by Lutz, where the fear of being seen by others is phrased as fear of shame or embarrassment (Lutz 1988: 188). And in China eyes and the sense of sight are a common focus of attention and concern. I often heard children being coached by their parents or teachers abut how to observe an object. Good observational ability *(guancha nengli)* is highly valued, and so is good vision, as evidenced by the daily eye exercises that students must do in school.

## The Reciprocation of Respect and Disrespect

In China social order is preserved by the obligation of all individuals (with the exception of children) to respect each other and protect each other's faces under normal circumstances. Conversely, if someone does something disrespectful to you, then you are entitled to be disrespectful to him, and to his face. In fact your success in doing so helps you recover your own lost respect and lost face.

In other shame-socialized cultures there is a similar principle of the reciprocation of respect and disrespect. Among the Kaluli of Papua New Guinea, for example, norms of reciprocity prevail. Not only are gifts reciprocated, but so are injuries and insults. If one individual injures or insults another, the latter is seen as having lost something and, according to the norms of reciprocity, he is entitled to redress. In many cases he will even up the score by staging a counterattack on the man who attacked him. Interestingly, the Kaluli even socialize their children to feel entitled to the redress of losses afflicting them. When Kaluli children become angry because they have lost something, their mothers often relieve their children's anger by giving them food which is explicitly termed a reciprocating item (Schieffelin 1983). Such parental strategies are similar to those of the Chinese, who tend to yield to the indignant demands for food or drink made by their young children.

The strategies of both the Chinese and the Kaluli teach children that, if they lose or lack something, an indignant or angry reaction on their part will earn them compensation for the missing item.

In the Mediterranean there is also a logic of reciprocity to disrespect. Campbell describes how in Greece if a family is outraged by someone, then it must retaliate in order to preserve its reputation (Campbell 1966: 144, 149). Bourdieu makes a similar observation but notes that the status of the offender and the person offended are important. If the offender is of equal or higher status than the person offended, then the person offended must retaliate against the offender in order to preserve his honor. However, if the offender is of lower status than the person offended, then the person who is offended must accept the offense. If the higher-status offended person were to retaliate, he would dishonor and humiliate himself. This is because fighting with someone is a way to acknowledge that his status equals yours, since it demonstrates your belief that he is capable and worthy of a fight. So if a high-status person fights someone beneath him, his status is lowered to a level commensurate with that of his opponent (Bourdieu 1966: 200, 205–7, 211).

Respect, like insults and offense, is reciprocated. Wikan describes how she was initially puzzled when a group of Omani women failed to criticize and confront one among them who was committing one of the most serious moral violations: adultery. The women explained their refusal to confront their adulterous friend by saying that she had not done them any harm, and had always been kind and hospitable to them. Thus, they had no cause to shame her. This suggests that the Omani believe you can attack another person's self-esteem only if that person has injured you, a more extreme version of the Chinese belief that an attack on your face is one justification, though not the only one, for attacking someone else's face. Also, as Wikan notes, the adulterous woman's hospitality to her friends further constrained them from criticizing her (Wikan 1984). This is also true in China. The person who is helpful to others is more likely to be forgiven if he is found to have committed a shameful act, and the person who is selfish is much more likely to be the target of attempts to criticize him, shame him, and attack his face. Gilmore found that helpfulness and hospitality were central to the system of respect in Spain in that those demonstrating these virtues were accorded esteem while the miserly man would be called "shameless" (Gilmore 1987a: 94–95).

Goffman uses the findings on reciprocity of respect and disrespect in face societies to support his general theory on such reciprocity and his analysis of the different strategies actors use to preserve or restore the "equilibrium" of mutual respect when it has been disturbed by one individual offending another. One means of restoring equilibrium is for someone who offends another person to show, following the insult, that the insult was neither serious nor intentional. For example, the offender may pretend that the offending remark was actually made in jest. Another means of restoring the equilibrium of respect is for the offender either to offer compensation to the victim of his offense, or for the offender to self-castigate and offer to do penance for his offense (Goffman 1967: 19–23). The latter strategy—the self-punishment of the offender—is one approach common in China in the form of self-criticism.

### The Sources of Honor and Shame

One of the important differences between the various shame cultures lies in the sources of honor and shame. These sources derive sometimes from the moral domain, and sometimes from what I call the competence domain. What kinds of action belong in the competence domain varies from culture to culture. Before discussing the differences in the sources of shame and honor in different cultures, some definitions are necessary. I will begin with competence versus morality, a distinction easy to show using examples but difficult to define in words. Essentially, morality and competence differ in the nature of the standards that characterize them. There are some standards to which individuals in a given society are thought capable, through their volitional action, of conforming. The standards are such that a given act may fail to conform to the standards but cannot exceed them. The standards usually refer to the behavior of individuals toward each other and toward society. This is morality. With competence there are no clear standards, or if there are standards, they are ones that cannot necessarily be met by all individuals and that can be exceeded by some. (In some cases the standards are specific to each individual— what others expect of the individual based on his reputation.) With competence, standards are directed toward the nature of how one acts, rather than whether or not one has acted out a particular action.

One of the things that seems particularly distinctive about the sources of shame and honor in China is the diversity of domains from which these derive. Immorality can lead to loss of face, but so can incompetence. For example, adultery is considered immoral, and the revelation of an individual's adultery can lead to loss of face. Singing poorly in public is a sign of incompetence, especially if people had thought you could sing well, and this too leads to loss of face. That both incompetence and immorality lead to loss of face (discussed in Chapter 4) is a characteristic of Chinese face also noted by other analysts (H.C. Hu 1944).

The moral domain is a common source of shame and honor in other societies but the domain of competence, at least in the Chinese sense, is not. Failure to perform some skill well—singing, speaking English, answering your students' questions, and so on—is a common source of shame in China but figures little, if at all, in many accounts of shame in other societies, a fact that may reflect the distinctiveness of the Chinese tradition of meritocracy. In the literature on Mediterranean societies, competence is an issue, but it is competence in performing acts linked to sexuality and to femininity and masculinity. The desire to prove competence and avoid incompetence in such matters is stronger, in the Mediterranean, for men rather than for women. Men must prove that they are "real men" by displaying their sexual virility and by protecting their own women—sisters, wives, and daughters—from the sexual advances of other men. Men who fail in their sexual displays, or fail to protect their women, are seen as failed men and, accordingly, are shamed and emasculated (Gilmore 1987b). Competence at being masculine and manly is also related to honor and shame in China since, as pointed out in Chapter 4, men whose weakness is displayed lose face. However, conformity to gender expectations is only one source of shame in China, whereas in the Mediterranean it is the primary source. The centrality of sexual and gender performance to shame and honor in the Mediterranean is what most defines shame and honor in that region and distinguishes its shame/honor complex from those of other cultures (Gilmore 1987b; Asano-Tamanoi 1987; Brandes 1987).

## The Burden of Higher Status and the Paradox of Power

One of the distinguishing characteristics of shame-socialized cultures is that in such cultures a prime means of disciplining an individual for violations of social norms is to reduce his status. This is accomplished through shame. The offender is shamed by society and loses the respect of others in society as well as, at least temporarily, the status that goes with it. Of course, one of the consequences of a moral system enforced through attacks on offenders' status is that those who are not thought highly of to begin with will not be very vulnerable to being shamed and disciplined, while those of higher status will be more vulnerable. Thus in shame-socialized and face cultures there is a price to be paid for having status: and that is, the potential loss of that status. The higher a person's status, the more he can be made to lose. This places the higher-status individual under a greater burden to conform to society's moral norms, and makes him more vulnerable to being shamed, and to feeling shame, if he fails. This is what I call the paradox of power.

Of course, non–shame-socialized cultures may also attack an offender's status, punishing him by fining him or by removing him from the social position from which he derived his social standing. But the loss a high-status person suffers from this punishment is not necessarily greater than the loss suffered by a low-status person (in fact, the opposite often turns out to be the case), whereas a high-status person who is humiliated in a shame-socialized culture almost automatically loses more than a low-status person. This is because, in a shame-socialized culture, it is the revelation to the public of the nature of the offense and the identity of the offender that constitutes the punishment. This revelation is more damaging to someone with a virtuous reputation. And since the whole system of shame depends on a link between what is thought about an individual—his reputation—and status, those with good reputations are likely to be of higher status and those of higher status will most likely have good reputations. Thus for a given offense, those of good reputations and higher status will suffer greater punishment proportionately—greater loss of status and greater shame—than the lower-status person, who has little to start with and little to lose. An interesting result of this paradox is that while status in a non–shame-socialized culture is a resource for one's defense, in a shame-socialized culture it is the offender's greatest liability. The only real way people of high status in a shame-socialized culture can use their status to protect themselves is to capitalize on their position to prevent public knowledge of their offenses, or to deny or distort the true nature of what they actually did. (Brandes, for example, describes how wealth makes it easier for the wealthy to hide their sexual improprieties—Brandes 1987: 127–28.) If this sounds similar to the status-protection methods of Western politicians, it is not accidental. Western politicians derive much of their power, and in fact their position, from what the public thinks of them. The Western political sphere therefore functions in a manner very similar to the whole of society in a shame-socialized culture.

What even further intensifies the burden of high status in many shame-socialized and face cultures is that those of higher status are either more obligated to conform to society's moral norms than those of lower status, or they are expected to conform to moral norms that are stricter than those to which those of lower status are held accountable. (Again, this is reminiscent of the higher standards to which, for example, American elected officials are held accountable.) Moral standards are not universal throughout the culture, but are relative to one's status. In addition to the heavier moral obligations, those of higher status in countries such as China are also under a greater burden to perform competently and to display their talents successfully.

The one protection enjoyed by those of higher status in shame-socialized cultures is that, in everyday situations or when they have committed minor transgressions of moral norms or displayed minor incompetence, others in society are more obligated to refrain from shaming them—in China, obligated to protect their faces—than is true in the case of lower status people. (This phenomenon appears to hold true in some non-shame-socialized cultures as well. As Goffman describes, the higher a British civil servant's position, the more regard must be taken of his feelings when firing him—Goffman 1967: 10.) But in the case of major incompetence or immorality, this obligation does not hold, and it is especially in such circumstances that the paradox of power is most evident.

### Evidence for the Paradox of Power

China is one of the best examples of the paradox of power, and the description of this paradox forms one of the major themes of this study. (Another discussion of the paradox of power can be found in H.C. Hu 1944. See also M. Yang 1945: 167–72.) To review, briefly: First, face, and its use for purposes of social control in homes, schools, and the workplace, depends on people judging each other. Even the person of superior status gains his reputation, and loses face, through what others think of him. Thus the requirements of face legitimize in some measure the evaluations of inferiors with regard to their superiors and the right of inferiors to criticize an immoral superior. Second, those of higher status are more likely to be the targets of evaluation. Their high status is based on others witnessing and acknowledging—often in a performative context—their merits and virtues. Paradoxically, this means that their immoralities and incompetence are more closely scrutinized as well. The role of those of higher status as the evaluative targets of Chinese society is especially reflected in the tendency to hold those of superior status—parents and teachers, for example—responsible for the successes or failures of their juniors, such as children or students. Third, more is expected of higher-status persons, and since the failure to perform according to expectation is a prime way to lose face, those of higher status are more vulnerable to losing face and feeling shame. Fourth, the judgment of a superior that his inferior has failed does not threaten the inferior's social standing, at least not relative to the superior. The inferior who judges the superior to have failed, however, can look down on the superior, reducing the latter to a level equal to or beneath the former and alienating him from his own status group. Finally, those of higher status are under a greater obligation to uphold certain societal virtues. They have, for example, a higher obligation to show respect for face and to conform to the Chinese norms against aggression and fighting. It is humiliating for them to argue with an inferior. As a result, those of lower status are, relative to superiors, freer to argue with others, including their superiors. And children and adolescents, who are not yet held accountable for protecting others' faces, can get away with criticizing their elders, even if such criticizing threatens their elders' faces.

The paradox of power is manifest as well in other societies. Thai culture, like Chinese culture, also has a strong concept of face. What is especially important to the Thais is to maintain a positive public appearance, and to avoid inappropriate actions that would lead to a loss of the esteem of others (Jackson 1989: 30–32). In Thai culture more is expected of those who are of higher status, and they are under greater pressure to uphold their family name. The higher-status persons are held to stricter moral standards; Jackson argues that this explains why homosexuality is tolerated among the nonelite but not among those of high status (Jackson 1989: 47–48, 64–65, 67–68). This is an example of what is described above as moral norms being relative to status, rather than applied equally to all persons regardless of status.

In the Mediterranean the paradox of power is most evident in gender status. Masculinity is more difficult for a man to achieve than femininity is for a woman. And men may have more status than women, but they are always in greater danger of losing the status they have. This may be true universally, but it is especially true in the Mediterranean, where honor and the defense of masculinity are so closely linked. In Mediterranean cultures, men are always in danger of acting, or being acted upon, so as to damage their masculinity and turn them into symbolic women (Gilmore 1987b: 9–11). Men are also under a greater burden than women because they are responsible not only for their own actions but also for those of their wives, sisters, and daughters. Just as the failures of Chinese children and students reflect on their parents and teachers, so the violations of sexual norms committed by women reflect on the honor of their male relatives—fathers, brothers, and husbands. Some analysts have even asserted that it is the male relatives, and not the woman at all, who are held accountable for the woman's sexual improprieties (Campbell 1966: 146; Peristiany 1966b: 182; Wikan 1984: 641–42; Gilmore 1987a: 96–97; Gilmore 1987b: 10–11). Such views of women, which allow them no responsibility for their own actions, certainly reinforce a patronizing attitude toward women, just as the parallel views toward children in China, cited above, reinforce the low status of the young. But at the same time, the greater responsibilities of those of higher status—here, men in the Mediterranean, those who are older in China—make them more vulnerable to "failure" and to being shamed for failure, their own or that of those for whom they are responsible. This is a paradox of their power.

Finally, anthropologists working in shame-socialized cultures have reported class-linked attitudes toward aggression. In southern Spain, Gilmore found, for example, that male and female workers who stand up to the police or similar authorities are admired. Men who do so are praised for their masculinity (Gilmore 1987a: 97). Swartz writes that among the Swahili women he studied, elite women view gentleness as a virtue, whereas lower-status women respect those who are bold and aggressive (Swartz 1988: 34). The relations between those of differing status are also governed by rules favorable to aggression by those of inferior status against their superiors. Bourdieu writes that among the group he studied to fight back against a man who is of lower status than you is humiliating to *you*. Thus a man of superior status is constrained from fighting against other men in a way that a man of lower or middle status is not (Bourdieu 1966: 197–200, 205–7). Such constraints on those of higher status are similar to those in China, where (as described in Chapter 4) it is degrading to an individual to argue or fight with someone of lower status.

## *Closing Observation*

When I stepped off the plane in China in late August of 1988, I could never have anticipated the profound protest movement that was to erupt in spring of the following year. But I lived through that movement and its aftermath. Many characteristics of the protests seemed strikingly similar to the way in which students challenged authority in the classroom. There was the same righteous indignation, the same feeling of duty to rebuke corrupt superiors, the same effort to delegitimate superiors by criticizing them for their incompetence and immorality. The Chinese leaders deemed the protests the result of foreign agitation, as well as of misguided youth. But the above analysis suggests that this was not so. The actions of the student protesters were legitimated by values indigenous to Chinese culture. Thus the government's use of force to stop the protests may have worked in the short run, but the manifestations of the Chinese paradox of power will inevitably return.

# References

Asano-Tamanoi, Mariko. 1987. "Shame, Family, and State in Catalonia and Japan." In *Honor and Shame and the Unity of the Mediterranean,* ed. David D. Gilmore, pp. 104–20. Washington, DC: American Anthropological Association.

Baker, Hugh D.R. 1979. *Chinese Family and Kinship.* New York: Columbia University Press.

Barlow, Tani E., and Donald M. Lowe. 1987. *Teaching China's Lost Generation: Foreign Experts in the People's Republic of China.* San Francisco: China Books and Periodicals.

Benedict, Ruth. 1974. *The Chrysanthemum and the Sword: Patterns of Japanese Culture.* New York: New American Library.

Bennett, Gordon A., and Ronald N. Montaperto. 1980. *Red Guard: The Political Biography of Dai Hsiao-ai.* Gloucester, MA: Peter Smith.

Borthwick, Sally. 1983. *Education and Social Change in China: The Beginnings of the Modern Era.* Stanford: Hoover Institution Press.

Bourdieu, Pierre. 1966. "The Sentiment of Honour in Kabyle Society," trans. Philip Sherrard. In *Honour and Shame: The Values of Mediterranean Society,* ed. J.G. Peristiany, pp. 193–241. London: Wiedenfeld and Nicolson.

Brandes, Stanley. 1987. "Reflections on Honor and Shame in the Mediterranean." In *Honor and Shame and the Unity of the Mediterranean,* ed. David D. Gilmore, pp. 121–34. Washington, DC: American Anthropological Association.

Campbell, J.K. 1966. "Honour and the Devil." In *Honour and Shame: The Values of Mediterranean Society,* ed. J.G. Peristiany, pp. 141–70. London: Wiedenfeld and Nicolson.

Chan, Anita, Richard Madsen, and Jonathan Unger. 1984. *Chen Village: The Recent History of a Peasant Village in Mao's China.* Berkeley: University of California Press.

Chang Chung-li. 1963. "Merit and Money." In *The Chinese Civil Service, Career Open to Talent?* ed. Johanna M. Menzel, pp. 22–27. Boston: D.C. Heath.

Chen, Jack. 1975. *Inside the Cultural Revolution.* New York: Macmillan.

Chen, Theodore Hsi-en. 1974. *The Maoist Educational Revolution.* New York: Praeger.

Chiang Yee. 1946. *A Chinese Childhood.* 3d ed. London: Methuen.

Chu, Don-chean. 1980. *Chairman Mao: Education of the Proletariat.* New York: Philosophical Library.

Cleverley, John. 1985. *The Schooling of China.* Sydney: George Allen and Unwin.

Creighton, Millie R. 1990. "Revisiting Shame and Guilt Cultures: A Forty-Year Pilgrimage." *Ethos* 18, pp. 279–307.

De Vos, George A. 1973. *Socialization for Achievement: Essays on the Cultural Psychology of the Japanese*. Berkeley: University of California Press.

Dittmer, Lowell. 1974. *Liu Shao-ch'i and the Chinese Cultural Revolution: The Politics of Mass Criticism*. Berkeley: University of California Press.

Edwards, Mikel G., and Yueping Sun. 1988. "China." In *World Education Encyclopedia*. Vol. 1, ed. George Thomas Kurian, pp. 212–37. New York: Facts on File.

Ethridge, James M. 1990. *China's Unfinished Revolution: Problems and Prospects Since Mao*. San Francisco: China Books and Periodicals.

Fairbank, John King. 1986. *The Great Chinese Revolution, 1800–1985*. New York: Harper and Row.

Gao Yuan. 1987. *Born Red: A Chronicle of the Cultural Revolution*. Stanford: Stanford University Press.

Gardner, Howard. 1989. *To Open Minds: Chinese Clues to the Dilemma of Contemporary Education*. New York: Basic Books.

Gilmore, David D. 1982. "Anthropology of the Mediterranean Area." *Annual Review of Anthropology* 11, pp. 175–205.

———. 1987a. "Honor, Honesty, Shame: Male Status in Contemporary Andalusia." In *Honor and Shame and the Unity of the Mediterranean*, ed. David D. Gilmore, pp. 90–103. Washington, DC: American Anthropological Association.

———. 1987b. "Introduction: The Shame of Dishonor." In *Honor and Shame and the Unity of the Mediterranean*, ed. David D. Gilmore, pp. 2–21. Washington, DC: American Anthropological Association.

Goffman, Erving. 1967. *Interaction Ritual: Essays on Face-to-Face Behavior*. New York: Pantheon.

Goldman, Merle. 1981. *China's Intellectuals: Advise and Dissent*. Cambridge: Harvard University Press.

Goodenough, Ward Hunt. 1963. *Cooperation in Change*. New York: Russell Sage Foundation.

Guo Moruo. 1979 [1928]. *Shaonian shidai* (Early Youth). Beijing: Renmin wenxue chubanshe (People's Literature Press).

Han Minzhu, and Hua Sheng, eds. 1990. *Cries for Democracy: Writings and Speeches from the 1989 Chinese Democracy Movement*. Princeton: Princeton University Press.

He Qiu. 1950. *Xiaoxue jiaoshi shouce* (Elementary School Teacher's Handbook). Shanghai: Shiyong chubanshe (Practical Press).

Ho, David Y.F. 1986. "Chinese Patterns of Socialization: A Critical Review." In *The Psychology of the Chinese People*, ed. Michael Harris Bond, pp. 1–37. Hong Kong: Oxford University Press.

Ho, Ping-ti. 1962. *The Ladder of Success in Imperial China: Aspects of Social Mobility, 1368–1911*. 2d printing, with revisions, 1967. New York: Columbia University Press.

Holden, Reuben. 1964. *Yale in China: The Mainland, 1901–1951*. New Haven: Yale in China Association.

Houn, Franklin W. 1965. *Chinese Political Traditions*. Washington, DC: Public Affairs Press.

Hsu, Francis L.K. 1963. "Patterns of Downward Mobility." In *The Chinese Civil Service, Career Open to Talent?* ed. Johanna M. Menzel, pp. 41–48. Boston: D.C. Heath.

————. 1967. *Under the Ancestor's Shadow: Kinship, Personality and Social Mobility in China.* 2d ed. Stanford: Stanford University Press.

————. 1981. *Americans and Chinese: Passage to Differences.* 3d ed. Honolulu: University of Hawaii Press.

Hsu, Immanuel C.Y. 1975. *The Rise of Modern China.* 2d ed. New York: Oxford University Press.

Hu, C.T. 1984. "The Historical Background: Examinations and Control in Premodern China." *Comparative Education* 20, pp. 7–26.

Hu, Hsien Chin. 1944. "The Chinese Concepts of 'Face.'" *American Anthropologist.* 46, pp. 45–64.

Hucker, Charles O. 1959. "Confucianism and the Chinese Censorial System." In *Confucianism in Action,* ed. David S. Nivison and Arthur F. Wright, pp. 182–208. Stanford: Stanford University Press.

Jackson, Peter A. 1989. *Male Homosexuality in Thailand: An Interpretation of Contemporary Thai Sources.* Elmhurst, NY: Global Academic.

Kracke, E.A., Jr. 1963. "Family vs. Merit in the Examination System." In *The Chinese Civil Service, Career Open to Talent?* ed. Johanna M. Menzel, pp. 1–8. Boston: D.C. Heath.

Kwong, Julia. 1988. *Cultural Revolution in China's Schools, May 1966–April 1969.* Stanford: Hoover Institution Press.

Lao Hu. 1989. "Giving Precedence to Others." *China Daily,* January 28.

Lao Wang (columnist). 1989. "Dui fumu de aihu guanhuai ying zuochu jiji fanying" (One Should Make a Positive Response to Parents' Loving Concern). *Jiazhang bao* (Parents' Newspaper), September 29.

Lebra, Takie Sugiyama. 1983. "Shame and Guilt: A Psychocultural View of the Japanese Self." *Ethos* 11, pp. 192–209.

Lewis, John Wilson. 1963. *Leadership in Communist China.* Ithaca, NY: Cornell University Press.

Liang Heng and Judith Shapiro. 1983. *Son of the Revolution.* Vintage Books edition, 1984. New York: Vintage Books.

Li Defu, ed. 1986. *Zhongxue banzhuren shouce* (Middle School Class Teacher's Handbook). Hubei: Hubei jiaoyu chubanshe (Hubei Education Press).

Liu, Hui-Chen Wang. 1959. *The Traditional Chinese Clan Rules.* Locust Valley, NY: J.J. Augustin.

Lutz, Catherine A. 1988. *Unnatural Emotions: Everyday Sentiments on a Micronesian Atoll and Their Challenge to Western Theory.* Chicago: University of Chicago Press.

Mao Zedong. 1965 [1942]. "Rectify the Party's Style of Work." In *Selected Works of Mao Tse-tung.* Vol. 3, pp. 35–51. Peking [Beijing]: Foreign Languages Press.

————. 1967. *Mao zhuxi yulu* (Quotations from Chairman Mao). n.p.: Zhongguo renmin jiefangjun zong zhengzhi bu (The People's Liberation Army General Political Department).

————. 1976. *Quotations from Chairman Mao Tse-tung.* Peking [Beijing]: Foreign Languages Press.

Marsh, Robert M. 1961. *The Mandarins: The Circulation of Elites in China, 1600–1900*. Glencoe, IL: Free Press.

Menzel, Johanna M., ed. 1963. *The Chinese Civil Service, Career Open to Talent?* Boston: D.C. Heath.

Mosher, Steven W. 1983. *Broken Earth: The Rural Chinese*. New York: Free Press.

n.a. 1987a. *Yuwen, disance* (Chinese, Book Three). Hubei: Renmin jiaoyu chubanshe (People's Education Press).

n.a. 1987b. "Tanxin ting" (The Heart-to-Heart Talk Pavilion). *Jiating* no. 9: 30–31.

n.a. 1989a. "Nide haizi kong xue ma?" (Does Your Child Dread School?). *Jiazhang bao* (Parents' Newspaper), September 29.

n.a. 1989b. "Rock Star Rolls to Success." *China Daily*, February 27.

Peristiany, J.G. 1966a. *Honour and Shame: The Values of Mediterranean Society*, ed. J.G. Peristiany. London: Wiedenfeld and Nicolson.

———. 1966b. "Honour and Shame in a Cypriot Highland Village." In *Honour and Shame: The Values of Mediterranean Society*, ed. J.G. Peristiany, pp. 173–90. London: Wiedenfeld and Nicolson.

Piers, Gerhart, and Milton B. Singer. 1953. *Shame and Guilt: A Psychoanalytic and a Cultural Study*. Springfield, IL: Charles C. Thomas.

Potter, Sulamith Heins, and Jack Potter. 1990. *China's Peasants: The Anthropology of a Revolution*. Cambridge: Cambridge University Press.

Pye, Lucian W. 1968. *The Spirit of Chinese Politics: A Psychocultural Study of the Authority Crisis in Political Development*. Cambridge, MA: MIT Press.

———. 1988. *The Mandarin and the Cadre: China's Political Cultures*. Ann Arbor: Center for Chinese Studies, University of Michigan.

Rosen, Stanley. 1982. *Red Guard Factionalism and the Cultural Revolution in Guangzhou (Canton)*. Boulder, CO: Westview.

Ross, Heidi Ann. 1987. "'Making Foreign Things Serve China.' A Historical-ethnography of a Chinese Foreign Language Middle School." Ph.D. dissertation in Education, University of Michigan.

Schieffelin, Edward L. 1983. "Anger and Shame in the Tropical Forest: On Affect as a Cultural System in Papua New Guinea." *Ethos* 11, pp. 181–91.

Schurmann, H.F. 1959. "Organization and Response in Communist China." *The Annals of the American Academy of Political and Social Science* 321, pp. 51–61.

Selden, Mark. 1969. "The Yenan Legacy: The Mass Line." In *Chinese Communist Politics in Action*, ed. A. Doak Barnett, pp. 99–151. Seattle: University of Washington Press.

Shirk, Susan L. 1982. *Competitive Comrades: Career Incentives and Student Strategies in China*. Berkeley: University of California Press.

Solomon, Richard H. 1969. "Mao's Effort to Reintegrate the Chinese Polity: Problems of Authority and Conflict in Chinese Social Processes." In *Chinese Communist Politics in Action*, ed. A. Doak Barnett, pp. 271–361. Seattle: University of Washington Press.

Sui Bian. 1988. "Colleges Try to Help Troubled Students." *China Daily*, November 8.

Sun Tianming. 1989. "Wo zenyang xuehui dang ge hao fuqin" (How I Learned to Be a Good Father). Jiazhang bao (Parents' Newspaper), September 29.

Swartz, Marc J. 1988. "Shame, Culture, and Status among the Swahili of Mombasa." *Ethos* 16, pp. 21–51.

Tao Dun. 1987. *Yige zhishifenzi de zishu* (An Intellectual's Self-Narrative). Shandong: Shandong renmin chubanshe (Shandong People's Press).

Thurston, Anne F. 1987. *Enemies of the People*. New York: Alfred A. Knopf.

Tong Te-kong and Li Tsung-jen. 1979. *The Memoirs of Li Tsung-jen*. Boulder, CO: Westview.

Unger, Jonathan. 1982. *Education under Mao: Class and Competition in Canton Schools, 1960–1980*. New York: Columbia University Press.

Wakeman, Frederic, Jr. 1975. *The Fall of Imperial China*. New York: Free Press.

Wang Rong. 1989. "A Place to Go When the Going Gets Tough. . . ." *China Daily*, January 1.

Whyte, Martin King. 1974. *Small Groups and Political Rituals in China*. Paperback edition, 1975. Berkeley: University of California Press.

Whyte, Martin King, and William L. Parish. 1984. *Urban Life in Contemporary China*. Chicago: University of Chicago Press.

Wikan, Unni. 1984. "Shame and Honour: A Contestable Pair." *Man* (N.S.)19, pp. 635–52.

———. 1987. "Public Grace and Private Fears: Gaiety, Offense, and Sorcery in Northern Bali." *Ethos* 15, pp. 337–65.

Wolf, Margery. 1970. "Child Training and the Chinese Family." In *Family and Kinship in Chinese Society*, ed. Maurice Freedman, pp. 37–62. Stanford: Stanford University Press.

———. 1974. "Chinese Women: Old Skills in a New Context." In *Woman, Culture, and Society*, ed. Michelle Zimbalist Rosaldo and Louise Lamphere, pp. 157–72. Stanford: Stanford University Press.

Wright, Mary Clabaugh. 1957. *The Last Stand of Chinese Conservatism: The T'ung-Chih Restoration, 1862–1874*. Stanford: Stanford University Press.

Yang, C.K. 1959. "The Chinese Family in the Communist Revolution." In *Chinese Communist Society: The Family and the Village*. Paperback reprint edition, 1965. C. K. Yang, author. Cambridge, MA: MIT Press.

Yang, Martin C. 1945. *A Chinese Village: Taitou, Shantung Province*. Paperback edition, 1965. New York: Columbia University Press.

Yi Mu and Mark V. Thompson. 1989. *Crisis at Tiananmen: Reform and Reality in Modern China*. San Francisco: China Books and Periodicals.

Yu Xinyan. 1984. "'Lao' shi shenmo yisi" ("What Does 'Old' Mean"). *Zhongxuesheng* (Middle School Student), no. 6: 52–55.

Zhang Yewen. 1985. "Kuanrong, ci ai de Sun Laoshi" (Tolerant and Kind Teacher Sun). In *Wode laoshi* (My Teacher), comp. Lin Conglong and Hou Xiaoqiong, pp. 245–47. Sichuan: Sichuan jiaoyu chubanshe (Sichuan Education Press).

Zhang Zhi. 1983. *Fang Zhimin jiangjun zhuan* (Biography of General Fang Zhimin). n.p.: Jiefangjun chubanshe (People's Liberation Army Press).

Zhao Qinjian. 1984. "Zize cai neng ziqiang" (Only by Reproaching Oneself Can One Strengthen Oneself). *Zhongxuesheng* (Middle School Student), no. 7: 59.

Zhou Ruizhen. 1989. "Yiwei yizhi xinling chuangshang de dashi" (A Master Curing the Wounds of the Heart). *Hubei qingnian* (Hubei Youth), no. 2: 14–16.

# Index

power, paradox of. *See* paradox of power
praise, 180
  and discipline, 105
  and face, 77, 79
  and therapy, 180, 182

*qiaobuqi*. *See* looking down on
questions
  significance of, 63–64, 99,126

reciprocity
  *see also* face, and reciprocity, dynamics of
  between children and parents, 141–142, 149–154
  between students and teachers, 120–121
reputation, 31, 43–45, 70, 84, 166
  *see also* fame; glory
  in shame-socialized cultures, 198–200
respect. *See* face, and reciprocity, dynamics of

self-criticism, 35–36, 79–81, 110
sexuality
  *see also* dating
  parental control of, 147–148
  and studying, 147, 180
  university control of, 72–73, 118
shame, 166, 191–203
  defined, 191
  sensitivity to, 67–69, 154–155, 191–193
  and social control, 192–193, 198–200
  and staring, 194–195
shame cultures, 190–191
shame-socialized cultures, 191–203
  characterization of, 191–194
  and reputation, 198–200

showing off (*chu fengtou*), 80-81
  and competitions, 111–112
spanking. See *da*
staring, 3, 81–82
  and shame, 194–195
student protest of 1989, 31, 53, 59, 88, 203
study (*xue*)
  meanings of, 24–25

talk reason (*jiang daoli*), 33–34, 107
*tan lian ai. See* dating
teacher/student relationship, 114–136
  attempts to transform, 115–117
  contemporary, 117–121
  and criticism, 28–30, 31–32, 51, 55–57, 60–64, 89, 91–92, 123–127, 130, 189–190
  feelings about, 174
  and parent/child relationship, 120–121
  traditional, 114–115
teaching
  feelings about, 176–177
Thailand
  paradox of power in, 201–202
therapy
  methods of, 177–185
Third Affiliated Middle School
  description of, 6–8
  identified, 4
  observations at, 4–5
  representativeness of, 187–190
tuition-paying students. *See jiedusheng*

*war* (play, socialize), 173–174
*zhengmian jiji jiaoyu* (positive and active education),105–106, 108–110
*zibei. See* inferiority, sense of one's own

**Martin Schoenhals** is a cultural anthropologist who specializes in China, the anthropology of education, and psychological anthropology. He conducted his University of Pennsylvania dissertation fieldwork during 1988–89 at a People's Republic of China middle school, and this book reports the results of the research. The 1989 Chinese Democracy Movement occurred during Schoenhals' fieldwork, and the anthropological analysis of the Movement has become an additional focus of his scholarship.

Schoenhals is assistant professor of anthropology in the Department of Sociology and Anthropology at Dowling College.

For Product Safety Concerns and Information please contact our EU
representative  GPSR@taylorandfrancis.com
Taylor & Francis Verlag GmbH, Kaufingerstraße 24, 80331 München, Germany

www.ingramcontent.com/pod-product-compliance
Lightning Source LLC
Chambersburg PA
CBHW070413270326
41926CB00014B/2801